PATHWAYS

Listening, Speaking, and Critical Thinking

4

Paul MacIntyre

Keith S. Folse / Series Consultant

NATIONAL GEOGRAPHIC LEARNING | **HEINLE CENGAGE Learning**

Australia • Brazil • Japan • Korea • Mexico • Singapore • Spain • United Kingdom • United States

Pathways 4
Listening, Speaking, and Critical Thinking
Paul MacIntyre
Keith S. Folse / Series Consultant

Publisher: Sherrise Roehr

Executive Editor: Laura Le Dréan

Acquisitions Editor: Tom Jefferies

Associate Development Editor:
  Marissa Petrarca

Director of Global Marketing: Ian Martin

Marketing Manager: Caitlin Driscoll

Marketing Manager: Katie Kelley

Marketing Manager: Emily Stewart

Director of Content and Media Production:
  Michael Burggren

Content Project Manager: Daisy Sosa

Manufacturing Manager: Marcia Locke

Manufacturing Buyer: Marybeth Hennebury

Cover Design: Page 2 LLC

Cover Image: JIM BRANDENBURG/MINDEN
  PICTURES/National Geographic Image
  Collection

Interior Design: Page 2 LLC

Composition: Cenveo Publisher Services/
  Nesbitt Graphics, Inc.

For permission to use material from this text or product,
submit all requests online at **www.cengage.com/permissions**
Further permissions questions can be emailed to
permissionrequest@cengage.com

Library of Congress Control Number: 2011944915

International Student Edition:

ISBN-13: 978-1-111-34778-9

ISBN-10: 1-111-34778-6

U.S. Edition:

ISBN-13: 978-1-111-34779-6

ISBN-10: 1-111-34779-4

Package-ISBN:

ISBN-13: 978-1-133-30766-2

ISBN-10: 1-133-30766-3

National Geographic Learning
20 Channel Center Street
Boston, MA 02210
USA

Cengage Learning is a leading provider of customized learning solutions with office locations around the globe, including Singapore, the United Kingdom, Australia, Mexico, Brazil, and Japan.

Cengage Learning products are represented in Canada by Nelson Education, Ltd.

Visit National Geographic Learning online at **elt.heinle.com**

Visit our corporate website at **www.cengage.com**

Printed in the United States of America
4 5 6 7 8 19 18 17 16 15

ACKNOWLEDGMENTS

The author and publisher would like to thank the following reviewers:

UNITED STATES **Adrianne Aiko Thompson**, Miami Dade College, Miami, Florida; **Gokhan Alkanat**, Auburn University at Montgomery, Alabama; **Nikki Ashcraft**, Shenandoah University, VA; **Karin Avila-John**, University of Dayton, Ohio; **Shirley Baker**, Alliant International University, California; **John Baker**, Oakland Community College, Michigan; **Evina Baquiran Torres**, Zoni Language Centers, New York; **Michelle Bell**, University of South Florida, Florida; **Nancy Boyer**, Golden West College, California; **Carol Brutza**, Gateway Community College, Connecticut; **Sarah Camp**, University of Kentucky, Center for ESL, Kentucky; **Maria Caratini**, Eastfield College, Texas; **Ana Maria Cepero**, Miami Dade College, Florida; **Daniel Chaboya**, Tulsa Community College, Oklahoma; **Patricia Chukwueke**, English Language Institute – UCSD Extension, California; **Julia A. Correia**, Henderson State University, Connecticut; **Suzanne Crisci**, Bunker Hill Community College, Massachusetts; **Katie Crowder**, University of North Texas, Texas; **Lynda Dalgish**, Concordia College, New York; **Jeffrey Diluglio**, Center for English Language and Orientation Programs: Boston University, Massachusetts; **Tim DiMatteo**, Southern New Hampshire University, New Hampshire; **Scott Dirks**, Kaplan International Center at Harvard Square, Massachusetts; **Margo Downey**, Center for English Language and Orientation Programs: Boston University, Massachusetts; **John Drezek**, Richland College, Texas; **Anwar El-Issa**, Antelope Valley College, California; **Anrisa Fannin**, The International Education Center at Diablo Valley College, California; **Jennie Farnell**, University of Connecticut, American Language Program, Connecticut; **Mark Fisher**, Lone Star College, Texas; **Celeste Flowers**, University of Central Arkansas, Arkansas; **John Fox**, English Language Institute, Georgia; **Pradel R. Frank**, Miami Dade College, Florida; **Sally Gearheart**, Santa Rosa Jr. College, California; **Karen Grubbs**, ELS Language Centers, Florida; **Joni Hagigeorges**, Salem State University, Massachusetts; **Valerie Heming**, University of Central Missouri, Missouri; **Mary Hill**, North Shore Community College, Massachusetts; **Harry L. Holden**, North Lake College, Texas; **Ingrid Holm**, University of Massachusetts Amherst, Massachusetts; **Marianne Hsu Santelli**, Middlesex County College, New Jersey; **Katie Hurter**, Lone Star College – North Harris, Texas; **Justin Jernigan**, Georgia Gwinnett College, Georgia; **Barbara A. Jonckheere**, American Language Institute at California State University, Long Beach, California; **Susan Jordan**, Fisher College, Massachusetts; **Maria Kasparova**, Bergen Community College, New Jersey; **Gail Kellersberger**, University of Houston-Downtown, Texas; **Christina Kelso**, Austin Peay State University, Tennessee; **Daryl Kinney**, Los Angeles City College, California; **Leslie Kosel Eckstein**, Hillsborough Community College, Florida; **Beth Kozbial Ernst**, University of Wisconsin-Eau Claire, Wisconsin; **Jennifer Lacroix**, Center for English Language and Orientation Programs: Boston University, Massachusetts; **Stuart Landers**, Missouri State University, Missouri; **Margaret V. Layton**, University of Nevada, Reno Intensive English Language Center, Nevada; **Heidi Lieb**, Bergen Community College, New Jersey; **Kerry Linder**, Language Studies International New York, New York; **Jenifer Lucas-Uygun**, Passaic County Community College, New Jersey; **Alison MacAdams**, Approach International Student Center, Massachusetts; **Craig Machado**, Norwalk Community College, Connecticut; **Andrew J. MacNeill**, Southwestern College, California; **Melanie A. Majeski**, Naugatuck Valley Community College, Connecticut; **Wendy Maloney**, College of DuPage, Illinois; **Chris Mares**, University of Maine – Intensive English Institute, Maine; **Josefina Mark**, Union County College, New Jersey; **Connie Mathews**, Nashville State Community College, Tennessee; **Bette Matthews**, Mid-Pacific Institute, Hawaii; **Marla McDaniels Heath**, Norwalk Community College, Connecticut; **Kimberly McGrath Moreira**, University of Miami, Florida; **Sara McKinnon**, College of Marin, California; **Christine Mekkaoui**, Pittsburg State University, Kansas; **Holly A. Milkowart**, Johnson County Community College, Kansas; **Warren Mosher**, University of Miami, Florida; **Lukas Murphy**, Westchester Community College, New York; **Elena Nehrebecki**, Hudson Community College, New Jersey; **Bjarne Nielsen**, Central Piedmont Community College, North Carolina; **David Nippoldt**, Reedley College, California; **Lucia Parsley**, Virginia Commonwealth University, Virginia; **Wendy Patriquin**, Parkland College, Illinois; **Marion Piccolomini**, Communicate With Ease, LTD, Pennsylvania; **Carolyn Prager**, Spanish-American Institute, New York; **Eileen Prince**, Prince Language Associates Incorporated, Massachusetts; **Sema Pulak**, Texas A & M University, Texas; **James T. Raby**, Clark University, Massachusetts; **Anouchka Rachelson**, Miami-Dade College, Florida; **Lynn Ramage Schaefer**, University of Central Arkansas, Arkansas; **Sherry Rasmussen**, DePaul University, Illinois; **Amy Renehan**, University of Washington, Washington; **Esther Robbins**, Prince George's Community College, Pennsylvania; **Helen Roland**, Miami Dade College, Florida; **Linda Roth**, Vanderbilt University English Language Center, Tennessee; **Janine Rudnick**, El Paso Community College, Texas; **Rita Rutkowski Weber**, University of Wisconsin – Milwaukee, Wisconsin; **Elena Sapp**, INTO Oregon State University, Oregon; **Margaret Shippey**, Miami Dade College, Florida; **Lisa Sieg**, Murray State University, Kentucky; **Alison Stamps**, ESL Center at Mississippi State University, Mississippi; **Peggy Street**, ELS Language Centers, Miami, Florida; **Lydia Streiter**, York College Adult Learning Center, New York; **Nicholas Taggart**, Arkansas State University, Arkansas; **Marcia Takacs**, Coastline Community College, California; **Tamara Teffeteller**, University of California Los Angeles, American Language Center, California; **Rebecca Toner**, English Language Programs, University of Pennsylvania, Pennsylvania; **William G. Trudeau**, Missouri Southern State University, Missouri; **Troy Tucker**, Edison State College, Florida; **Maria Vargas-O'Neel**, Miami Dade College, Florida; **Amerca Vazquez**, Miami Dade College, Florida; **Alison Vinande**, Modesto Junior College, California; **Christie Ward**, Intensive English Language Program, Central Connecticut State University, Connecticut; **Colin S. Ward**, Lone Star College- North Harris, Texas; **Denise L. Warner**, Lansing Community College, Michigan; **Wendy Wish-Bogue**, Valencia Community College, Florida; **Cissy Wong**, Sacramento City College, California; **Kimberly Yoder**, Kent State University, ESL Center, Ohio.

ASIA **Teoh Swee Ai**, Universiti Teknologi Mara, Malaysia; **Nor Azni Abdullah**, Universiti Teknologi Mara, Malaysia; **Thomas E. Bieri**, Nagoya College, Japan; **Paul Bournhonesque**, Seoul National University of Technology, Korea; **Michael C. Cheng**, National Chengchi University; **Fu-Dong Chiou**, National Taiwan University; **Derek Currie**, Korea University, Sejong Institute of Foreign Language Studies, Korea; **Christoph A. Hafner**, City University of Hong Kong, Hong Kong; **Wenhua Hsu**, I-Shou University; **Helen Huntley**, Hanoi University, Vietnam; **Rob Higgens**, Ritsumeikan University, Japan; **Shih Fan Kao**, JinWen University of Science and Technology; **Ikuko Kashiwabara**, Osaka Electro-Communication University, Japan; **Richard S. Lavin**, Prefecturla University of Kumamoto, Japan; **Mike Lay**, American Institute, Cambodia; **Byoung-Kyo Lee**, Yonsei University, Korea; **Lin Li**, Capital Normal University, China; **Hudson Murrell**, Baiko Gakuin University, Japan; **Keiichi Narita**, Niigata University, Japan; **Huynh Thi Ai Nguyen**, Vietnam USA Society, Vietnam; **James Pham**, IDP Phnom Penh, Cambodia; **Duncan Rose**, British Council, Singapore; **Simone Samuels**, The Indonesia Australia Language Foundation Jakarta, Indonesia; **Wang Songmei**, Beijing Institute of Education Faculty, China; **Chien-Wen Jenny Tseng**, National Sun Yat-Sen University; **Hajime Uematsu**, Hirosaki University, Japan

AUSTRALIA **Susan Austin**, University of South Australia, **Joanne Cummins**, Swinburne College; **Pamela Humphreys**, Griffith University

LATIN AMERICA AND THE CARIBBEAN **Ramon Aguilar**, Universidad Tecnológica de Hermosillo, México; **Livia de Araujo Donnini Rodrigues**, University of São Paolo, Brazil; **Cecilia Avila**, Universidad de Xapala, México; Beth Bartlett, Centro Cultural Colombo Americano, Cali, Colombia; **Raúl Billini**, Colegio Loyola, Dominican Republic; **Nohora Edith Bryan**, Universidad de La Sabana, Colombia; **Raquel Hernández Cantú**, Instituto Tecnológico de Monterrey, Mexico; **Millie Commander**, Inter American University of Puerto Rico, Puerto Rico; **Edwin Marín-Arroyo**, Instituto Tecnológico de Costa Rica; **Rosario Mena**, Instituto Cultural Dominico-Americano, Dominican Republic; **Elizabeth Ortiz Lozada**, COPEI-COPOL English Institute, Ecuador; **Gilberto Rios Zamora**, Sinaloa State Language Center, Mexico; **Patricia Veciños**, El Instituto Cultural Argentino Norteamericano, Argentina

MIDDLE EAST AND NORTH AFRICA **Tom Farkas**, American University of Cairo, Egypt; **Ghada Hozayen**, Arab Academy for Science, Technology and Maritime Transport, Egypt

Scope and Sequence

Unit	Academic Pathways	Vocabulary	Listening Skills
1 **Urban Challenges** *Page 1* **Academic Track:** Interdisciplinary	**Lesson A:** Listening to a Lecture Discussing Pros and Cons of Tourism **Lesson B:** Listening to a Conversation Between Classmates Presenting a Problem and Proposing Solutions	Understanding Meaning from Context Using a Dictionary Using New Vocabulary to Complete a Text	Predicting Content Listening for Main Ideas Listening for Details **Pronunciation:** Pronouncing the Letter *t*
2 **Protecting Our Planet** *Page 21* **Academic Track:** Life Science	**Lesson A:** Listening to a Guided Tour Brainstorming Ideas about Conservation **Lesson B:** Listening to a Student Debate Participating in a Debate	Understanding Meaning from Context Using a Dictionary Using New Vocabulary to Complete a News Story Using New Vocabulary to Discuss Unit Content	Note-taking Listening for Main Ideas Evaluating Arguments in a Debate **Pronunciation:** Pronouncing –*s* endings
3 **Beauty and Appearance** *Page 41* **Academic Track:** Sociology, Aesthetics	**Lesson A:** Listening to a News Report Conducting a Survey **Lesson B:** Listening to an Informal Conversation Giving a Group Presentation	Understanding Meaning from Context Using New Vocabulary to Ask and Answer Questions Using a Dictionary Using New Vocabulary to Complete a Conversation Understanding Suffixes	Listening for Key Concepts Listening for Main Ideas Listening for Details Predicting Content Note-Taking Listening for Specific Information **Pronunciation:** Pronouncing /η/ and /ηk/
4 **Energy Issues** *Page 61* **Academic Track:** Interdisciplinary	**Lesson A:** Listening to a Guest Speaker Role-Playing a Town Meeting **Lesson B:** Listening to a Study Group Discussion Creating and Using Visuals in a Presentation	Understanding Meaning from Context Using a Dictionary Using New Vocabulary to Complete an Interview Using New Vocabulary to Discuss Themes of the Unit	Predicting Content Listening for Main Ideas Outlining Listening for Key Concepts Listening for Details **Pronunciation:** Stressing Two-Word Compounds
5 **Migration** *Page 81* **Academic Track:** Life Science, Biology	**Lesson A:** Listening to a Radio Show Talking about your Family History **Lesson B:** Listening to a Conversation Between Friends Doing a Research Presentation	Understanding Meaning from Context Using a Dictionary Choosing the Right Definition Using New Vocabulary to Complete an Article Using New Vocabulary to Discuss Personal Opinions	Predicting Content Listening for Key Concepts Note-Taking Predicting Content Listening for Main Ideas **Pronunciation:** Using Question Intonation

Grammar	Speaking Skills	Viewing	Critical Thinking Skills
The Passive Voice Using an Agent in Passive Voice Sentences	Introducing a Topic Agreeing or Disagreeing **Student to Student:** Apologizing for Interrupting **Presentation Skills:** Making Eye Contact	**Video:** *Tuareg Farmers* Viewing to Confirm Predictions Viewing for Main Ideas	Inferring Information Not Stated in a Conversation Understanding Visuals Organizing Ideas for a Discussion Using New Vocabulary in a Discussion Using a Graphic Organizer **Critical Thinking Focus:** Identifying the Lecture Topic
Restrictive Adjective Clauses Non-Restrictive Adjective Clauses	Introducing Examples Brainstorming Responding to and Refuting an Argument **Student to Student:** Expressing Encouragement **Presentation Skills:** Speaking with Confidence	**Video:** *Crocodiles of Sri Lanka* Note-Taking while Viewing Using Video Information to Role-play	Expressing Individual Ideas Using New Grammar and Vocabulary Restating Information from Notes Understanding Visuals Organizing Ideas for a Discussion Expressing and Explaining Opinions Arguing a Point of View **Critical Thinking Focus:** Evaluating Arguments in a Debate
Compound Adjectives Tag Questions	Paraphrasing Asking for Clarification **Student to Student:** Asking about Personal Opinions **Presentation Skills:** Preparing Your Notes	**Video:** *Skin Mask* Predicting Content Viewing for Main Ideas Sequencing Events	Expressing and Explaining Opinions about Beauty Paraphrasing and Explaining Quotations Creating Sentences and Using New Grammar Discussing Survey Results Organizing a Group Presentation **Critical Thinking Focus:** Understanding Quotations
The Future Perfect The Future Perfect Progressive	Emphasizing Important Information Expressing Approval and Disapproval **Student to Student:** Conceding a Point **Presentation Skills:** Fighting Nervousness	**Video:** *Solar Power* Viewing for Specific Information Viewing for Main Ideas	Discussing Unit Content Using New Vocabulary Using a Graphic Organizer to Take Notes Understanding Visuals Evaluating Pros and Cons of Energy Sources Analyzing and Ranking Statements and Providing Reasons **Critical Thinking Focus:** Using an Outline to Take Notes
Using Past Modals to Make Guesses about the Past Using Past Modals to Make Inferences	Expressing Surprise Expressing Hopes **Student to Student:** Expressing Interest **Presentation Skills:** Preparing for Audience Questions	**Video:** *Wildebeest Migration* Understanding and Interpreting Visuals Sequencing Events Note-Taking	Making Inferences about Unit Content Presenting Theories and Evidence about Early Humans Using a Graphic Organizer Understanding Visuals Restating Information from a Listening **Critical Thinking Focus:** Understanding Scientific Theories

Scope and Sequence

Unit	Academic Pathways	Vocabulary	Listening Skills
6 **Tradition and Progress** *Page 101* **Academic Track:** Interdisciplinary	**Lesson A:** Listening to a Student Presentation Interviewing a Classmate **Lesson B:** Listening to a Study Group Discussion Evaluating Web Sources	Understanding Meaning from Context Using a Dictionary Choosing the Right Definition Using New Vocabulary to Complete an Article Using New Vocabulary to Discuss Personal Experiences	Listening for Main Ideas Completing an Idea Map While Listening Note-Taking **Pronunciation:** Linking Consonants to Vowels
7 **Money in Our Lives** *Page 121* **Academic Track:** Economics	**Lesson A:** Listening to a Radio Interview Discussing Values **Lesson B:** Listening to a Conversation Between Friends Preparing a Budget	Understanding Meaning from Context Using a Dictionary Choosing the Right Definition Using New Vocabulary to Complete an Article Using New Vocabulary to Relate to Personal Experiences	Listening for Main Ideas Listening for Details Listening for Information to Complete an Outline **Pronunciation:** Vowel-to-Vowel Linking
8 **Health and Fitness** *Page 141* **Academic Track:** Health and Medicine	**Lesson A:** Listening to a Question-and-Answer Session Discussing Environmental Health Concerns **Lesson B:** Listening to a Conversation Between Friends Sharing Advice about Health and Fitness	Understanding Meaning from Context Using a Dictionary Understanding Collocations Using New Vocabulary to Complete an Article Identifying Synonyms for New Vocabulary Words	Listening for Main Ideas Listening for Details Listening for Information to Complete a Chart Note-Taking **Pronunciation:** Dropped Syllables
9 **Mind and Memory** *Page 161* **Academic Track:** Psychology/ Brain Science	**Lesson A:** Listening to a TV Show Giving a Short Persuasive Speech **Lesson B:** Listening to a Conversation Between Classmates Using Memory Skills to Recall Information	Understanding Meaning from Context Using New Vocabulary to Complete an Article Using New Vocabulary to Discuss Opinions Using a Dictionary Understanding Collocations	Listening for Main Ideas Note-Taking Listening for Details Listening for Information to Complete an Outline **Pronunciation:** Using Word Stress to Clarify Information
10 **Food Concerns** *Page 181* **Academic Track:** Interdisciplinary **Independent Student Handbook** *Page 201*	**Lesson A:** Listening to a PowerPoint Lecture Role-Playing a Debate **Lesson B:** Listening to an Informal Conversation Creating a PowerPoint Presentation	Understanding Meaning from Context Using a Dictionary Using New Vocabulary to Complete an Article	Listening for Main Ideas Synthesizing Information Listening for Details Note-Taking **Pronunciation:** Syllable Stress

Grammar	Speaking Skills	Viewing	Critical Thinking Skills
Verb + Gerund Verb + Object + Infinitive	Using Fillers Expressing a Lack of Knowledge **Student to Student:** Congratulating the Group **Presentation Skills:** Varying Your Voice Volume	**Video:** *Farm Restoration* Viewing for Main Ideas Viewing for Specific Information Note-Taking	Understanding and Using Buzzwords in a Conversation Interviewing Classmates and Analyzing Feedback Relating Unit Content to Personal Opinions Comparing and Contrasting Cultures Using Unit Content Analyzing and Discussing Web Sites **Critical Thinking Focus:** Evaluating Numbers and Statistics
Using Connectors to Add and Emphasize Information Using Connectors of Concession	Showing that You are Following a Conversation Digressing from the Topic **Student to Student:** Asking Sensitive Questions **Presentation Skills:** Dealing with Difficult Questions	**Video:** *The Black Diamonds of Provence* Viewing for Main Ideas Note-Taking While Viewing	Orally Summarizing Information from Notes Relating Unit Content to Personal Experiences Applying New Grammar to Discussions about Finance Understanding and Analyzing Visuals Interpreting Information about Budgets **Critical Thinking Focus:** Summarizing
Phrasal Verbs Three-Word Phrasal Verbs	Expressing Uncertainty Showing Understanding Sharing Advice **Student to Student:** Going First **Presentation Skills:** Relating to Your Audience	**Video:** *Paraguay Shaman* Applying Prior Knowledge to Video Content Viewing for Main Ideas Viewing for Specific Details	Proposing Solutions for Health Problems Relating Unit Content to Personal Experiences Evaluating a Health-Related Lawsuit Using New Grammar and Vocabulary while Role-Playing a Scenario Expressing and Explaining Opinions **Critical Thinking Focus:** Asking Questions for Further Research
Subject-Verb Agreement with Quantifiers Present Participle Phrases	Enumerating Checking Background Knowledge **Student to Student:** Joining a Group **Presentation Skills:** Using Gestures	**Video:** *Animal Minds* Viewing for Main Ideas Viewing for Specific Information Sequencing Events	Making Comparisons about Human and Animal Intelligence Practicing Memory-Building Techniques Making Inferences Organizing Ideas for a Presentation Using New Grammar to Summarize Unit Content **Critical Thinking Focus:** Questioning Results
Causative Verbs Subjunctive Verbs with *That* Clauses	Confirming Understanding Giving Recommendations **Student to Student:** Expressing Opinions **Presentation Skills:** Preparing Visuals for Display	**Video:** *Slow Food* Viewing for Main Ideas Viewing to Complete Direct Quotations	Proposing Solutions for Food Shortages Expressing Opinions about Unit Content Deducing Meaning from Context Understanding Visuals Creating Effective Visuals **Critical Thinking Focus:** Remaining Objective

Each unit consists of two lessons which include the following sections:

Building Vocabulary
Using Vocabulary
Developing Listening Skills
Exploring Spoken English
Speaking (called "Engage" in Lesson B)

An **academic pathway** is clearly labeled for learners, starting with formal listening (e.g., lectures) and moving to a more informal context (e.g., a conversation between students in a study group).

The **"Exploring the Theme"** section provides a visual introduction to the unit and encourages learners to think critically and share ideas about the unit topic.

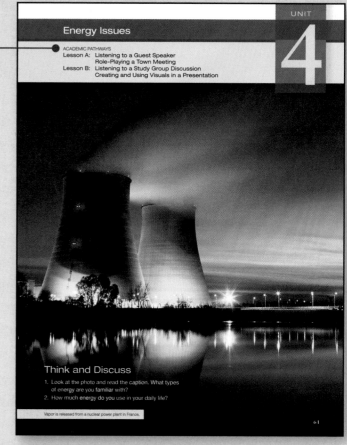

UNIT
4

Energy Issues

ACADEMIC PATHWAYS
Lesson A: Listening to a Guest Speaker
           Role-Playing a Town Meeting
Lesson B: Listening to a Study Group Discussion
           Creating and Using Visuals in a Presentation

Think and Discuss

1. Look at the photo and read the caption. What types of energy are you familiar with?
2. How much energy do you use in your daily life?

Vapor is released from a nuclear power plant in France.

61

Exploring the Theme:
Energy Issues

A | Look at the photos and read the captions. Then answer the questions.

1. How do you think energy use has changed over time?
2. In the future, do you think you will be using more or less electricity than you do now? Why do you think so?
3. Would you be willing to live next to a large energy facility such as a nuclear power plant or wind farm? Explain your answer.

Big Power, Big Risks

By the year 2030, the demand for energy is expected to be double what it was in the year 2000. Providing the enormous quantity of energy the world needs is a difficult task, and there is often risk for workers, the public, and the environment.

In this village, lights shine from nearly every house. However, the world is still far away from providing inexpensive electricity. In fact, about one in four people still have no electricity at all.

Wind power provides energy to farms and homes in Abilene, Texas.

62 | UNIT 4   ENERGY ISSUES | 63

Key academic and high-frequency vocabulary
is introduced, practiced, and expanded throughout
each unit. Lessons A and B each present and
practice 10 terms.

A **"Developing Listening Skills"** section follows a before, during, and after listening approach to give learners the tools necessary to master listening skills for a variety of contexts.

Listening activities encourage learners to listen for and consolidate key information, reinforcing the language, and allowing learners to think critically about the information they hear.

A | Meaning from Context. Read and listen to the news report about the Deepwater Horizon oil spill. Notice the words in blue. These are words you will hear and use in Lesson A.

On April 20, 2010, one of the worst oil spills in history began in the Gulf of Mexico. The spill occurred at an oil rig, called the Deepwater Horizon, which is owned by the BP company. A buildup of pressure caused natural gas to shoot up suddenly from the ocean floor. The gas triggered a terrible explosion and a fire on the oil rig. After the explosion, the crew abandoned the platform and escaped in lifeboats. Unfortunately, eleven workers were never found.

A beach in the United States is covered with oil after the Deepwater Horizon oil spill.

For weeks, no one was sure just how much oil was being released into the Gulf of Mexico. Gradually, information about the damage from the oil spill emerged. It was discovered that between 50,000 to 60,000 barrels of oil a day were flowing into the Gulf. Experts from BP and other organizations tried to stop the spill, but it continued for nearly three months. By the time the leak was stopped, the beautiful blue waters of the Gulf had been contaminated with nearly 5 million barrels of oil.

The disaster did serious harm to the fishing and tourism industries in the southern United States. Pictures of birds that had been exposed to the thick oil appeared daily in the news. The American public reacted angrily, and the spill created a huge controversy. Some people even wanted to stop oil companies from drilling in the Gulf of Mexico. BP set aside 20 billion dollars to compensate fishermen, hotel owners, and store owners whose businesses were impacted by the spill.

B | Match each word in blue from exercise **A** with its definition. Use your dictionary to help you.

1. triggered (v.) _____
2. abandoned (v.) _____
3. released (v.) _____
4. emerged (v.) _____
5. experts (n.) _____
6. contaminated (v.) _____
7. exposed (v.) _____
8. reacted (v.) _____
9. controversy (n.) _____
10. compensate (v.) _____

a. to pay someone to replace lost money or things
b. became known; appeared
c. responded to
d. caused an event to begin to happen
e. left a place, thing, or person permanently
f. people who are very skilled or who know a lot about a particular subject
g. entered the surrounding atmosphere or area; freed
h. a disagreement, especially about a public policy or moral issue that people feel strongly about
i. made something dirty, harmful, or dangerous because of chemicals or radiation
j. placed in a dangerous situation

Before Listening

Predicting Content. Work with a partner. Look at the map and diagram. Discuss the questions.

1. Use your dictionary and look up these terms: *containment, radiation, radioactive, half-life.* How do you predict these words will be used in the lecture?
2. Locate the containment structure in the diagram. Why do you think this structure is important? Explain your ideas.

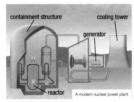

A modern nuclear power plant

Listening: A Guest Speaker

Critical Thinking Focus: Using an Outline to Take Notes

Using an outline can help you take organized and clear notes. In an outline, indicate main ideas with Roman numerals (I, II, III) and capital letters (A, B, C). Indicate details with numbers. As information becomes more specific, move it to the right.

A | Listen to the introduction to a lecture about the Chernobyl nuclear disaster. Read the outline as you listen.

> I. Background
>   A. 1970s & 1980s: Soviet Union developed nuclear technology
>   B. 1986: 25 plants w/ safety probs.
> II. Chernobyl disaster
>   A. Causes
>   1. Mistakes during safety test
>   2. No containment building to limit fire and radiation
>   B. Result: explosion → people dead

B | Discussion. With a partner, discuss the questions. Refer to the outline in exercise **A**.

1. What topics did the introduction cover?
2. Which items are main ideas? Which items are details?

C | Listening for Main Ideas. Listen to the entire lecture and answer the questions.

1. Check (✔) each effect of the explosion that the speaker mentions.
   ___ a. People were forced to leave their homes.
   ___ b. Animals died from exposure to radiation.
   ___ c. Young people became ill with thyroid cancer.
   ___ d. Billions of dollars were spent on health and cleanup costs.
   ___ e. Modern nuclear power plants are built with containment structures.
2. What happened to the town of Pripyat?
   a. It was abandoned.
   b. It burned to the ground.
   c. It was turned into a tourist attraction.
3. What is surprising about Chernobyl today?
   a. The residents of Pripyat have returned.
   b. Many animals have come back to the area.
   c. The radiation from the explosion has disappeared.

D | Outlining. Listen again. Continue the outline from exercise **A** on page 66. Complete the outline with details from the lecture. (See page 206 of the *Independent Student Handbook* for more information on outlining.)

> C. The Chernobyl plant today
>   1. Still extremely _____
>   2. There are plans to build a _____
> D. Radioactivity
>   1. Many areas still contaminated with cesium _____
>   2. Half-life of _____ years
> E. The exclusion zone today
>   1. _____ people live there
>   2. Animals have returned, for ex. _____

After Listening

Discussion. With a partner, answer the questions. Use your notes as well as your own ideas.

1. Describe the town of Pripyat before and after the disaster.
2. These days, a small number of tourists travel to Chernobyl. Would you go there if you had the opportunity?

Language Function

Emphasizing Important Information

Here are some expressions used to emphasize important information.

Don't forget that . . .
Let me stress that . . .
I want to emphasize that . . .
I would like to stress that . . .

I would like to point out that . . .
You need to remember that . . .
It is important to note/remember that . . .

A | In the lecture about Chernobyl, the speaker used a number of useful expressions to emphasize her point. Listen to the excerpts and fill in the missing expressions.

1. _____ Chernobyl had no containment structure. This building would have limited the fire and contained the radioactivity.

2. Thyroid cancer can be cured, but _____ survivors must spend a lifetime taking medication.

3. _____, however, that it will be decades before large numbers of people are allowed to come back and live in the exclusion zone.

Wild horses, called Przewalski horses, walk through the Chernobyl exclusion zone. These horses are extinct in the wild and can only be found in a few nature reserves and in the Chernobyl exclusion zone.

B | Form a group with two other students. Choose one of the types of energy below and read the facts. Then tell the members of your group what you know about your energy source. Add your own ideas. Emphasize the fact that you think is the most interesting.

> Oil prices are rising. For example, it cost me almost $60 to put gas in my car yesterday. Last year, it would have cost me only $40. Still, it is important to remember that . . .

Oil
- The price of oil is rising.
- Oil spills pollute the environment.
- The top three oil-producing countries in the world are Saudi Arabia, Russia, and the United States.

Coal
- Coal deposits in the United States contain more energy than all the world's oil reserves combined.
- Coal is a relatively inexpensive energy source.
- Coal mining is dangerous. Between 1969 and 2000, more than 20,000 coal miners were killed.

Wind
- Wind power is clean, but is sometimes very noisy.
- The world will never run out of wind.
- Denmark gets 20 percent of its electricity from wind power.

• The **"Exploring Spoken English"** section allows students to examine and practice specific grammar points and language functions from the unit while enabling them to sharpen their listening and speaking skills.

• Lesson A closes with a **full page of "Speaking" activities** including pair and group work activities, increasing learner confidence when communicating in English.

• **A variety of activity types** simulate the academic classroom, where multiple skills must be applied simultaneously for success.

SPEAKING

Role-Playing a Town Meeting

A | Form a group with three other students. You will role-play a city council meeting about building a nuclear power plant. Read the situation and the role cards. Assign two students to each role.

Situation: The city council has approved a plan to build a nuclear power plant in your city. A small group of residents are against the plan. They are going to meet with city council members to discuss their concerns.

Role #1: Residents against the Nuclear Power Plant

1. Nuclear power plants aren't safe. We don't want a nuclear accident to happen here.

2. Nuclear power plants produce waste that is dangerous for many years.

3. People who live near a nuclear power plant might get cancer.

Role #2: City Council Members

1. Nuclear safety technology has greatly advanced in recent years.

2. France, Belgium, and Slovakia rely on nuclear power for more than 50 percent of their electricity. There have been no big nuclear accidents in those countries.

3. Nuclear power could help us stop using oil.

B | Work with the group member who shares your role. Think of more arguments to support your point. In addition, try to think of responses to the other side's arguments.

> I think they will say that . . .
> If they say that, we should emphasize that . . .

C | Role-Playing. Role-play the discussion in your group. Use expressions of emphasis when appropriate.

> Thank you for meeting with us. We have a few concerns about this nuclear power plant.
> I understand. First of all, let me stress that we will do everything possible to make this power plant safe.

Student to Student: Conceding a Point

In a debate or discussion, people often argue from different points of view. If an argument is very convincing to you, you can let the other person know that you agree with their point or that you accept that their point is true. Here are some expressions to concede a point.

Good point.
Fair enough.
I'll give you that.

● The **"Viewing" section** works as a content-bridge between Lesson A and Lesson B and includes two pages of activities based on a fascinating video from National Geographic.

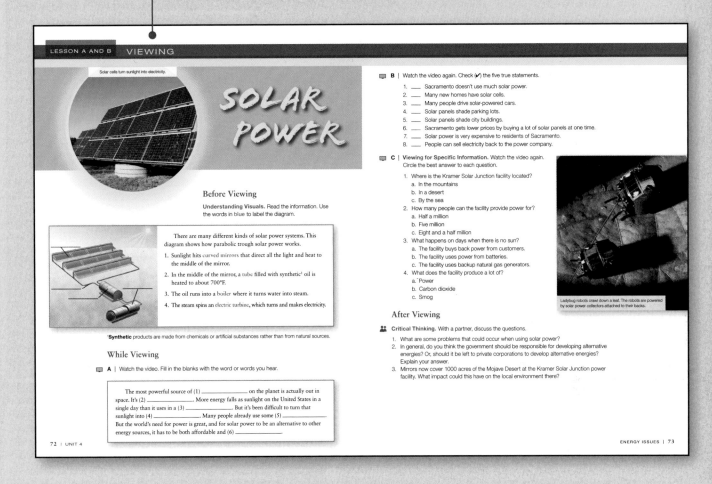

LESSON A AND B   VIEWING

Solar cells turn sunlight into electricity.

SOLAR POWER

Before Viewing

Understanding Visuals. Read the information. Use the words in blue to label the diagram.

There are many different kinds of solar power systems. This diagram shows how parabolic trough solar power works.

1. Sunlight hits curved mirrors that direct all the light and heat to the middle of the mirror.

2. In the middle of the mirror, a tube filled with synthetic[1] oil is heated to about 700°F.

3. The oil runs into a boiler where it turns water into steam.

4. The steam spins an electric turbine, which turns and makes electricity.

[1]**Synthetic** products are made from chemicals or artificial substances rather than from natural sources.

While Viewing

A | Watch the video. Fill in the blanks with the word or words you hear.

The most powerful source of (1) _____ on the planet is actually out in space. It's (2) _____. More energy falls as sunlight on the United States in a single day than it uses in a (3) _____. But it's been difficult to turn that sunlight into (4) _____. Many people already use some (5) _____. But the world's need for power is great, and for solar power to be an alternative to other energy sources, it has to be both affordable and (6) _____.

B | Watch the video again. Check (✔) the five true statements.

1. ____ Sacramento doesn't use much solar power.
2. ____ Many new homes have solar cells.
3. ____ Many people drive solar-powered cars.
4. ____ Solar panels shade parking lots.
5. ____ Solar panels shade city buildings.
6. ____ Sacramento gets lower prices by buying a lot of solar panels at one time.
7. ____ Solar power is very expensive to residents of Sacramento.
8. ____ People can sell electricity back to the power company.

C | **Viewing for Specific Information.** Watch the video again. Circle the best answer to each question.

1. Where is the Kramer Solar Junction facility located?
   a. In the mountains
   b. In a desert
   c. By the sea
2. How many people can the facility provide power for?
   a. Half a million
   b. Five million
   c. Eight and a half million
3. What happens on days when there is no sun?
   a. The facility buys back power from customers.
   b. The facility uses power from batteries.
   c. The facility uses backup natural gas generators.
4. What does the facility produce a lot of?
   a. Power
   b. Carbon dioxide
   c. Smog

Ladybug robots crawl down a leaf. The robots are powered by solar power collectors attached to their backs.

After Viewing

Critical Thinking. With a partner, discuss the questions.

1. What are some problems that could occur when using solar power?
2. In general, do you think the government should be responsible for developing alternative energies? Or, should it be left to private corporations to develop alternative energies? Explain your answer.
3. Mirrors now cover 1000 acres of the Mojave Desert at the Kramer Solar Junction power facility. What impact could this have on the local environment there?

72 | UNIT 4

ENERGY ISSUES | 73

● **A DVD for each level** contains 10 authentic videos from National Geographic specially adapted for English language learners.

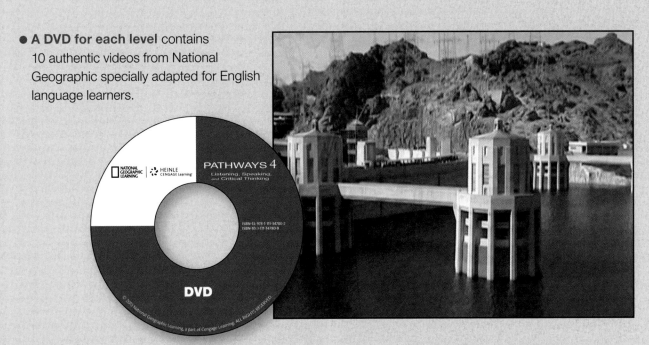

NATIONAL GEOGRAPHIC LEARNING · HEINLE CENGAGE Learning

PATHWAYS 4
Listening, Speaking, and Critical Thinking

ISBN-13: 978-1-111-34780-2
ISBN-10: 1-111-34780-8

DVD

© 2012 National Geographic Learning, a part of Cengage Learning. ALL RIGHTS RESERVED.

Critical thinking activities are integrated in every unit, encouraging continuous engagement in developing academic skills.

An **"Engage" section** at the end of the unit challenges learners with an end-of-unit presentation project. Speaking tips are offered for formal and informal group communication, instructing students to interact appropriately in different academic situations.

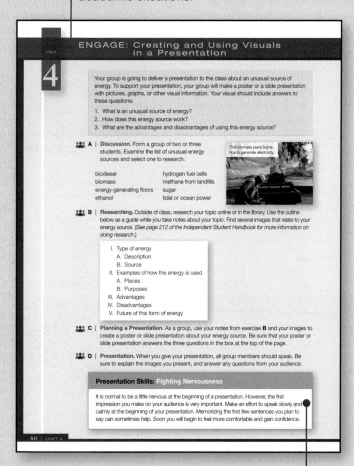

"Presentation Skills" boxes offer helpful tips and suggestions for successful academic presentations.

A 19-page **"Independent Student Handbook"** is conveniently located in the back of the book and provides helpful self-study strategies for students to become better independent learners.

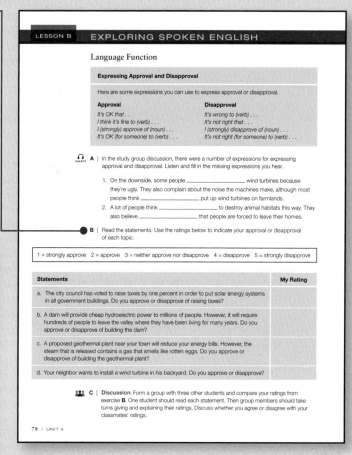

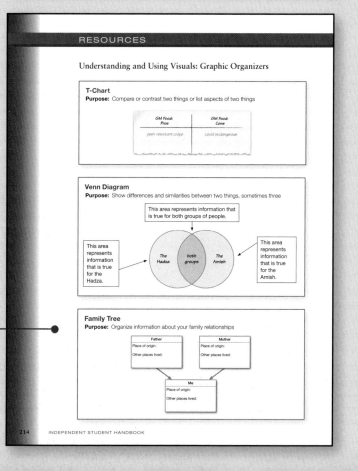

For the Teacher:

Perfect for integrating language practice with exciting visuals, **video clips from National Geographic** bring the sights and sounds of our world into the classroom.

A **Teacher's Guide** is available in an easy-to-use format and includes teacher's notes, expansion activities, and answer keys for activities in the student book.

The Assessment CD-ROM with Exam*View*® is a test-generating software program with a data bank of ready-made questions designed to allow teachers to assess students quickly and effectively.

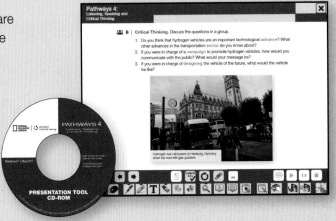

Bringing a new dimension to the language learning classroom, the **Classroom Presentation Tool CD-ROM** makes instruction clearer and learning easier through interactive activities, audio and video clips, and Presentation Worksheets.

For the Student:

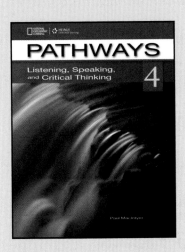

The **Student Book** helps students achieve academic success in and outside of the classroom.

Audio CDs contain the audio recordings for the exercises in the student books.

ELT Powered by MyELT, the **Online Workbook** has both teacher-led and self-study options. It contains 10 National Geographic video clips, supported by interactive, automatically graded activities that practice the skills learned in the student books.

Visit elt.heinle.com/pathways for additional teacher and student resources.

LISTENING AND TEXT

5-7,10: Adapted from "Vanishing Venice," by Cathy Newman: National Geographic Magazine, August 2009, **14-16:** Adapted from, "The Singapore Solution," by Mark Jacobson: National Geographic Magazine, January 2010, **19:** Adapted from "Urban Fishing Catches on in Rebounding Rivers" by James Owen: National Geographic Daily News, May 17, 2010, **25:** Adapted from "Forests of the Tide," by Kennedy Warne: National Geographic Magazine, February 2007, **26-27:** Adapted from "Last One," by Verlyn Klinkenborg: National Geographic Magazine, January 2009, **34:** Adapted from "Freshwater Hero," National Geographic Web site, **35:** Adapted from "Wolf Wars" by Douglas Chadwick: National Geographic Magazine, March 2010, **36-37:** Adapted from "Hunters: For the Love of the Land," by Robert M. Poole: National Geographic Magazine, November 2007, **46-47:** Adapted from "The Enigma of Beauty," by Cathy Newman, National Geographic Magazine, January 2000, **46-47:** Adapted from "New 'Golden' Ratios for Facial Beauty," by Pamela Pallett et al., National Institute of Health, January 25, 2010, **56-57:** Adapted from "Dreamweavers," by Cathy Newman: National Geographic Web site, January 1, 2003.

56-57: Adapted from "Artificial Spider Silk Could Be Used for Armor, More," by Brian Handwerk: National Geographic Daily News, January 14, 2005, **64:** Adapted from "Is Another Deepwater Disaster Inevitable?," by Joel K. Bourne, Jr.: National Geographic Magazine, October 2010, **66-67:** Adapted from "The Long Shadow of Chernobyl," by Richard Stone: National Geographic Magazine, April 2006, **84-87:** Adapted from "Human Journey" by James Shreeve: National Geographic Magazine, March 2006, **84-87:** Adapted from "From Africa to Astoria by Way of Everywhere," by James Shreeve: National Geographic Web site, August 17, 2009, **96-97:** Adapted from "Heartbreak on the Serengeti" by Robert M. Poole: National Geographic Magazine, February 2006, **104:** Adapted from "The Hadza," by Michael Finkel: National Geographic Magazine, December 2009, **106-107, 111:** Adapted from "Bhutan's Enlightened Experiment" by Brook Larmer: National Geographic Magazine, March 2008, **110:** Adapted from "Spread of the Amish" by National Geographic Staff: National Geographic Blog Central, July 8, 2009, **114:** Adapted from "Disappearing Languages: Enduring Voices Project," National Geographic Web site, January 2011, **115-117:** Adapted from "Native Lands," by Charles Bowden: National Geographic Magazine, August 2010, **118:** Adapted from " 'Spectacular' Three-Cat Monolith Unearthed in Mexico," by Ker Than: National Geographic Daily News, August 1, 2011, **118:** Adapted from "Machu Picchu's Mysteries Continue to Lure Explorers," by Kelly Hearn and Jason Golomb: National Geographic Web site, **124, 126-127:** Adapted from "Living it Up, Paying it Down," by Mary McPeak: National Geographic Magazine, February 2005, **144, 146-147** Adapted from "The Pollution Within," by David Ewing Duncan: National Geographic Magazine, October 2006, **156-157:** Adapted from "Yosemite Climbing," by Mark Jenkins: National Geographic Magazine, May 2011, **165-167:** Adapted from "Minds of Their Own," by Virginia Morrell: National Geographic Magazine, March 2008; **175:** Adapted from "Young Chimp Outscores College Students in Memory Test," by Malcolm Ritter: National Geographic News, December 3, 2007, **176-177** Adapted from "Remember This" by Joshua Foer: National Geographic Magazine, November 2007, **184, 186-187, 189:** Adapted from "Food: How Altered?," by Jennifer Ackerman: National Geographic Magazine, May 2002, **184:** Adapted from "Food Ark," by Charles Siebert: National Geographic Magazine, July 2011, **194-197:** Adapted from "The Global Food Crisis: The End of Plenty," by Joel K. Bourne, Jr.: National Geographic Magazine, June 2009

PHOTOS

1: Richard Levine/Alamy, **3:** Jodi Cobb/National Geographic Image Collection, **3:** Fritz Hoffmann/National Geographic Image Collection, **4:** Atelier Tekuto, **4:** Andy Z/Used under license from Shutterstock.com, **4:** Frances Roberts/Alamy, **5:** Jo Chambers/Shutterstock.com, **6:** Jodi Cobb/National Geographic Image Collection, **9:** Caitlin Mirra/Shutterstock.com, **11:** Mike Theiss/National Geographic Image Collection, **12:** Frans Lemmens/SuperStock, **13:** Matt Fletcher/Lonely Planet Images/Alamy, **13:** Rich Carey/Shutterstock.com, **14:** Caro/Alamy, **14:** Toshifumi Kitamura/AFP/Getty Images, **16:** Joseph Calev/Shutterstock.com, **19:** James Owen, **21:** Brian J. Skerry/National Geographic Image Collection, **22:** Pi-Lens/Shutterstock.com, **22:** Jason Lugo/iStockphoto.com, **22-23:** Beverly Joubert/National Geographic Image Collection, **24:** All Canada Photos/SuperStock, **25:** Tim Laman/National Geographic Image Collection, **26:** John A. Anderson/Shutterstock.com, **26:** Joel Sartore/National Geographic Image Collection, **28:** Gary Meszaros/Photo Researchers, Inc., **29:** Alexandr Pakhnyushchyy/iStockphoto.com, **29:** CraigRJD/iStockphoto.com, **32:** BsChan/Shutterstock, **33:** Null/FLPA/Alamy, **34:** Joel Sartore/National Geographic Image Collection, **35:** Len Tillim/iStockphoto.com, **36:** Bruno Barbey, Magnum/National Geographic Image Collection, **40:** Perrush/Shutterstock.com, **41:** George Steinmetz/National Geographic Image Collection, **42:** GoGo Images/Jupiter Images, **42:** Greg Dale/National Geographic Image Collection, **42-43:** Mike Theiss/National Geographic Image Collection, **44:** Justin Guariglia/National Geographic Image Collection, **45:** esolla/iStockphoto, **46:** Reprinted from Vision Research, Vol 50, No 2, 25th January 2010, Pallett et al, "New 'Golden' ratios for facial beauty" with permission from Elsevier, **47:** Peter Zagar/National Geographic Image Collection, **49:** Demid Borodin/Shutterstock, **50:** Todd Gipstein/National Geographic Image Collection, **52:** Sarah Leen/National Geographic Image Collection, **52:** Joe McNally/National Geographic Image Collection, **53:** photobywayne/Alamy, **53:** Sarah Leen/National Geographic Image Collection, **54:** John Macdougall/AFP/Getty Images, **55:** Cary Wolinsky/National Geographic Image Collection, **56:** Designer: Alex Soza/Photographer: Peter Svendsen, **56:** Tom Vickers/Splash/Newscom, **56:** Yoshikazu Tsuno/AFP/Getty Images, **58:** Natali Glado/Shutterstock.com, **60:** AJ Wilhelm/National Geographic Image Collection, **60:** Mike Theiss/National Geographic Image Collection, **61:** Hervé Lenain/Hemis/Corbis, **62-63:** Joel Sartore/National Geographic Image Collection, **63:** James M Phelps, Jr/Shutterstock.com, **63:** Michael Utech/Vetta Collection/iStockphoto, **64:** Tyrone Turner/National Geographic Image Collection, **65:** Brendan Howard/Shutterstock.com, **68:** Gerd Ludwig/National Geographic Image Collection, **69:** huyangshu/Shutterstock.com, **69:** nito/Shutterstock.com, **69:** oorka, 2009/Used under license from Shutterstock.com, **72:** Tobias Machhaus/Shutterstock.com, **73:** George Steinmetz/National Geographic Image Collection, **74:** Samuel Acosta/Shutterstock.com, **74:** Image copyright Belinda Pretorius, 2010 Used under license from Shutterstock.com, **75:** Annie Griffiths/National Geographic Image Collection, **79:** Angela Hampton/Angela Hampton Picture Library/Alamy, **80:** Sarah Leen/National Geographic Image Collection, **81:** Norbert Rosing/National Geographic Image Collection, **82:** Bill Bachman/Alamy, **83:** Joe Mcnally/National Geographic Image Collection, **84:** Jim Richardson/National Geographic Image Collection, **86:** Anthony Peritore, **86:** Piero Gherardi, **86:** Valerie Chazottes Louvat, **86:** Lisa Hopgood, **89:** image copyright Paul Banton/used under license from www.shutterstock.com, **89:** mmm/Shutterstock.com, **92:** Beverly Joubert/National Geographic

continued on p.226

Urban Challenges

ACADEMIC PATHWAYS

Lesson A: Listening to a Lecture
           Discussing Pros and Cons of Tourism
Lesson B: Listening to a Conversation between Classmates
           Presenting a Problem and Proposing Solutions

Think and Discuss

1. What are some of the problems that modern cities face?
   How can cities solve these problems?
2. Would you move to a city that is dealing with challenges
   such as overcrowding? Explain.

In New York City, people walk by a mural by a Brazilian graffiti artist.

Exploring the Theme:
Urban Challenges

A | Look at the map and map key. Then answer the questions.

1. What is the largest city in the world? What are some other large cities?
2. What do you notice about the location of cities in relation to large bodies of water?
3. By 2040, more than half of the world's population will live in urban areas. Imagine this map for the year 2040. How will it look different?

B | Look at the photos and read the captions. Then discuss the questions.

1. Why are millions of people leaving the countryside and moving into crowded cities?
2. What are the causes of traffic jams in large cities? How can cities solve this problem?

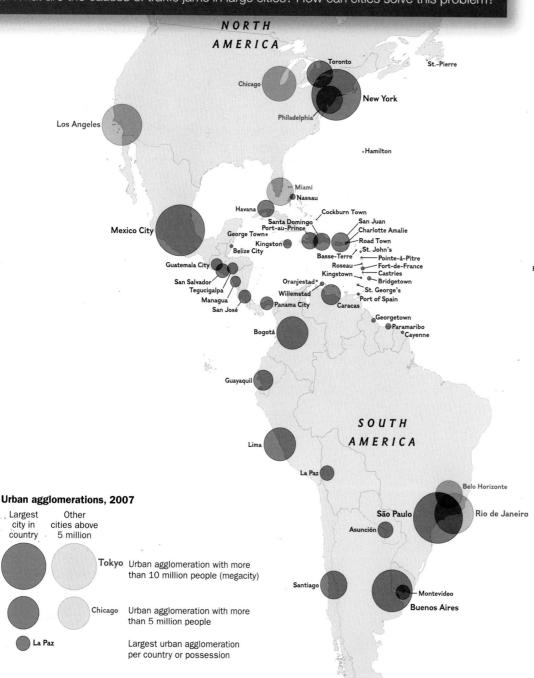

Urban agglomerations, 2007

Largest city in country

Other cities above 5 million

Tokyo — Urban agglomeration with more than 10 million people (megacity)

Chicago — Urban agglomeration with more than 5 million people

La Paz — Largest urban agglomeration per country or possession

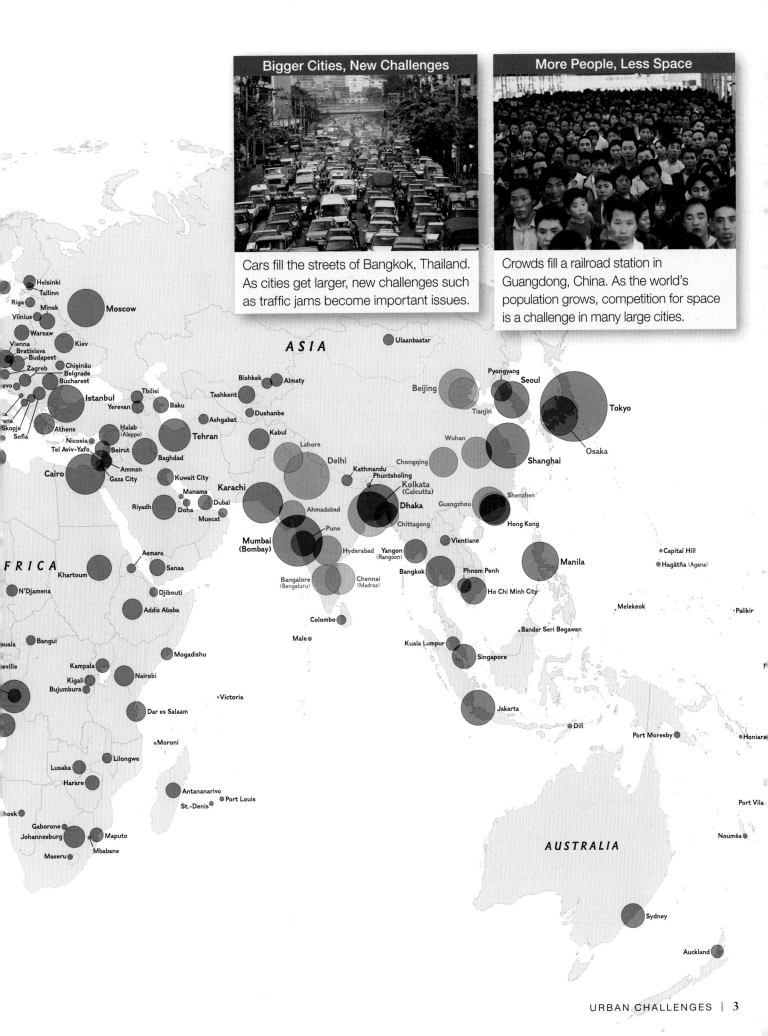

Bigger Cities, New Challenges

Cars fill the streets of Bangkok, Thailand. As cities get larger, new challenges such as traffic jams become important issues.

More People, Less Space

Crowds fill a railroad station in Guangdong, China. As the world's population grows, competition for space is a challenge in many large cities.

ASIA

AFRICA

AUSTRALIA

Helsinki
Tallinn
Riga
Minsk
Vilnius
Moscow
Warsaw
Vienna
Kiev
Bratislava
Budapest
Zagreb
Chișinău
Belgrade
evo
Bucharest
Skopje
Istanbul
Tbilisi
Sofia
Athens
Yerevan
Baku
Nicosia
Tel Aviv-Yafo
Ḥalab (Aleppo)
Beirut
Tehran
Cairo
Amman
Gaza City
Baghdad
Kuwait City
Riyadh
Manama
Doha
Dubai
Muscat
Bishkek
Almaty
Tashkent
Dushanbe
Ashgabat
Kabul
Lahore
Delhi
Kathmandu
Phuntsholing
Karachi
Ahmadabad
Pune
Mumbai (Bombay)
Hyderabad
Bangalore (Bengaluru)
Chennai (Madras)
Colombo
Male
Ulaanbaatar
Beijing
Pyongyang
Seoul
Tianjin
Tokyo
Wuhan
Osaka
Chongqing
Shanghai
Kolkata (Calcutta)
Dhaka
Shenzhen
Chittagong
Guangzhou
Hong Kong
Vientiane
Yangon (Rangoon)
Bangkok
Phnom Penh
Ho Chi Minh City
Manila
Capital Hill
Hagåtña (Agana)
Melekeok
Palikir
Bandar Seri Begawan
Kuala Lumpur
Singapore
Jakarta
Dili
Port Moresby
Honiara
Port Vila
Nouméa
Sydney
Auckland

Khartoum
N'Djamena
Asmara
Sanaa
Djibouti
Addis Ababa
uala
Bangui
Mogadishu
eville
Kampala
Kigali
Nairobi
Bujumbura
Dar es Salaam
Victoria
Moroni
Lusaka
Lilongwe
Harare
Antananarivo
St.-Denis
Port Louis
hoek
Gaborone
Johannesburg
Maputo
Maseru
Mbabane

🎧 track 1-2 **A** | **Meaning from Context.** Read and listen to the information about the ways that some cities are meeting new challenges. Notice the words in blue. These are words you will hear and use in Lesson A.

Finding affordable land for housing is a **challenge** in many of the world's largest cities. Some **residents** of Tokyo, Japan, have found a solution to this problem. They are building homes on pieces of land as small as 344 square feet (32 square meters). These "micro-homes" allow people to live close to central Tokyo and cost much less than other homes in the city. Many micro-homes have several floors and big windows that **maximize** sunlight.

Many cities have problems with air pollution and smog[1]. What can big cities do to **regulate** the amount of air pollution and smog **generated** by cars and factories? An Italian company has come up with an **innovative** tool to reduce pollution: smog-eating cement. The cement contains a substance that **converts** pollution into harmless chemicals. The harmless chemicals wash off roadways when it rains. Smog-eating materials are also being used in roof tiles in Los Angeles, California, the smoggiest city in the United States.

Cities must find creative ways to build public parks, gardens, and outdoor areas when space is limited. In New York City, the High Line was an unattractive black steel **structure** that once supported railroad tracks. Today, the High Line has been **restored** as an elevated urban park. The park was **financed** by donations, and now it is one of the most inviting public spaces in the city. Visitors can walk through the gardens, relax on the sundeck, and attend public art exhibits and special events.

[1]**Smog** is a combination of smoke and fog that can damage the health of humans, plants, and animals.

B | Match each sentence beginning to its ending to complete each definition. Use context clues from exercise **A** to understand the words in blue. Use your dictionary to help you.

1. The **residents** of a house or area are ___
2. To **finance** something means ___
3. If you **maximize** something, ___
4. A **challenge** is ___
5. An **innovation** is ___
6. If you **restore** an old painting, ___
7. To **regulate** something means ___
8. When you **generate** something, ___
9. A **structure** is ___
10. To **convert** one thing into another means ___

a. you repair and clean it.
b. to change it so that it can be used for another purpose.
c. the people who live there.
d. you produce it, or cause it to be produced.
e. something new and creative.
f. you increase it as much as possible.
g. something that has been built.
h. a difficult job that requires effort.
i. to control the way it is done.
j. to pay for it.

A | Using a Dictionary. Complete the chart with the correct form of each word. Use your dictionary to help you. *(See page 209 of the Independent Student Handbook for more information on using a dictionary.)*

	Noun	Verb	Adjective
1.	challenge	*challenge*	
2.		convert	
3.		finance	
4.		generate	
5.			innovative
6.		maximize	
7.		regulate	
8.	resident		
9.		restore	
10.	structure		

B | Read a tour guide's explanation of an unusual challenge facing the city of Venice, Italy. Fill in each blank with the correct form of a word from exercise **A** above.

Welcome to Venice, everybody! To start our tour today, I want to tell you about a (1) _____ we face in our beautiful city: floods. You see, a large portion of Venice was built on a salt marsh.[1] City planners had to find a way to (2) _____ space and use every part of the marsh. Builders placed hundreds of wooden logs deep into the marsh. Then they placed building foundations[2] on top of the logs. By doing this, they were able to (3) _____ the salt marsh into land for farming. But the salt marsh is like a giant sponge. The weight of the city pushes down on the salt marsh and buildings slowly sink into the water. High tides, called *acqua alta*, are also a problem. Now, Venice floods on a regular basis. Venetian (4) _____ are used to the floods, but our old and beautiful buildings suffer. Many (5) _____ are damaged by the water and the (6) _____ of these buildings is very expensive.

The city is now building water barriers that will stop seawater from flooding the city. This (7) _____ project is called MOSE, and it will be completed soon. The cost of this project is already more than seven billion dollars. Some people argue that the project violates government (8) _____ and is illegal. Others believe that the water barriers will interfere with the beauty of the city and will cause tourists to leave. Let's hope this does not happen, because tourism (9) _____ business for shops, restaurants, and hotels. (10) _____ support is necessary to help pay for the MOSE project. So thank you for coming to Venice!

[1]A **salt marsh** is an area of flat, wet ground that is sometimes covered by salt water.
[2]A **foundation** is a layer of bricks or concrete that a structure is built on.

Before Listening

Predicting Content. Look at the photo of tourists in Venice. Can you guess how many tourists visit Venice each year? How do tourists help the city? How do they hurt it? Discuss your ideas with a partner. (*See page 202 of the Independent Student Handbook for more information on predicting.*)

Thousands of tourists fill the streets of Venice.

Listening: A Lecture

Critical Thinking Focus: Identifying the Lecture Topic

Lecture introductions often have two parts. In the first part, the speaker provides background information about the topic, or reviews what was covered in earlier lectures. In the second part of the introduction, the speaker announces the specific topic they plan to discuss and explains how they will present the information. Correctly identifying the lecture topic can help you organize your lecture notes.

track 1-3 **A** | Listen to the lecture introduction. Which *specific* topic is this lecture about? Circle the correct answer.

1. The problem of flooding
2. The MOSE project
3. Problems caused by tourists

track 1-4 **B** | **Listening for Main Ideas.** Listen to the lecture and complete the main ideas about the problems and benefits of tourism. (*See page 203 of the Independent Student Handbook for more information on listening for main ideas.*)

Problems of Tourism	Benefits of Tourism
1. City services _____	1. Generates _____
2. Higher prices for _____	2. Money helps city _____
3. Higher _____ in tourist areas	3. Many Venetians have jobs related to _____
4. Bad _____ problem	
5. The city's population is _____	

C | With a partner, compare your answers from exercise **B**. Did you both list the same main ideas?

🎧 **D | Listening for Details.** Listen again and answer the questions about details in the lecture.

track 1-4

1. How many tourists visited Venice in one holiday weekend?
   a. 60,000
   b. 80,000
   c. 21 million
2. What is NOT found in the Rialto Market area?
   a. Grocery stores
   b. Souvenir shops
   c. A beach
3. What did a 1999 law make it easier to do?
   a. Convert residences to hotels or guest houses
   b. Increase the cost of garbage collection
   c. Create affordable housing for young people
4. What is the population of Venice today?
   a. Around 120,000
   b. Around 80,000
   c. Around 60,000
5. What did the speaker say about the unemployment rate in Venice?
   a. It is higher than in the rest of Italy.
   b. It is lower than in the rest of Italy.
   c. It is lower in the summer than in other seasons.

After Listening

A | Making Inferences. Discuss these questions with a partner.

1. Based on the lecture, what is the attitude of Venetian residents toward tourists? Use information from the listening to support your answer.
2. What is the lecturer's attitude about Venice's future?
3. Look at the cartoon. Do you think it is funny? Discuss the ways in which it relates to the lecture you just heard.

B | Form a group with two or three other students. Look at the cartoon. As a group, create a caption for the cartoon. Share your caption with the class.

Language Function

> **Introducing a Topic**
>
> During a presentation or a formal conversation, we often use special phrases and expressions to introduce a topic. These expressions help listeners to identify main ideas and follow along with a presentation or conversation. Here are some common phrases to introduce a new topic.
>
> | | |
> |---|---|
> | *To begin with . . .* | *Let me add that . . .* |
> | *I'd like to focus on . . .* | *Another point I want to make is . . .* |
> | *Today's topic is . . .* | *Today, we're going to cover . . .* |
> | *Let's move on to . . .* | *What I want to do today is . . .* |

track 1-5 **A** | In the lecture, the speaker used a number of expressions for introducing a topic. Listen to the sentences and fill in the expressions.

1. OK, everyone, _____ continue our discussion about cities and the challenges they face . . .

2. So, _____, let's review a few of the points we've discussed so far.

3. _____ there is a serious housing problem in Venice.

4. _____ that many people in Venice have jobs related to tourism.

B | Reread the expressions for introducing a topic. Which expressions are for introducing topics at the beginning of a talk? Which expressions are for introducing topics later on in a talk? Write each expression in the correct column.

Introducing a Topic at the Beginning of a Talk	Introducing a Topic Later on in a Talk

C | You have learned about two of Venice's challenges. Imagine that you are explaining one of the challenges to a new student. Choose one of the roles below and explain the problem to a partner. Use expressions for introducing a topic in your discussion.

> **Student A:** Flooding in Venice (Refer to exercise **B**, page 5.)
>
> **Student B:** Tourism in Venice (Refer to pages 6–7 and CD 1, Track 4.)

Grammar

The Passive Voice

We use the active voice to emphasize the agent, or the "doer," of an action:
> During the acqua alta, **people wear boots** instead of shoes.

We use the passive voice when the agent of a sentence is not known or is not important. Instead, the passive voice emphasizes the object of the action.
> During the acqua alta, **boots are worn** instead of shoes.

The passive voice consists of a form of *be* + the past participle of the verb.

Verb Tense	Passive Voice
Simple present	*During the Carnival celebration, masks **are worn**.*
Simple past	*The walkways **weren't set up** today.*
Future	*The barriers **will be (are going to be) constructed**.*
Present continuous	*Flood barriers **are being constructed**.*
Present perfect	*Their house **hasn't been sold**.*
Modal, simple present	*The house **can't be converted** into a hotel.*

A | Complete each sentence with the passive voice of the verb in parentheses. Use the correct verb tense.

1. New Orleans _____ badly _____ (damage) during Hurricane Katrina in 2005.
2. Eighty percent of the city _____ (flood).
3. Some parts of New Orleans _____ still _____ (rebuild).
4. There have been many meetings to discuss how a similar disaster _____ (can, avoid) in the future.
5. A conference on this subject _____ (hold) next year.
6. Meanwhile, tourists are returning to New Orleans, and many conventions _____ (hold) there every year.

Hurricane Katrina flooded the city of New Orleans, Louisiana.

B | Study the diagram of the MOSE flood barrier project in Venice. Work with a partner to complete the conversation about the diagram. Complete the sentences with the active or passive voice of the verb in parentheses. Use the correct tense.

How It Works:
1. Hollow steel gates filled with water lie in areas built into the Venice lagoon floor.
2. When a flood is predicted, air is pumped into the gates. This makes the gates float and allows them to rise within a half hour.
3. Fully elevated, the gates separate the sea from the lagoon. When the flood stops, water flows back into the gates to cover them.

1. **A:** Where _will_ the barriers _be constructed_ (construct)?

   B: They _____ (construct) in the three places where water enters the Venice lagoon from the Adriatic Sea.

2. **A:** What _____ the barriers _____ (consist) of?

   B: They _____ (consist) of 78 giant gates, 92 feet (28 meters) wide and 65 feet (20 meters) across.

3. **A:** What _____ the gates _____ (attach) to?

   B: They _____ (attach) to giant concrete bases lying on the sea floor.

4. **A:** When _____ the gates _____ (raise)?

   B: Whenever a high tide _____ (predict) and there is a danger of flooding in the city.

5. **A:** How _____ the gates _____ (raise)?

   B: Air _____ (pump) into hollow panels in the gate. This _____ (force) the gate to rise and form a barrier against the waves.

6. **A:** When _____ the project _____ (complete)?

   B: If everything goes as planned, it _____ (complete) in 2012.

C | **Understanding Visuals.** Work with your partner and practice the conversation from exercise **B**. Then discuss the MOSE diagram with your partner. Based on the diagram, do you think the MOSE barrier will stop floods? Explain your opinions.

Discussing Pros and Cons of Tourism

A | **Critical Thinking.** Form a group with two or three other students. Look at the list of topics below. How does tourism affect each of these areas? Discuss your ideas with your group. Add your own topics to the list.

Over nine million international tourists visit Rio de Janeiro, Brazil, each year.

> Public transportation
> Culture (arts, restaurants, and museums)
> Tourist attractions
> Cleanliness
> Job opportunities for residents
> The cost of living
> The city's reputation
> Other: _____

B | **Organizing Ideas.** With your group, select a city that you know well. Make notes in the chart about the positive effects (pros) and negative effects (cons) that tourism has on your chosen city.

City	_____
Positive Effects (Pros)	_____ _____ _____ _____ _____ _____
Negative Effects (Cons)	_____ _____ _____ _____ _____

C | **Discussion.** With your group, use your chart from exercise **B** to talk about the effects of tourism on your chosen city. Does tourism have more positive effects or more negative effects?

Student to Student: Apologizing for Interrupting

Sometimes in pair or group conversations people accidentally interrupt other people. Here are some expressions you can use to apologize for interrupting.

Sorry.
Go ahead.
I'm sorry. I didn't mean to cut you off.
Sorry. What were you going to say?
Oops. Please finish what you were saying.

TUAREG
FARMERS

Mali — Gossi lake

The Tuareg people were nomads, but today some of them are farmers.

Before Viewing

A | Predicting Content. Lesson A discussed some challenges faced by people in cities. The video you are going to watch is about a problem faced by farmers in Mali. With a partner, look at the map and the photos on pages 12 and 13 and answer the questions.

1. Some Tuareg farmers live next to Lake Gossi. Why do you think they live there?
2. Some elephants stay at Lake Gossi during the dry season. Why do you think they stay there?
3. What problems can you imagine between the farmers and elephants at Lake Gossi? Write three problems you think you might see in the video.

_____

_____

_____

B | Using a Dictionary. You will hear these words and phrases in the video. Work with your partner and match each word or phrase with the correct definition. Use your dictionary to help you.

1. catastrophe (n.) _c_
2. brush fence (n.) _e_
3. drought (n.) _d_
4. nightmare (n.) _a_
5. nomad (n.) _b_

a. a frightening dream; a terrible experience
b. a person who has no permanent home, but moves constantly in search of water and food
c. an unexpected event that causes great suffering
d. an unusually long time during which no rain falls
e. a barrier made from short, strong bushes

While Viewing

A | Look at the problems you listed in exercise **A** in the Before Viewing section. Watch the video. Check the problem(s) the video talks about.

B | **Viewing for Main Ideas.** Watch the video again. What do the farmers do to keep elephants out of their gardens? Check (✔) *Yes* for the things you see and *No* for the things you don't see.

Lake Gossi in Mali has no rain for many months of the year.

Solutions to the Elephant Problem	Yes	No
1. They dig deep holes for the elephants to fall into.	X	
2. They build fences around the gardens to keep the elephants out.	X	
3. They shine lights at the elephants and make a lot of noise.	X	
4. They use guns to shoot at the elephants.		X
5. They put the elephants in trucks and take them far away.		X
6. They grow food for the elephants outside of the gardens.		X

After Viewing

A | Complete each sentence using the passive voice of the verb in parentheses.

1. The water ___is shared___ (share) between the people and the elephants.
2. Water ___is carried___ (carry) from the lake to the gardens in goatskins.
3. The elephants ___are attracted___ (attract) to the gardens because there is little food available during the dry season.
4. Last night was a nightmare for the farmers. Many crops and trees ___were destroyed___ (destroy).
5. The same struggle ___has been repeated___ (repeat) every year since Omar was a child.

B | **Critical Thinking.** Form a group with two or three other students. Look at your answers to exercise **B** in the While Viewing section. There are six ideas in the list, but the farmers don't try all of them. Discuss the other ideas. Why do you think the farmers don't try these ideas?

Elephants need huge amounts of water and food.

A | Using a Dictionary. Work with a partner. Match each word with its definition. Use your dictionary to help you.

1. internalize (v.) ____
2. conform (v.) ____
3. ethnic (adj.) ____
4. debatable (adj.) ____
5. enforce (v.) ____
6. compatible (adj.) ____
7. economy (n.) ____
8. dominate (v.) ____
9. prohibit (v.) ____
10. unique (adj.) ____

a. relating to a group of people who have the same culture, race, traditions, or background
b. able to exist together
c. to make sure that a rule is obeyed
d. one of a kind
e. to have control of or power over an area
f. to make a belief part of your way of thinking
g. to forbid
h. a topic that can be questioned and is not certain
i. the system by which a country's trade, industry, and money are organized
j. to behave in the same way as most other people

B | Read the article and fill in each blank with the correct form of a word from exercise **A**. Then listen and check your answers.

track 1-6

Singapore is one of Asia's most interesting countries. It is surprising that such a small nation has such a powerful (1) _____. Many people believe that Singapore's economic success is because of the leadership of Lee Kuan Yew, Singapore's first Prime Minister. His ideas have (2) _____ the politics of Singapore for decades.

Singapore's model of success is unlike that of any other country. The model is a (3) _____ combination of two ideas: the encouragement of business and the enforcement of strict laws. To follow this model, the people of Singapore have learned to live and work together in an orderly way. There are laws that encourage cooperation between (4) _____ groups, and like all laws in Singapore, they are strictly (5) _____.

Spitting, selling chewing gum, and littering are all (6) _____ by law. While these laws may surprise some visitors, many Singaporeans have (7) _____ them, and for the most part, they follow the rules and laws without thinking about them.

Most Singaporeans believe that strict laws are (8) _____ with an orderly and secure society. They are willing to (9) _____ to rules and laws if it will make life in Singapore more pleasant. Some Singaporeans and some people from other countries, however, may feel that the benefits of these laws are (10) _____.

Residents of Singapore

Lee Kuan Yew

A | Using a Dictionary. Complete the chart with the correct form of a word from exercise **A** on page 14. Then complete each sentence with the correct form of the word. Use your dictionary to help you.

	Noun	Verb	Adjective
1.			debatable
2.		enforce	
3.	economy		
4.		prohibit	

1. Dogs are _____ on public beaches and in many parks.
2. The two candidates for president are going to hold a public _____.
3. In the United States, a law against chewing gum would not be _____.
4. When my father lost his job, our family was forced to _____.

B | Work with a partner. Read the statements about Singapore. Guess if they are true or false. Circle **T** for *true* or **F** for *false*. Then check your answers at the bottom of the page.

1. The cream-colored giant squirrel is a **unique** animal that lives only in Singapore.   **T**   **F**

2. The largest **ethnic** group in Singapore is Malay.   **T**   **F**

3. In 2010, Singapore's **economy** had the highest growth rate in the world.   **T**   **F**

4. In Singapore, eating ice cream in public is **prohibited** by law.   **T**   **F**

5. Singapore has a special government agency that **enforces** anticorruption laws.   **T**   **F**

C | Self-Reflection. Form a group with two or three other students. Discuss the following questions.

1. Do you have a goal such as graduating from school that has **dominated** your actions? In what way has this goal affected you?
2. What is an important value or belief you have **internalized**?
3. Talk about a time when you chose to **conform** to what other people were doing. Do you think you made the right choice, or did you regret it later?
4. Are strict laws **compatible** with your ideas of personal freedom? Explain.

ANSWERS:
1. T 2. F (The largest ethnic group in Singapore is Chinese.)
3. F (It had the second-highest growth rate.) 4. F (It is not prohibited.) 5. T

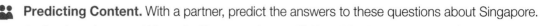

Before Listening

👥 **Predicting Content.** With a partner, predict the answers to these questions about Singapore.

1. Look at the map. Where is Singapore located? How big do you think it is? How many large cities does it have?

2. Look at the photo at the bottom of the page. Why do you think the Merlion was chosen as the symbol of Singapore? Brainstorm some ideas.

Listening: A Conversation between Classmates

🎧 **A** | **Listening for Main Ideas.** Read the statements below. Then listen to the conversation about
track 1-7 Singapore. Circle **T** for *true* or **F** for *false*.

1. The word *Singapore* means "lion city."	**T**	**F**
2. Singapore is rich in natural resources.	**T**	**F**
3. Nearly all the people of Singapore belong to one ethnic group.	**T**	**F**
4. Singapore is a small country with a large economy.	**T**	**F**
5. The spirit of *kiasu* is about enjoying life every minute.	**T**	**F**
6. Singapore has a strict system of laws.	**T**	**F**

👥 **B** | Compare your answers to exercise **A** with a partner. Revise the false statements to make them true.

🎧 **C** | **Listening for Details.** Listen again. Fill in the missing information.
track 1-7

1. Singapore started off as a _____ village.
2. Modern Singapore was founded in the year _____.
3. The size of Singapore is about _____ square miles (697 square kilometers).
4. Singapore is _____ percent urbanized.
5. Singapore's economy was ranked the _____ most innovative economy in the world.
6. Lee Kuan Yew's ideas dominated Singapore politics for _____ years.
7. *Kiasu* means "afraid to _____."

After Listening

👥 **Discussion.** With a partner, discuss the questions.

1. Do you have the spirit of *kiasu*? Explain.

2. In Singapore you can be fined for spitting on the ground and for forgetting to flush a public toilet. Do you think these types of laws would be helpful in your city? Explain.

The Merlion is the symbol of Singapore.

Pronunciation

Pronouncing the letter *t*

The letter *t* at the end of a word can be pronounced in different ways. Here are three common ways to pronounce *t* at the end of a word:

1. When a word that ends in *t* is followed by a word that begins with a vowel, the *t* is pronounced as a quick *d* sound.
   a o u e y
   that again   *it is*   *what are*

2. When *t* is followed by a word that begins with a consonant (other than *t* or *d*), hold your teeth and tongue in a *t* position, but do not release any air.
   not now   *what really*   *that language*

3. When *t* is followed by a word beginning with the sound /y/, such as *you* or *your*, the *t* is pronounced *ch*.
   what you   *that you*   *at your*

track 1-8

A | Look at the following word pairs. How is the final *t* of the first word pronounced? Check (✔) your answer.

	d	no air	*ch*			*d*	no air	*ch*
1. at you	☐	☐	☒	5. thought your	☐	☐	☒
2. upset about	☒	☐	☐	6. not yet	☐	☒	☐
3. hit us	☒	☐	☐	7. eight o'clock	☒	☐	☐
4. what now	☐	☒	☐	8. not really	☐	☒	☐

track 1-9

B | Listen and check your answers to exercise **A**. Then listen again and repeat the phrases.

C | With a partner, practice the following dialogs. Pay attention to the underlined words and be sure to pronounce *t* correctly. When you finish, switch roles and repeat.

1. **A:** I didn't hear <u>what you</u> said. *ch*
   B: I'm sorry. I'll say it again.

2. **A:** Do you <u>want some</u> coffee? *no air*
   B: No thanks. But how about some tea?

3. **A:** Is it lunchtime?
   B: <u>Not yet</u>. *d*

4. **A:** What are you going to do with those papers?
   B: I'm going to <u>put them</u> in the trash. *no air*

5. **A:** What are you so <u>upset about</u>? *d*
   B: I got a bad grade on that science test.

Language Function

Agreeing or Disagreeing

We use many different expressions to agree or disagree with something that someone has said. Some expressions are mild (gentle). Others are stronger and said with more feeling.

	Agree		**Disagree**
mild	*I agree.*	mild	*I'm not so sure (about that).*
↓	*I think so too.*	↓	*That's debatable.*
	I think you're right.		*I disagree.*
	Exactly!		*I don't think so.*
strong	*No kidding!*	strong	*No way!*
	You can say that again!		*That's crazy!*

track 1-10 **A** | In the conversation about Singapore, the classmates used a number of expressions for agreeing and disagreeing. Listen to the conversation again and write the expressions you hear.

1. **Man:** You know, the Singaporeans I've met all work very hard. They seem to want to be number one in everything.
   Woman: _____.

2. **Man:** I think that the laws seem way too strict, don't you?
   Woman: Actually, no. _____.

3. **Woman:** In my opinion, I'd rather have strict laws and safe streets than lenient laws and more crime.
   Man: Hmmm. _____. I think it's a debatable point.
   But _____ that Singapore is an interesting place.

 B | With a partner, practice the sentences in exercise **A**. Replace the responses with other expressions from the box that have the same meaning.

C | Work with your partner. Read the statements below about different urban challenges. Do you agree or disagree with each statement? Discuss your ideas with your partner.

> There should be a $200 fine for using a cell phone while driving.

> I agree. I think there should also be a fine for text messaging while driving.

1. It is the government's responsibility to provide free housing for homeless people.
2. Billboards by the side of the road are ugly and distracting. They should be illegal.
3. Pets should be allowed in restaurants, shops, and movie theaters.
4. Everyone should be allowed to own firearms.
5. Smoking should be prohibited in all public places, both indoors and outdoors.
6. It is impossible for people from different ethnic groups to live together in peace.
7. In crowded cities, the government has the right to limit the number of cars a family can have.

Grammar

Using an Agent in Passive Voice Sentences

In passive voice sentences, the agent of the action is not mentioned when:

- The agent is understood and would be redundant.
  The garbage hasn't been collected yet. (Agent: *by the garbage collectors*)

- The agent is unknown.
  A policeman was shot yesterday.

- The speaker doesn't want to state the agent.
  The president admitted that mistakes were made.

You should include the agent in passive sentences when it is important that people know the "doer" of the action. In these types of sentences, the agent follows the word *by.*
*Grass has been planted **by volunteers** in all the public parks.*

A | Read the paragraph. Circle the passive voice verb forms. Underline any agents.

Cleaning Up Europe's Urban Rivers

Keeping rivers clean is a challenge for most large cities. In the 1900s, rivers in many cities were polluted by harmful chemicals and raw sewage from nearby industries. Fish were often missing from urban rivers completely. Today, some large European cities are successfully keeping their rivers clean. More and more, fishermen are catching fish in rivers flowing through cities such as London, Paris, and Stockholm. Even fish that require very clean water to live, such as salmon and trout, are being caught. Why are the fish returning? A couple of reasons have been suggested. One reason is the disappearance of industries that used to pollute the rivers. Tough new pollution laws and water rules have also helped make rivers cleaner. Not all the rivers have been cleaned up, but the signs of recovery are promising for Europe's urban rivers.

A man fishes in a London river.

B | With a partner, review your answers in exercise **A**. Locate sentences where the passive voice is used without an agent. Why hasn't an agent been used? Decide on a reason.

C | **Discussion.** Select a tourist attraction or landmark in your favorite city. Form a group with two or three other students. Tell the members of your group about this place. Use the passive voice as appropriate. Answer the following questions:

- Where is this place or attraction?
- When was it designed and built?
- What is it used for?
- Will it be changed in the future? How?

ENGAGE: Presenting a Problem and Proposing Solutions

In this presentation, you and a partner will present a problem affecting your city and propose solutions to the problem. You and your partner will use a graphic organizer to help organize your ideas.

A | With a partner, discuss problems affecting your city. Use your own knowledge and experience. If necessary, look at a local newspaper for information about local problems.

B | **Using a Graphic Organizer.** With your partner, choose one of the problems you discussed in exercise **A**. Create a Spider Map like the one below to help you organize your ideas. Write the problem in the center circle of the Spider Map. Discuss the causes of the problem and list them in the Spider Map. Then discuss different ways to solve each problem and add the solutions to the Spider Map. (*See page 214 of the Independent Student Handbook for more information about using graphic organizers.*)

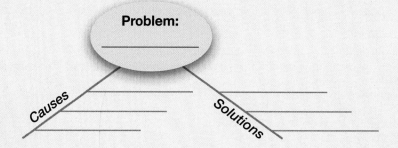

C | **Planning a Presentation.** Decide who will present each part of the presentation and practice out loud. Try to include new vocabulary from this unit and the passive voice.

D | **Presentation.** With your partner, present your problem and solutions to the class.

> We would like to talk about the problem of youth gangs. The causes are quite complicated. To begin with . . .

> One way to solve this problem is to start an after-school program at the Community Center.

Presentation Skills: Making Eye Contact

When you are giving a presentation, it is important to make eye contact with the audience. Try to make eye contact a natural part of your presentation. If you are using notes during your presentation, do not read directly from your notes. Instead, look down only when you need help to remember your next point. Look around the room at your listeners and make eye contact with the individuals in the audience.

Protecting Our Planet

ACADEMIC PATHWAYS
Lesson A: Listening to a Guided Tour
Brainstorming Ideas about Conservation
Lesson B: Listening to a Student Debate
Participating in a Debate

Think and Discuss

1. Look at the photo and read the caption. What do you imagine this scene looked like 50 or 60 years ago? What caused the change?
2. What are some reasons that animals become extinct?
3. Who do you think should be responsible for protecting endangered species? Governments? Companies? Citizens?

An endangered turtle floats over a dead coral reef.

Exploring the Theme:
Protecting Our Planet

A | Look at the photos and read the caption. Then discuss the questions.

1. Lions and other types of big cats are dying at a rapid rate. What do you think is the biggest threat to these animals?
2. If a plant species becomes extinct, what effect does this have on the environment?

B | Look at the chart. Then discuss the questions.

1. Which group is the most threatened? Which is the least?
2. Which categories of species are common in your country?

Protecting Our Plants and Animals

Around the planet, human impact has resulted in the destruction of animal and plant life. Now conservationists are trying to save these plants and animals from extinction. Once a plant or animal is extinct, there will be no living members of that species left on the planet.

Percentage of Threatened Species by Category

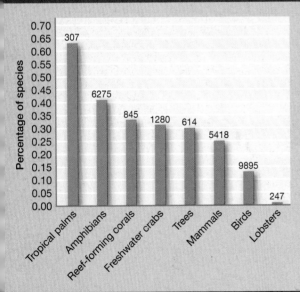

Each year, The International Union for Conservation of Nature studies plants and animals. Many of the species studied are threatened or at risk of dying. The graph shows the percentage of threatened species in each category. The numbers at the top of the graph show how many species were studied.

An African lion rests near a tree in Botswana. Over the past 20 years, nearly 30 percent of all African lions have died.

track 1-11 **A** | **Meaning from Context.** Read and listen to the information about saving the whales. Notice the words in blue. These are words you will hear and use in Lesson A.

Save the Whales!

Of the 70 species of whales and dolphins, nearly all have been affected by human activities.

Does that mean that all whales are endangered?

Not all, but many. Most species of baleen[1] whales, such as blue and humpback whales, have been significantly reduced. Their status today is the result of commercial whaling in the 19th and 20th centuries, when whales were exploited for meat and oil. Of the eleven baleen species, nine are currently endangered. We have evidence that many toothed whales are also in danger of dying. Threats to whales include hunting, habitat[2] destruction, and pollution.

Northern right whales are the rarest of all large whales. Scientists believe that only several hundred live in the wild.

What kinds of conservation efforts are taking place?

Many ongoing conservation strategies are helping whale populations. For example, the International Whaling Commission (IWC) ordered a stop to commercial whaling. Unfortunately, a number of countries have chosen to violate the rule and continue to kill whales.

Can whale populations recover?

Although it may be too late for some species, there are some indications that conservation efforts are working. For example, the California gray whale, which was near extinction, has made an amazing recovery. Gray whales were removed from the Endangered Species List.

How can I help save the whales?

You can help by learning about whales and their habitats. Donate your time to conservation organizations, and alter your behavior so that you create as little waste as possible. If we all participate in these efforts, we can help protect these magnificent animals.

[1] Instead of having teeth, **baleen** whales have plates in their mouths that separate food from the water.
[2] The **habitat** of an animal or plant is the natural environment in which it lives and grows.

B | Work with a partner. Match each word in blue from exercise **A** with its definition.

1. status (n.)   c
2. exploited (v.)   i
3. threats (n.)   g
4. ongoing (adj.)   b
5. strategies (n.)   a
6. violate (v.)   h
7. recover (v.)   e
8. indications (n.)   d
9. alter (v.)   j
10. evidence (n.)   f

a. plans to achieve a goal, over a long period
b. continuing to happen
c. a state or condition at a particular time
d. signs that something will happen or is true
e. to get stronger and return to an earlier, healthy state
f. facts or physical signs that prove something is true
g. situations or activities that could cause harm or danger
h. to do the opposite of an agreement or law
i. developed or profited from (e.g., resources)
j. to change

A | **Using a Dictionary.** Complete the chart with the correct form of each word. Use your dictionary to help you.

	Noun	Verb	Adjective
1.		exploit	
2.	threat		
3.		recover	
4.	indication		

B | Read the article and fill in each blank with the correct form of a word from exercise **A** on page 24.

Satellite Photos Reveal Damaged Mangrove Forests
by Staff Writers

WASHINGTON, D.C.— A recent study by the U.S. Geological Survey shows that mangrove forests cover much less land than previously believed. The research team led by Chandra Giri used more than 1000 satellite images to examine the (1) _____ of mangrove forests worldwide. Giri's team discovered that mangrove forests cover 12 percent less land than previously estimated by the United Nations Food and Agriculture Organization.

A man kayaks through a mangrove forest.

(2) _____ from satellite photos (3) _____ that these important coastal forests are disappearing. Mangrove forests are found along the coastlines of 118 different tropical countries. These forests, which consist of trees, shrubs, and palms, protect coastlines and villages against hurricanes and tsunamis, and provide a habitat for many types of ocean wildlife. Human (4) _____ of wood, housing construction, and shrimp farming have all contributed to the destruction of many mangrove forests. Only about seven percent of mangrove forests worldwide are protected by law.

(5) _____ efforts are required to help mangrove forests (6) _____. Recommended (7) _____ include replanting trees, passing laws to protect endangered forests, and forcing individuals or companies that (8) _____ the law to pay fines. Educating citizens, teachers, and public officials about the importance of conservation is also a key step in protecting mangrove forests.

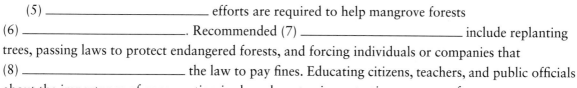

C | **Discussion.** With a partner, discuss the questions.

1. Do you agree that people who alter or destroy mangrove forests should pay a fine? Explain.
2. How can you participate in the efforts to save endangered plants and animals?
3. Which is more important: saving mangrove forests or helping businesses that destroy mangrove forests but help the local economy? Explain.

Before Listening

A | **Predicting Content.** Form a group with two or three other students. Look at the photos and read the caption. Then discuss the questions.

The dusky seaside sparrow was a bird species of southern Florida.

1. What kind of habitat do you think this bird lived in?
2. The dusky seaside sparrow is now extinct. What do you think are some possible causes for its extinction?

Note-Taking

People generally speak more quickly than they can write. To take good notes quickly while listening to a lecture, write only the most important ideas.

- Write only the key words.
- Don't write complete sentences.
- Use abbreviations (short forms) and symbols when possible.
- Indent specific information, such as examples.

---

track 1-12 **B** | Listen to the first part of a guided tour and look at the student's notes below. Notice the use of key words, indentation, abbreviations, and symbols.

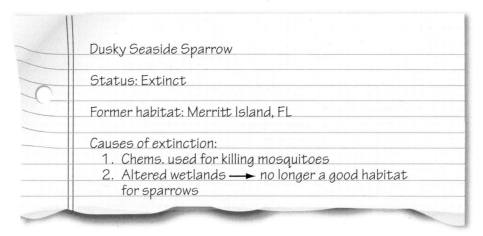

Dusky Seaside Sparrow

Status: Extinct

Former habitat: Merritt Island, FL

Causes of extinction:
 1. Chems. used for killing mosquitoes
 2. Altered wetlands ⟶ no longer a good habitat
    for sparrows

C | Work with a partner. Using the notes from exercise **B**, retell the first part of the lecture in complete sentences. Use your own words.

Listening: A Guided Tour

🎧 track 1-13 **Note-Taking.** Listen to the guided tour and complete the notes. Be sure to use key words, abbreviations, and symbols. Notice the indentations. Listen again if necessary. (*See page 206 of the Independent Student Handbook for more information on taking notes.*)

Endangered Species Act (ESA) - 1973

    Protects animals and their _____

        Ex.: _____

    Ongoing conflict between _____ and _____

        Ex.: _____

    ESA protects _____; ranchers feel law violates _____

Endangered Species Today

    Situation today is ___*worse*___ than in 1973

    1. ___/___ species listed as ___*river*___ or ___*forest*___

    2. Since 1973 only ___*39*___ species removed from list

    3. BUT only ___*/X*___ removed because they recovered;

       ___*9 species*___ became extinct, others listed by accident

    4. ___*300*___ more species may soon be added to list

Conclusion

    Even w/ ESA in place, _____

After Listening

A | Use your notes from above to answer the questions.

1. What is the main topic of the talk?
   a. Why the dusky seaside sparrow became extinct *—Intro*
   b. The difficulties of protecting both animals and their habitats
   c. Reasons that the Endangered Species Act isn't working
2. What does the Endangered Species Act protect?
   a. Endangered animals and their habitats
   b. Endangered animals but not their habitats
   c. Animal habitats but not endangered animals
3. What has happened since the passage of the Endangered Species Act?
   a. The number of species that are endangered has decreased.
   b. There is more cooperation between landowners and the government.
   c. The number of species that are endangered has stayed the same.

B | **Discussion.** Work with a partner. How might the extinction of the dusky seaside sparrow have been prevented? Explain your ideas.

Language Function

Introducing Examples

We use many expressions to introduce examples. Most of them are placed directly before the example.

> I've visited many national parks, **for example,** Yellowstone and Yosemite.
> There's a wide variety of animals there—**for instance,** bison and wolves.

> Alligators thrive in habitats **such as** the Everglades swamp.
> The Everglades is home to many species of wildlife, **including** the Florida panther and the American alligator.

A few expressions may be placed after the examples, especially in casual speech.

> I've visited many national parks—Yellowstone and Yosemite, **for example.**
> There's a wide variety of animals there—bison and wolves, **for instance.**

🎧 track 1-14 **A** | In the guided tour, the speakers used expressions to introduce examples. Listen and fill in the expressions you hear.

1. That's why the Endangered Species Act, which was passed in the United States in 1973, protects both endangered animals and their habitats. _for example_, the steelhead trout lives in rivers and streams on the west coast of the United States. . .

2. There's an ongoing conflict between some landowners and the government. Take the case of the gray wolf, _for instance_.

3. Reports on topics _such as_ habitat loss, deforestation, and overfishing show that the situation for many species is far worse now than it was in 1973.

4. Meanwhile, another 300 species may soon be added to the list, _including_ a plant, the Las Vegas buckwheat, and an insect, the Miami blue butterfly.

The Miami blue butterfly

B | Collaboration. Work with a partner. Each student should choose a different box. Use the information in the boxes to talk about each animal. Create sentences that include a statement and examples. Explain the information to your partner. Use expressions for introducing examples.

Student A

Statements	Examples
1. Bee populations are decreasing in many areas of the world.	China Brazil North America Europe
2. This decrease is caused by a number of factors.	viruses habitat loss climate change
3. It's important to follow strategies to protect bees.	Educate the public about the role of bees. Pay farmers to protect bee habitats. Use nontoxic chemicals.

Student B

Statements	Examples
1. Many people are afraid of bats, but bats help the environment in important ways.	Bats eat insects that destroy crops. Fruit-eating bats pollinate[1] plants.
2. Human activities threaten bats.	Machines kill bats. Development destroys their habitat. People kill them.
3. We can take steps to help bats survive.	Explain how bats help the environment. Build a bat house (similar to a bird house). Pass laws to protect bats and their habitats.

[1] To **pollinate** a plant or tree, insects place pollen in the plant or tree so seeds can be made.

C | Self-Reflection. Complete these sentences with an expression for introducing examples and your own ideas. Then share your sentences with your partner.

1. I plan to travel to many different places _____.
2. I have seen many types of animals _____.
3. I have visited some wonderful museums _____.

Grammar

Restrictive Adjective Clauses

We use adjective clauses, also called relative clauses, to modify a noun. There are two types of adjective clauses: restrictive and non-restrictive. Restrictive adjective clauses give information that is essential for identifying the noun.

Adjective clauses start with relative pronouns. *Who, whose, whom,* and *that* are used for people. *Which* and *that* are used for things. A relative pronoun can be the subject or object of its adjective clause. When the relative pronoun is the object of a restrictive adjective clause, it can be omitted.

Sentences with adjective clauses are formed by combining two simple sentences as follows:

Relative pronoun as subject

*Chandra Giri is a scientist. **She** used satellite images to study mangrove forests.*

*Chandra Giri is a scientist **who** used satellite images to study mangrove forests.*

Relative pronoun as object

*The meeting was about conservation efforts in national parks. We attended **it.***

*The meeting **that** we attended was about conservation efforts in national parks.*

A | Combine the two sentences. Change the second sentence to an adjective clause.

1. The police discovered the body of a deer. It had been killed illegally.

   _____

2. The woman belongs to a bird-watching club. I met her yesterday.

   _____

3. I know a woman. She keeps two tigers as pets.

   _____

4. I think it was a grizzly bear. It tore open all my trash bags.

   _____

5. There are too many people. They don't care about endangered species.

   _____

B | **Collaboration.** Complete these sentences with your own ideas. Use adjective clauses. Then discuss your sentences with a partner.

1. I'm fascinated by animals that _____.

2. I enjoyed talking to the person whom/that _____.

3. Let me tell you about the vacation that _____.

Brainstorming Ideas about Conservation

> **Brainstorming**
>
> Brainstorming helps us connect ideas and come up with new ideas about a topic.
>
> To brainstorm in a group, follow these steps:
>
> - Assign one group member to be a secretary. The secretary will take notes for the group.
> - Choose a topic. Say as many ideas about the topic as you can. Do not stop to organize your thoughts or correct errors. The secretary will write down all of the ideas.
> - After you have finished brainstorming, look over the list and add any related ideas that you may have missed.

A | **Brainstorming.** Form a group with two or three other students. Look at the list of habitats in the chart. With your group, brainstorm and complete the chart with examples of plants and animals that live in each place. Then brainstorm about the dangers that the plants and animals face in each habitat.

Habitat	Animals	Dangers
ice	polar bear, seal, walrus, penguin	
desert		
rain forest		
ocean		
Other: _____		

B | **Discussion.** Work with your group. Use the brainstorming list from exercise **A**. Have a group discussion about the dangers that plants and animals face in each habitat.

> Melting ice is dangerous for animals in the ice habitat—polar bears, for example.

> And animals in the ice habitat are also hunted for their fur.

Crocodiles of Sri Lanka

Before Viewing

A | Predicting Content. Work with a partner. What is the biggest problem for the crocodiles of Sri Lanka? Brainstorm some ideas.

B | Using the Dictionary. Some words have more than one meaning. With a partner, read these sentences from the video. Notice the words in blue. Then read the definitions. There are two definitions for each word. Match each word with the definition that fits the sentence from the video. Use your dictionary to help you.

_____ 1. The only chance the **mugger** has in the wild is here, in Yala.
    a. a criminal who robs others in public
    b. a crocodile of southern Asia

_____ 2. If they die out here, they're probably gone **for good**.
    a. forever, permanently
    b. so that things will be better

_____ 3. The winner gets the prize—his **pick** of the females.
    a. a sharp, pointed tool
    b. a choice

_____ 4. Muggers have been acting out this **ritual** for more than 100 million years.
    a. a procedure for a religious ceremony
    b. an activity or behavior that happens often

While Viewing

A | **Note-Taking.** Watch the first two minutes of the video. Complete the notes with words from the box.

captive	crocodiles	farms	habitat	human	India	mugger

1. Increased _____human_____ populations ➔ less _____habitat_____ for animals
2. India: big problem for _____crocodiles_____
3. Rom Whitaker wants to save the _____mugger_____ crocodile
4. Indian wetlands are now _____farms_____
5. Madras Crocodile Bank—world's largest _____captive_____ pop. of muggers
6. Can't let them go—no place for them in _____India_____

B | **Note-Taking.** Watch the next two minutes of the video. Complete the notes with one or two words you hear.

1. Past: wild muggers throughout Indian _____subcontinent_____
2. Today: _____only few_____ thousand left
3. _____30_____ years ago: wild muggers in Sri Lanka
4. _____rom_____ is going to look for them.
5. Yala National Park—world's largest pop. of _____wild_____ muggers

Yala National Park, Sri Lanka

C | With your partner, discuss your answers to the question in exercise **A** in the Before Viewing section. Were you correct?

D | **Note-Taking.** Watch the rest of the video and take notes. Then use your notes to answer the questions.

1. Rom wants to know if the Yala muggers are thriving. Why can't he find out from other researchers?
2. Why is Rom observing the muggers at night? What is he doing?
3. Do the males spend a lot of time fighting? Why do they fight? Are many of them killed?

After Viewing

A | **Collaboration.** With a partner, think of four questions you would like to ask Rom Whitaker about the future of the mugger crocodiles.

B | Work with a group of two or three students. One student in the group should pretend to be Rom Whitaker. The other students will ask the questions they wrote in exercise **A**. The student playing Rom Whitaker should answer each question as if he or she is Rom Whitaker.

A | **Meaning from Context.** Read and listen to the interview. Notice the words in blue. These are words you will hear and use in Lesson B.

track 1-15

Q: What does a fish biologist do?

A: Well, lots of things. I teach at a university and research ways to **maintain** fish populations. I spend a lot of time trying to raise **funds** for research and contacting **authorities** to get permission for the research I want to do. And I get to travel around the world and educate people about **sustainable** fishing.

Q: What is the **focus** of your research?

A: My interest is to protect large freshwater[1] fish and their habitats. Forty percent of the freshwater fish in North America are in danger of extinction. That's 700 endangered species. And that's just in North America! Each year, when I join other biologists for our **annual** meeting, someone reports on the extinction of another species. That's hard to hear.

Q: Don't you get discouraged?

A: On the **contrary**, it just makes me want to work harder. I've always loved water, and I've always loved fish. I'm inspired to do what I can to help them survive.

Q: If you could tell people to do one thing to help save freshwater fish, what would it be?

A: Get involved! **Contribute** as much time as you can. Volunteer to help clean up a river, or write letters to politicians to make them aware of the **issues**. Above all, don't **ignore** the problem, because things are not going to get better without our help.

A biologist holds an endangered fish called the smoky madtom.

[1] **Freshwater** lakes and rivers contain water that is not salty.

B | **Using a Dictionary.** Work with a partner. Match each word from exercise **A** with its definition. Use your dictionary to help you.

1. maintain (v.) ___g___
2. funds (n.) ___j___
3. authorities (n.) ___i___
4. sustainable (adj.) ___e___
5. focus (n.) ___f___
6. annual (adj.) ___c___
7. contrary (n.) ___h___
8. contribute (v.) ___b___
9. issues (n.) ___a___
10. ignore (v.) ___d___

a. important problems that people are discussing or arguing about

b. to give money or time to make an effort successful

c. happening once a year

d. to pay no attention to

e. able to be kept at a certain level without causing damage to the animals or the environment

f. a topic that you are concentrating on or paying special attention to

g. to take care of something and keep it in good condition

h. the opposite of an idea or condition

i. people who have the power to make decisions and to make sure that laws are obeyed

j. amounts of money given to organizations or people to be spent for a purpose

A | Read the article and fill in each blank with the correct form of a word from exercise **A** on page 34. Use a dictionary if necessary.

The Yellowstone Wolf Project

Wolves were once common throughout North America, but by the mid-1930s, most had been killed. In 1995 and 1996, the United States Fish and Wildlife Service (1) _____ a plan to capture wolves from Canada and free them in Yellowstone National Park. This program, known as the Yellowstone Wolf Project, cost only $267,000 in government (2) _____. It was a huge success. Today, the Yellowstone wolf population has recovered and can (3) _____ itself.

Wolves in Yellowstone National Park

(4) _____ to the wishes of many farmers and ranchers, wolf populations have also been recovering in other parts of the western United States. As the number of wolves has grown, wolves have become the (5) _____ of a bitter debate. People cannot (6) _____ the fact that wolves occasionally kill sheep, cattle, and other farm animals. On the other hand, wolves hunt and help control populations of grazing animals such as elk, moose, and deer.

The presence of wolves brings financial benefits to Yellowstone Park. Tens of thousands of tourists visit Yellowstone (7) _____ to see the wolves. Those tourists provide money to help (8) _____ the park and keep it in good condition. Tourists also (9) _____ about 35 million dollars a year to the area around the park. The Yellowstone Wolf Project continues to be a complicated (10) _____ with strong arguments for and against the effort.

B | **Critical Thinking.** Form a group with two or three other students and discuss the questions.

1. In many places in the United States, wolves are protected by the Endangered Species Act. If wolf populations have recovered, should wolves continue to be protected by law? Why, or why not?

2. If a wolf attacks a farmer's sheep or cattle, should the farmer have the right to kill the wolf? Explain your opinion.

3. Do you think the government should pay farmers or ranchers whose animals are killed by wolves? Why, or why not?

Before Listening

👥 **Prior Knowledge.** With a partner, discuss the questions below.

Hunters and their dogs look for animals.

1. Ducks, quail, turkeys, and pheasants are popular birds to hunt. Elk and deer are popular four-legged animals to hunt. What other animals do you know that are hunted?

2. Have you ever gone hunting? If you have, did you like it? If you haven't, would you like to try it? Explain.

Listening: A Student Debate

Critical Thinking Focus: Evaluating Arguments in a Debate

In a debate, speakers take turns presenting arguments for or arguments against a controversial issue. Each speaker provides facts, examples, and statistics to prove that his or her argument is accurate. Each speaker also tries to show that the other speaker's arguments are incorrect, incomplete, or illogical. Members of the audience must listen and decide which speaker presented a stronger argument.

🎧 track 1-16 **A** | **Listening for Key Concepts.** Listen to two classmates debate about legalized hunting. Who speaks in favor of it? Who speaks against it?

🎧 track 1-16 **B** | **Note-Taking.** Listen again. Take notes on the speakers' arguments for and against hunting. Also take notes on their responses to each other's arguments.

Yumi's Arguments for Hunting	Yumi's Responses to Raoul
Hunting helps control animal pops.	

Raoul's Arguments against Hunting	Raoul's Responses to Yumi
Some hunters are irresponsible.	

👥 **C** | With a partner, compare your notes from exercise **B**. Restate the arguments for hunting and against hunting in your own words.

👥 **D** | **Discussion.** Refer back to the debate. Which speaker do you think presented the stronger argument? Explain your opinion to your partner.

After Listening

Critical Thinking. Form a group with two or three other students. Then answer the questions.

1. Do you think that hunting should be allowed in your area? If yes, what hunting rules would you make? If no, why not?
2. Some groups believe that teaching children and teenagers about hunting will make them responsible hunters as adults. Should the government try to convince more young people to take up hunting? Explain your opinion.

Pronunciation

Pronouncing -s endings

The letter *s* at the end of nouns, verbs, and possessives has three pronunciations. Put your hand on your throat and say *zeeeeeee*. This is a voiced sound, so you should feel a vibration in your throat. Now, put your hand on your throat and say *sssssss*. This is a voiceless sound, so there is no vibration in your throat.

track 1-17

After voiceless consonants, *s* is pronounced /s/: duc**ks**, hun**ts**, photograp**hs**
After voiced consonants and all vowels, *s* is pronounced /z/: bea**rs**, be**es**, mangrov**es**
After words ending in *ss*, *sh*, *ch*, *ce*, *se*, *ge*, or *x*, *s* is pronounced /ɪz/: grass**es**, buzz**es**, fish**es**, catch**es**

When a word ending in *s* is followed by a word that starts with a vowel, the two words are linked.

ducks in danger   hunts after dark   bears and deer   dollars annually

A | Look at the following words. How is the final *s* pronounced? Check (✔) your answer.

	/s/	/z/	/ɪz/			/s/	/z/	/ɪz/
1. government's	❏	❏	❏	5.	elks	❏	❏	❏
2. hunters	❏	❏	❏	6.	boys	❏	❏	❏
3. crashes	❏	❏	❏	7.	stamps	❏	❏	❏
4. whales	❏	❏	❏	8.	passes	❏	❏	❏

B | Listen and check your answers in exercise **A**. Then listen again and repeat the words you hear. Pay special attention to the pronunciation of the final *s*.

track 1-18

C | With a partner, practice saying the phrases in the box below. Be careful to link the final *s* sound with the first vowel of the next word. Then listen and check your pronunciation.

track 1-19

government's actions	hunters' activities	crashes into	whales ahead
elks' antlers	species of birds	stamps in use	passes out

Language Function

Responding to and Refuting an Argument

Speakers use specific expressions to respond to an argument in a debate or conversation. First, you must show that you have heard the other speaker's argument. Then, you should use a contrast word or phrase to signal that you have a different point of view. Here are some expressions you can use to respond to or refute an argument in a debate or conversation.

Yes, but . . .	*That's a good argument, but . . .*
Yeah, but . . .	*That may be true, but on the other hand . . .*
OK, but . . .	*You are right that . . .; however, . . .*

 A | In the listening, the classmates used a number of expressions for responding to and refuting an argument. Listen and fill in the expressions you hear.

1. **Yumi:** . . . without hunting, deer populations would be too large, and many animals would starve because there wouldn't be enough food to sustain them.
   Raoul: _____, I think you're ignoring an important point.

2. **Raoul:** So instead of allowing humans to hunt, we should allow populations of meat-eating animals to recover.
   Yumi: _____ don't forget that wolves and mountain lions don't just eat deer and elk.

3. **Raoul:** And in Shenandoah National Park in Virginia, authorities recently caught a group of hunters who were shooting black bears and selling their body parts for medicines.
   Yumi: _____ that these kinds of violations occur. However, they are rare.

B | With a partner, practice the sentences from exercise **A**. Then switch roles and read them again.

C | With your partner, take turns reading the statements below. Explain your opinion about each statement. Explain the reasons for your opinion. If you disagree with your partner, use the expressions in the Language Function box to respond to or refute your partner's arguments.

1. Human beings have always been hunters. Hunting and killing animals is natural for us.
2. We should stop fishing for a few years to allow fish populations to recover.
3. Just as humans have rights, I believe animals have rights, too.
4. The government does not have the right to stop people from hunting on their own land.
5. I don't care if the dusky seaside sparrow becomes extinct. It doesn't make any difference in my life.

> Hunting should be illegal because many people are hurt in hunting accidents each year.

> Yes, but more people are hurt in car accidents each year. Does that mean we should make driving illegal, too?

Grammar

Non-Restrictive Adjective Clauses

Unlike restrictive adjective clauses, non-restrictive adjective clauses provide extra information about a noun.

Adjective clauses following proper nouns, plural nouns, and unique nouns are typically non-restrictive. For example:

> The largest land animal in North America is the American bison, **which can be over six feet (two meters) tall.** (unique noun)
>
> John Muir, **who lived from 1838 to 1914,** was one of America's earliest conservationists. (proper noun)
>
> Lions, **whose roars can be heard for miles,** are quickly disappearing in the wild. (plural noun)

Often there is a slight pause between a non-restrictive clause and the preceding noun. When you are talking about things, use the pronoun *which*. Do not use *that*.

A | Combine the two sentences into one sentence using a non-restrictive adjective clause. Use the relative pronouns *who, which,* or *whose.* Insert commas as needed.

1. The dusky seaside sparrow became extinct due to changes to its habitat. It lived in the wetlands of southern Florida.

   The dusky seaside sparrow, which lived in the wetlands of southern Florida, became extinct due to changes to its habitat.

2. Sting works to protect the Amazon. He is a British celebrity.

   _____

3. Whales were hunted to near extinction. They are the largest animals on earth.

   _____

4. Wolves have been introduced into Yellowstone. It is America's oldest national park.

   _____

5. The hippopotamus is not an endangered species at this time. It lives in African rivers.

   _____

6. Businessman Ted Turner allows elk hunting on his land during part of the year. His ranch is very large.

   _____

B | **Collaboration.** With a partner, complete the following sentences. Use a non-restrictive adjective clause and your own information.

1. Not long ago I heard an interesting speaker named _____, who . . .
2. I have a _____ relationship with my neighbors, whose . . .
3. My favorite item, which I bought _____, is . . .

In this section, you will evaluate arguments for and against keeping wild animals in zoos. Then you will organize and prepare for a debate on this question.

A | Evaluating Arguments. Read the statements below. Are these arguments for or against keeping animals in zoos? Write **F** if the argument is *for zoos* or **A** if the argument is *against zoos*.

____ 1. Animals do not have rights, so it is acceptable for people to keep them in zoos.

____ 2. Zoos educate people about how to protect endangered species.

____ 3 In many zoos, animals are kept in small cages and cannot move around.

____ 4. It costs a lot of money to keep animals in zoos.

____ 5. It is fun to see interesting and unusual animals in zoos.

____ 6. Zoos protect animals that are hunted illegally, such as rhinos and elephants.

____ 7. People can be educated about animals without keeping animals in zoos.

____ 8. The artificial environment of a zoo is very stressful for many animals. They often stop eating.

B | With a partner, take turns reading and responding to the statements in exercise **A**. In your responses, use expressions for responding to and refuting an argument from the box on page 38.

C | Organizing Ideas. Your teacher will instruct you to prepare arguments for or against keeping animals in zoos. Write down notes to support your position. Try to predict the arguments the other speaker will make, and think of how you will answer them.

D | Presentation. Your teacher will pair you with a student who prepared the opposite side of the issue. You will hold a three to five minute debate in front of the class or a small group of classmates. The student who speaks in favor of zoos should begin.

Student to Student:
Expressing Encouragement

Here are some expressions you can use to wish another student good luck before a presentation.

Good luck!
Go for it!
Go get 'em!

Presentation Skills: Speaking with Confidence

When speaking in front of a group, it is important to appear confident. This will give the impression that you know your topic well, and that you believe in what you are saying. There are several things that you can do to feel more confident. Make sure you have organized your notes and have practiced your presentation at least once. Use hand gestures and body language when you can. Finally, remember to pause between sentences and to speak slowly and clearly.

Beauty and Appearance

ACADEMIC PATHWAYS
Lesson A: Listening to a News Report
          Conducting a Survey
Lesson B: Listening to an Informal Conversation
          Giving a Group Presentation

Think and Discuss

1. Look at the photo and read the caption. Does this advertisement make you want to buy clothing or beauty products? Explain.

2. How would you describe the items this man is wearing?

3. What surprises or interests you about this photo?

An advertisement for a fashion designer hangs on the side of a building in Milan, Italy.

Exploring the Theme:
Beauty and Appearance

A | Look at the photos and read the captions. Then discuss the questions.

1. What makes a person beautiful, in your opinion?
2. Do different people and cultures have different ideas about what is beautiful? Give some examples.

B | Look at the chart. Then discuss the questions.

1. Does it surprise you to find these five countries in the chart? Explain.
2. What country do you think would be next on the chart?

What is Beauty?

How much of a person's beauty is based on physical appearance? How much depends on what people wear or where they live? Some people go to spas to make themselves beautiful while others dress in unusual fashions. People around the world have different ideas about what makes someone beautiful.

Colorful jewelry and sandals are for sale at an outdoor stand in Colombia.

Making Yourself Beautiful

Cosmetic Surgeries
Number of Procedures
2,000,000
1,750,000
1,500,000
1,250,000
1,000,000
750,000
500,000
250,000
0
United States
China
Brazil
India
Mexico
Countries

Source: ISAPS Biennial Global Survey

Around the world, people are having cosmetic surgery—surgery that changes their appearance to make them more beautiful or attractive. A recent survey shows the five countries in the world with the most cosmetic surgery procedures.

A | **Meaning from Context.** Read and listen to the article. Notice the words in blue. These are words you will hear and use in Lesson A.

track 1-21

In the world of high-fashion models, you don't see the variations in body type that you find with random people on the street. In fact, the classic runway model is skinny, or thin. Many people are disturbed by extremely thin models in fashion shows and magazines. Some models have a height-to-weight ratio that is unhealthy. For example, a model with an unhealthy height-to-weight ratio might be around five feet six inches tall (173 centimeters tall) but weigh only 108 pounds (49 kilograms).

The modeling business is slowly evolving, and the type of model that designers prefer is changing. In the past, fashion shows consistently featured extremely skinny models. Now, healthy-looking models are also appearing on runways. In some countries—Australia, for example—the government has even asked fashion designers and magazines to stop hiring extremely thin models for fashion shows and photo shoots. Now when designers think about presenting their clothes in a fashion show, they often envision their clothes on people with different body types. As a result, people's perception of fashion models and their opinion of what constitutes beauty are starting to change.

A model walks down a runway at a fashion show.

B | Write each word in blue from exercise **A** next to its definition.

1. _____envision_____ (v.) to have or form a mental picture
2. _____evolving_____ (v.) gradually changing and developing
3. _____consistently_____ (adv.) always behaving or happening in the same way
4. _____ratio_____ (n.) the relationship between the size, amount, or number of two things; a proportion, e.g., 2:1
5. _____classic_____ (adj.) traditional or expected characteristics that remain the same over time
6. _____constitute_____ (v.) serves as
7. _____variation_____ (n.) differences in level, amount, quantity, and so on
8. _____random_____ (adj.) without a special reason or plan
9. _____disturbed_____ (v.) made someone feel upset or worried
10. _____perception_____ (n.) the way people think about a topic or the impression they have of it

A | Read the paragraph and fill in each blank with the correct form of a word from the box.

classic	constitute	disturb	envision	evolve

Have you ever considered cosmetic surgery? The idea of changing one's looks surgically (1) _____disturb_____ or even frightens many people. Still, people's feelings about cosmetic surgery have (2) _____evolved_____ over time. According to the International Society of Aesthetic Plastic Surgeons,[1] more than 8 million cosmetic surgeries were completed worldwide in 2009. The most popular type of cosmetic surgery was liposuction, a surgery where fat is removed from the body. Liposuction surgeries (3) _____constitute_____ about 19 percent of the total cosmetic surgeries in the world.

With modern cosmetic surgery, you (4) _____envision_____ what you want to look like and then use surgery to make it happen. For example, think about the (5) _____classic_____ beauties of the movies. Would you like Marilyn Monroe's nose, Audrey Hepburn's eyes, or Grace Kelly's chin? They can be yours—for a price. The average price for liposuction is nearly $3000 and a hair transplant may cost more than $4500. No one ever said beauty was cheap!

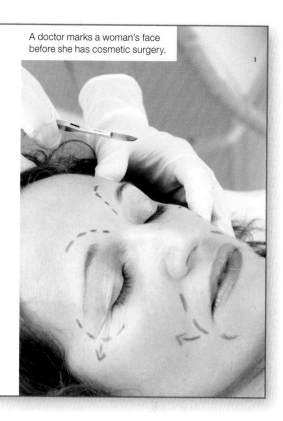

A doctor marks a woman's face before she has cosmetic surgery.

[1]**Aesthetic plastic surgery** is another way to refer to cosmetic surgery.

B | **Self-Reflection.** Form a group with two or three other students and discuss the questions.

1. What is your **perception** of cosmetic surgery? Explain your opinion.
2. Determine the **ratio** of men to women in your class or at your workplace.
3. Would you prefer to live in a city where the weather changes often or in a city where the weather is always **consistent**? Explain your answer.
4. Have you ever had a **random** meeting with a person who later became your friend? Talk about how you met.
5. Do you like to follow the same schedule every day or do you prefer a **variation** of your daily activities? Explain your answer.

Before Listening

Discussion. With a partner, discuss the questions.

1. Look at the two rows of photos. These photos were shown to people who participated in a study on beauty. In each row, select the photo that shows the most beautiful face, in your opinion. Do you and your partner agree?

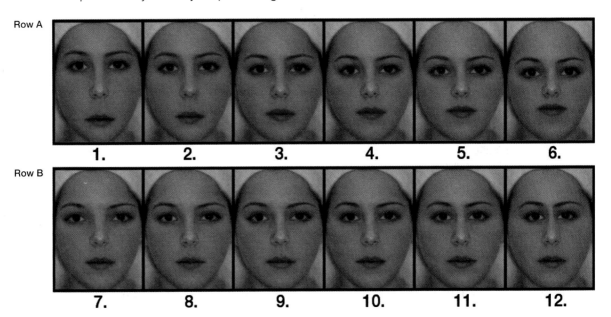

Row A

Row B

2. Look at the photos again. According to researchers, most people would choose Photo 4 and Photo 9 as the most beautiful faces. Did you choose these photos? Explain.

Listening: A News Report

A | Listening for Main Ideas. Listen to a news report about beauty. Match each scientist or group of scientists with the correct research results.

track 1-22

Scientists	Research Results
1. Judith Langlois ____	a. Men's ideas about beauty and attractiveness evolved over thousands of years.
2. Pamela M. Pallett Stephen Link Kang Lee ____	b. Symmetry is a key part of what makes a face beautiful.
3. Victor Johnston David Perrett ____	c. There is a "golden ratio" for the ideal distance between the eyes, the mouth, and the edge of the face.
4. Don Symons ____	d. Men prefer large eyes, full lips, and a small nose and chin.

track 1-22 **B | Listening for Details.** Listen again and circle the correct answer to each question or statement.

1. According to the research, most people think that a beautiful face is _____.
   a. a face with small eyes
   b. average and almost symmetrical
   c. disturbing to observers

2. The "golden ratio" for the length of a face states that the distance between the eyes and the mouth _____.
   a. is 36 percent of the length of the whole face
   b. is 56 percent of the length of the whole face
   c. is 66 percent of the length of the whole face

3. What facial features did scientists Victor Johnston and David Perrett think men find most beautiful?
   a. blue eyes, full lips, and a strong chin
   b. large eyes, full lips, and a small chin
   c. large eyes, thin lips, and a strong nose

4. What conclusion does the reporter, Gwen Silva, probably agree with?
   a. Beauty is in the eye of the beholder.
   b. There is no variation in the ideas about beauty between cultures.
   c. People from the same culture mostly agree on what makes someone beautiful.

After Listening

Critical Thinking. Form a group with two or three other students and discuss the questions.

1. Do you agree or disagree with the saying "Beauty is in the eye of the beholder"? Explain your opinions.
2. Scientists believe that a beautiful face is a symmetrical face. What other features make a face beautiful to you?
3. The news report said that perceptions of beauty vary from culture to culture. Can you give any examples of how perceptions of beauty vary between cultures?

Maori women of New Zealand perform a traditional dance. The Maori people believe that blue lips are beautiful.

Language Function

Paraphrasing

During lectures and conversations, speakers often need to paraphrase information. If you paraphrase, you express what was said in a different way. Paraphrasing is a useful way to restate information that may be new or difficult for listeners to understand. Here are some expressions you can use to paraphrase information.

I mean . . .	*Let me put it another way.*
In other words . . .	*To put it another way . . .*
That is (to say), . . .	

track 1-23

A | In the news report, there were a number of useful expressions for paraphrasing. Listen to the sentences from the news report and fill in the expressions.

1. An often-quoted expression is "Beauty is only skin deep." _____, someone can be beautiful on the outside, but be mean or unpleasant on the inside.

2. Another famous saying is "Beauty is in the eye of the beholder." _____, each person's idea of beauty is different.

3. In addition, the research shows that a beautiful face is a symmetrical face. _____, if both sides of the face are exactly the same, we consider a person beautiful.

Critical Thinking Focus: Understanding Quotations

Speakers sometimes use quotations when talking with others. A quotation is a sentence or phrase from another speaker that you repeat in your own speech. Quotations are often used to introduce the topic of a lecture, to emphasize an idea, or to end a conversation in an interesting way.

B | Read these quotations about beauty. In your own words, write what each quotation means.

1. Beauty is not in the face; beauty is a light in the heart. —Kahlil Gibran

   _____

2. It matters more what's in a woman's face than what's on it. —Claudette Colbert

   _____

3. I've never seen a smiling face that was not beautiful. —Author Unknown

   _____

4. Time is a great healer, but a poor beautician.[1] —Lucille S. Harper

   _____

[1]A **beautician** is a person who cuts hair and performs other beauty-related tasks for people.

C | Paraphrasing. Work with a partner. Take turns reading the quotations in exercise **B** on page 48. Explain each quotation to your partner using a paraphrasing expression.

> Beauty is not in the face; beauty is a light in the heart. In other words, a person's beauty doesn't come from the way they look. It comes from their personality.

Grammar

Compound Adjectives

Compound adjectives are made up of two words, but act as a single idea. Compound adjectives are used to modify nouns. Compound adjectives can be formed in many different ways.

Adjective + past participle	Adverb + past participle	Noun + past participle
a **kind-hearted** man	a **highly respected** firm	a **sun-dried** tomato
a **red-headed** assistant	**consistently applied** rules	a **sweat-soaked** shirt

A | Study the grammar box above. Then look at the words in the boxes below. With a partner, come up with a compound adjective that describes each noun. Choose one word from each box to form the compound adjective.

Box A

good	often	rose
highly	poorly	sugar

Box B

built	free	motivated
colored	looking	quoted

1. a ___poorly - built___ structure
2. a(n) ___often - quoted___ saying
3. ___Highly - motivated___ students
4. ___rose - colored___ glasses
5. a ___sugar - free___ cake
6. a ___good looking___ model

a red-headed office worker

B | Work with your partner. One student will be Student A and the other will be Student B. Read each sentence in your list to your partner. Your partner will restate the sentence using a compound adjective.

> I see a girl with brown eyes.

> I see a brown-eyed girl.

Student A

1. I have an interview for a job that is part time.
2. The chef is preparing a meal that makes my mouth water.
3. I gave Elena the vase that was made by hand.
4. I can't wear this shirt that is soaked with sweat.

Student B

5. I'm going to buy a bookshelf that is four feet tall.
6. If you are a person who looks good, you might be able to have a career as a model.
7. The author who is world famous is visiting my university.
8. In an emergency, it's good to know that the babysitter has a cool head.

C | **Discussion.** Form a group with two or three other students and discuss the questions. Try to use compound adjectives.

1. What are some world-famous companies that you can think of?
2. Who is the most highly-respected person you know?
3. What is an often-quoted saying from your language? Do you agree with the saying?
4. What are some time-saving tips for helping to complete errands? Share your ideas with your group.
5. What are some well-known magazines and newspapers in your area?

A magazine stand in Beijing, China sells popular beauty, fashion, and lifestyle magazines.

Conducting a Survey

A | Follow the instructions to conduct a survey of your classmates' ideas about beauty.

   1. Choose four of the following questions to include in your survey. Then write two new questions of your own.

> **Survey Questions**
> - Is it better to be beautiful, intelligent, or wealthy? Explain your choice.
> - Who do you think is the most beautiful woman alive today? Who is the most handsome man alive today?
> - What is the minimum age at which people should be allowed to have cosmetic surgery?
> - What is the most unusual item of clothing you own?
> - What do you spend more money on: clothing and beauty supplies, food, or electronics?
> - Are there any fashions today that you think are strange?

   2. On a piece of paper, make a chart similar to the one below. Write your questions.

Questions	Student 1: _____	Student 2: _____	Student 3: _____
What is the most unusual item of clothing you own?			

   3. Talk to three of your classmates. Ask each classmate the survey questions you have chosen. In your notebook, take notes on each person's answers.

B | Form a group with two or three other students. Discuss the survey results. What is interesting or surprising about the information you heard? How would you answer each question in the survey? Discuss your thoughts with your group.

> The people that I surveyed think being intelligent is more important than being beautiful or wealthy. I agree with that.

> **Student to Student: Asking about Personal Opinions**
>
> Asking about a person's opinion can help you learn more information about that person. Here are some expressions you can use to ask about personal opinions.
>
> *What about you? What do you think?*
> *What was your experience like?*

A person holds a skin mask of a woman's face.

Skin Mask

Before Viewing

A | Using a Dictionary. Look at the words in the box. You will hear these words and phrases in the video. Write each word or phrase from the box next to the correct definition. Use your dictionary to help you.

gooey	inject	mummy	silicone	special effects

1. _____silicone_____ (n.) a rubber-like material
2. _____gooey_____ (adj.) soft and sticky
3. _____mummy_____ (n.) a dead body wrapped in cloth as in ancient Egyptian tombs
4. _____special effects_____ (n.) in movies, unusual images or sounds created using special techniques
5. _____inject_____ (v.) to force a liquid into something

B | Predicting Content. Look at the photos on pages 52 and 53 and read the captions. How do you think a skin mask is made? Discuss your ideas with the class.

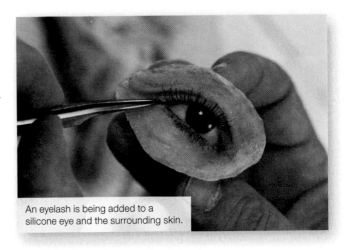

An eyelash is being added to a silicone eye and the surrounding skin.

While Viewing

A | Watch the video and choose the correct answer to each question.

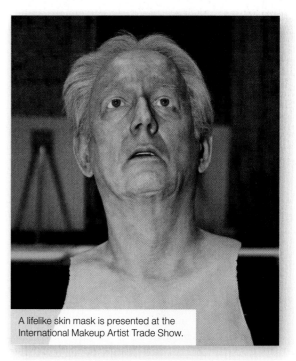

A lifelike skin mask is presented at the International Makeup Artist Trade Show.

1. Where are the people in the video?
   a. They are in a hospital.
   b. They are in a special-effects studio.
   c. They are in a room in Mike's home.

2. Why does the narrator say that Cassandra is brave?
   a. Because modeling for the skin mask is uncomfortable.
   b. Because she had cosmetic surgery on her face.
   c. Because she is the first model for a new type of skin mask.

3. How will the skin mask likely be used?
   a. To fool Cassandra's friends
   b. To demonstrate cosmetic surgery
   c. For special effects in a movie

B | **Sequencing Events.** Watch the video again. Put the steps for making a skin mask in the correct order from 1 to 9.

___6___ a. The artists create a series of positive and negative masks.

___8___ b. The mixture is injected into the master mold.

___1___ c. A cap is placed on Cassandra's hair.

___4___ d. Her face is wrapped in bandages.

___7___ e. The artists mix soft silicone and then color it with chemicals.

___2___ f. Vaseline is brushed over her eyebrows and eyelashes.

___9___ g. Makeup, eyebrows, and eyelashes are added to the skin mask.

___5___ h. The hardened material comes off.

___3___ i. Artists paint her face in quick-drying silicone.

After Viewing

Critical Thinking. With a partner, discuss the questions.

1. This skin mask is made by special-effects artists. How do you think a skin mask might be used for special effects in movies?

2. What are some other ways a skin mask could be used?

Model Cassandra Wheatley holds the completed silicone mask of her face.

track 1-24 **A** | **Using a Dictionary.** Read the sentences. Write the word from the box that can replace each word in parentheses. These are words you will hear and use in Lesson B. Use your dictionary to help you. Then listen and check your answers.

alternative	convince	derive	insert	textile
considerably	definite	exhibit	integrate	transport

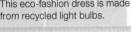

1. Joanne tried to ___convince___ (persuade) Steven to enter his design in the fashion show.

2. Eco-fashion is a(n) ___alternative___ (different) type of fashion that uses recycled materials.

3. The artist is going to ___exhibit___ (display) her latest work at a museum in Barcelona.

4. The workers in that ___textile___ (fabric) factory are treated fairly and paid well.

5. To sew the dress, ___insert___ (put) the needle into the fabric and make small stitches.

6. You can ___derive___ (make) a light, smooth fabric called rayon from plant cells.

7. The architect will ___integrate___ (combine) traditional and modern elements in the building he is designing.

8. My new job as a nurse pays ___considerably___ (a lot) more than my old job as an office worker.

9. They will ___transport___ (move) the trees to the park by truck.

10. The fashion show will be sometime in May, but the exact date is not yet ___definite___ (certain).

This eco-fashion dress is made from recycled light bulbs.

B | Read the information about eco-fashion. Fill in each blank with the correct form of a word from exercise **A**.

Q: What is eco-fashion?

A: Eco-fashion is all about making and wearing clothing that is safe and healthy for the environment, shoppers, and workers in the fashion industry. For example, some eco-fashion designers do not think clothes should be (1) ___transported___ long distances in trucks that use gasoline and create air pollution.

Q: Are eco-fashions made from traditional (2) ___textiles___ such as cotton?

A: Not always. Some eco-fashions combine or (3) ___integrate___ recycled or reused materials such as second-hand[1] clothes. Some fibers used in eco-fashion are even (4) ___derived___ from plastic bottles.

Q: What do eco-fashions look like?

A: Eco-fashion is very innovative! In fact, you might think that some of the most imaginative eco-fashion ideas are strange. At a recent eco-fashion show, designers (5) ___exhibited___ several new designs that used real plants. The designs included a ring with grass growing from it, a shirt collar made of living moss, and a handbag with a space in the center into which you can (6) ___insert___ a plant.

---

[1]**Second-hand** items are not new and have been owned by someone else.

A | Use the correct form of each word from the box to complete the information. Use each word only once.

alternative	convince	considerably	exhibit	insert	integrate	transport

The Cargolifter balloon can lift up to 75 tons.

If you don't already think clothing and textiles are amazing, here are a few examples that will (1) ___convince___ you that they truly are.

• The Cargolifter is a fabric balloon that is (2) ___considerably___ taller than most ballons. It is nearly as tall as a 20-story building. It can carry up to 75 tons. It is used to (3) ___transport___ trains from one place to another.

• A design laboratory has developed an "intelligent apron" that can understand what you say and help you in the kitchen. Electronics and a microphone are (4) ___integrated___ into the apron. The apron can turn on the stove, set a cooking timer, or show you a recipe on a screen.

• New York City's Museum of Modern Art recently (5) ___exhibited___ a number of (6) ___alternative___ items. One was "non-stop shoes." These shoes collect the energy you create in the day, and in the evening you can (7) ___insert___ an electric cord into them to power your electronic devices.

Understanding Suffixes

A suffix is placed at the end of a word in order to form a different word. The suffixes *-ive* or *-ative* are often added to words to form adjectives. It is often necessary to drop the final letter of the verb before you add a suffix.

> **imagine**   Do you prefer traditional fashion designs or **imaginative** ones?

B | **Using a Dictionary.** Use a word from the box below and the suffix *-ive* or *-ative* to complete the sentences. Use your dictionary to help you. (*See page 209 of the Independent Student Handbook for more information on suffixes.*)

act	addict	construct	cooperate	definite	derive

1. ___Cooperative___ learning is when students do coursework together.
2. We need to set a ___definitive___ date for our wedding.
3. Caffeine and nicotine are two ___addictive___ substances.
4. A person who does a lot of exercise has a(n) ___active___ lifestyle.
5. Criticism that is meant to help someone to improve is called ___constructive___ criticism.
6. ___derivative___ art is unoriginal; it copies elements from other artists' work.

Before Listening

Predicting Content. You are going to listen to three people talking about unusual fashions. Look at the photos. What do you think these items are? Discuss your ideas with a partner.

1. _____ 2. _____ 3. _____

Listening: An Informal Conversation

track 1-25 **A** | **Listening for Main Ideas.** Listen to the conversation. Look back at the photos. Under each photo, write the name or a brief description of the item.

track 1-25 **B** | **Note-Taking.** Listen again and complete the notes. (*See page 206 of the Independent Student Handbook for more information on note-taking.*)

> Antigravity jacket: part _____balloon_____ and part _____jacket_____
>
> Kevlar: _____man made_____ fiber, stronger than _____steel_____
>
> • used in _____Bullet proof vests_____ and _____ropes_____
>
> • developed in _____1960s_____
>
> Biosteel made from _____spider silk_____ protein produced in _____goat milk_____
>
> • possible uses: _____Rockets_____
>
> Wearable electronics integrate _____clothes_____ and _____electronics_____
>
> • Ex.: GPS sneakers allow parents to _____track lost children_____

C | Listening for Specific Information. Listen again. With a partner, answer the questions.

1. According to the conversation, where does Danish clothing designer Alex Soza get his ideas?
2. Which piece of clothing was modeled at the fashion show by an animal?
3. Why can't textile manufacturers raise large groups of spiders?
4. What does the man think about the future of wearable technology?

After Listening

Critical Thinking. With a partner, discuss the questions.

1. What are some uses for an antigravity jacket?
2. Goats and spiders are used in the production of Biosteel. Do you think it is acceptable to use animals for the purpose of creating new textiles? Explain your answer.
3. What could be some additional uses of GPS sneakers, besides helping parents to track their children?
4. Ten years from now, what other types of wearable electronics could people be wearing?

Pronunciation

Pronouncing /ŋ/ and /ŋk/

The /ŋ/ sound is often spelled with the letters *ng*.

/ŋ/   so**ng**, walki**ng**, ri**ng**

The sound /ŋk/ is usually spelled *nc* or *nk*.

/ŋk/   u**nc**le, a**nk**le

 A | Listen again to the words from the box and repeat the words after the speaker.

B | Collaboration. Work with a partner. Brainstorm words that have the /ŋ/ or /ŋk/ sound. Then write three questions using words from the pronunciation box or from your list. Take turns asking and answering your questions with your partner. Focus on the correct pronunciation of /ŋ/ and /ŋk/.

Language Function

Asking for Clarification

During a conversation, discussion, or a lecture, you may need to ask for clarification when you do not understand something. You may also need to ask speakers to define a word for you. Here are some expressions you can use to ask for a definition or for clarification.

(Sorry,) What does . . . mean?
What do you mean by . . . ?

What (exactly) is . . . ?
Could you explain . . . (for me, please)?

track 1-27 **A** | In the conversation, the speakers use a number of expressions to ask for clarification. Listen to the sentences and fill in the missing expressions.

1. **Sandra:** That antigravity jacket was like a piece of science fiction.

   Ana: Antigravity jacket? _____What exactly is_____ an antigravity jacket?

2. **David:** That jacket was interesting, I guess. But what amazed me was the vest made of Kevlar.

   Ana: _____Sorry what does_____ Kevlar _____mean_____?

3. **Ana:** Well, my friend was exhibiting some of her designs at an art gallery downtown, so I went there. She designs wearable electronics.

   Sandra: _____What do you mean by_____ wearable electronics?

B | Work with a partner. One student is Student A and the other is Student B. Your partner will read aloud a statement which includes an unknown word. Ask your partner for clarification about the word. Your partner will locate the definition from the box below and give you more information.

Many textiles are made from the silk of the *Bombyx mori*.

What is *Bombyx mori*?

Bombyx mori is the scientific name of the silk worm.

Student A

1. Next week Marjan is going to have **rhinoplasty**.
2. It cost 2 million dollars to develop a **prototype** of the electronic shoes.

Student B

3. I would never wear clothing made from spider webs because I have **arachnophobia**.
4. By law, children's pajamas must be **noncombustible**.

Definitions

Rhinoplasty is surgery to change the shape of the nose.
A **prototype** is the first model of a new product.
Arachnophobia is a great fear of spiders.
Noncombustible materials do not burn.

Grammar

Tag Questions

Tag questions help keep a conversation going. Tag questions are formed by adding a short question (or "tag") to the end of a statement. Affirmative statements have negative tags, and negative statements have affirmative tags. A listener can respond to tag questions by agreeing or disagreeing.

Questions	Responses	
*That's a very interesting dress, **isn't it**?*	*Yes, **it is**.*	*No, **it isn't**.*
*She wasn't thinking about becoming a fashion designer, **was she**?*	*Yes, **she was**.*	*No, **she wasn't**.*
*You haven't worn that before, **have you**?*	*Yes, **I have**.*	*No, **I haven't**.*
*This fabric won't tear easily, **will it**?*	*Yes, **it will**.*	*No, **it won't**.*

A | With a partner, complete the conversations with tag questions and appropriate answers. Then take turns asking and answering each question.

1. **Q:** Alex Soza is a very imaginative clothing designer, _isn't he?_
   A: Yes, _he is_.

2. **Q:** We've already discussed eco-fashion, _haven't we_?
   A: Yes, _we have_.

3. **Q:** You'd like to learn more about wearable electronics, _wouldn't you_?
   A: No, _I wouldn't_.

4. **Q:** You're not going to wear a wool sweater today, _Are you_?
   A: Yes, _I am_.

5. **Q:** It's not possible to make textiles from plastic bottles, _Is it_?
   A: Yes, _it is_.

6. **Q:** You had a good time at the fashion show, _hadn't you_?
   A: No, _I hadn't_.

B | **Role-Playing.** Work with your partner. Pretend that one student is a famous fashion designer and the other student is a news reporter. The news reporter should ask the designer questions about the designer's company, style, favorite textiles, or recent projects. Use your imagination to come up with questions and answers. Be sure to use tag questions when asking your questions.

> You live and work in Paris, don't you?

> Yes, I do. I've lived there for 20 years now.

ENGAGE: Giving a Group Presentation

You are going to prepare and give a group presentation about fashion trends from a particular country.

A | **Discussion.** Form a group with two or three other students. Discuss the differences in fashion that you see in your city or area.

B | **Brainstorming.** Your group is going to brainstorm about fashion trends in a particular city, country, or area. As a group, decide on the location you want to talk about. If necessary, do additional research to find out more about the styles and fashions that are popular. Take notes in the chart below to help you organize your ideas.

A clothing store in Kabul, Afghanistan

A clothing market in Oruro, Bolivia

What types of fabrics are popular?	
What clothing fashions are "in"?	
How do people wear their hair?	
What types of shoes do people prefer?	
What accessories do people like to wear?	
What other aspects of fashion are important?	

C | **Planning a Presentation.** In your group, compare your notes from exercise **B**. Work together to plan and organize your presentation. (*See page 211 of the Independent Student Handbook for more information on planning and organizing your presentation.*)

D | **Presentation.** Give your presentation. Be sure that each group member gets a chance to speak during the presentation.

Presentation Skills: Preparing Your Notes

Often you will use notes to help you remember what you want to say during a presentation. When you are preparing your notes, do not write out your presentation word-for-word. Instead, use key words, short sentences, or even pictures. Keep your notes organized and list points in the order you want to speak about them.

Energy Issues

ACADEMIC PATHWAYS

Lesson A: Listening to a Guest Speaker
           Role-Playing a Town Meeting
Lesson B: Listening to a Study Group Discussion
           Creating and Using Visuals in a Presentation

Think and Discuss

1. Look at the photo and read the caption. What types of energy are you familiar with?

2. How much energy do you use in your daily life?

Vapor is released from a nuclear power plant in France.

Exploring the Theme:
Energy Issues

A | Look at the photos and read the captions. Then answer the questions.

1. How do you think energy use has changed over time?
2. In the future, do you think you will be using more or less electricity than you do now? Why do you think so?
3. Would you be willing to live next to a large energy facility such as a nuclear power plant or wind farm? Explain your answer.

Wind power provides energy to farms and homes in Abilene, Texas.

Big Power, Big Risks

By the year 2030, the demand for energy is expected to be double what it was in the year 2000. Providing the enormous quantity of energy the world needs is a difficult task, and there is often risk for workers, the public, and the environment.

In this village, lights shine from nearly every house. However, the world is still far away from providing inexpensive electricity. In fact, about one in four people still have no electricity at all.

A | **Meaning from Context.** Read and listen to the news report about the Deepwater Horizon oil spill. Notice the words in blue. These are words you will hear and use in Lesson A.

On April 20, 2010, one of the worst oil spills in history began in the Gulf of Mexico. The spill occurred at an oil rig, called the Deepwater Horizon, which is owned by the BP company. A buildup of pressure caused natural gas to shoot up suddenly from the ocean floor. The gas triggered a terrible explosion and a fire on the oil rig. After the explosion, the crew abandoned the platform and escaped in lifeboats. Unfortunately, eleven workers were never found.

A beach in the United States is covered with oil after the Deepwater Horizon oil spill.

For weeks, no one was sure just how much oil was being released into the Gulf of Mexico. Gradually, information about the damage from the oil spill emerged. It was discovered that between 50,000 to 60,000 barrels of oil a day were flowing into the Gulf. Experts from BP and other organizations tried to stop the spill, but it continued for nearly three months. By the time the leak was stopped, the beautiful blue waters of the Gulf had been contaminated with nearly 5 million barrels of oil.

Deepwater Horizon oil spill, Gulf of Mexico

The disaster did serious harm to the fishing and tourism industries in the southern United States. Pictures of birds that had been exposed to the thick oil appeared daily in the news. The American public reacted angrily, and the spill created a huge controversy. Some people even wanted to stop oil companies from drilling in the Gulf of Mexico. BP set aside 20 billion dollars to compensate fishermen, hotel owners, and store owners whose businesses were impacted by the spill.

B | Match each word in blue from exercise **A** with its definition. Use your dictionary to help you.

1. triggered (v.) _____
2. abandoned (v.) _____
3. released (v.) _____
4. emerged (v.) _____
5. experts (n.) _____
6. contaminated (v.) _____
7. exposed (v.) _____
8. reacted (v.) _____
9. controversy (n.) _____
10. compensate (v.) _____

a. to pay someone to replace lost money or things
b. became known; appeared
c. responded to
d. caused an event to begin to happen
e. left a place, thing, or person permanently
f. people who are very skilled or who know a lot about a particular subject
g. entered the surrounding atmosphere or area; freed
h. a disagreement, especially about a public policy or moral issue that people feel strongly about
i. made something dirty, harmful, or dangerous because of chemicals or radiation
j. placed in a dangerous situation

A | Read the interview and fill in each blank with the correct form of the word from the box. Use each word only once.

abandon	controversy	expert	react	trigger

Q: Can mining for energy sources such as coal and oil cause natural disasters?

A: Some people think so. For example, in 1989, there was an earthquake in the city of Newcastle, Australia. Some (1) _____ said it was (2) _____ by coal mining in the area. Others thought there was no way that mining 2297 feet (700 meters) down could cause an earthquake 6 miles (10 kilometers) beneath the surface of the earth.

Newcastle, Australia

Q: How did the public (3) _____ to the experts' opinion?

A: Well, it created a great deal of (4) _____. A lot of people called for an end to coal mining in Newcastle. John Tate, the Lord Mayor of the city at the time, said there was no chance Newcastle would (5) _____ coal mining.

B | With a partner, practice the interview from exercise **A**. Then switch roles and practice again.

C | **Discussion.** Form a group with two or three other students and discuss the questions.

1. Eleven people died in the 1989 Newcastle earthquake. Should the coal-mining companies of Newcastle **compensate** the families of the workers who died? Explain your opinion.

2. What is your reaction when photos of an environmental disaster are **released**? Give an example.

3. The Deepwater Horizon oil spill **contaminated** the ocean and seashore. In your opinion, who is responsible for cleaning up the oil spill?

4. What could happen to animals, fish, and plants that are **exposed** to oil spills or dangerous gases from coal mines?

5. Following an environmental disaster, what do you think should happen if information **emerges** that shows the accident was caused by a company's or a government's negligence?[1]

[1]If someone is guilty of **negligence**, they have failed to do something that they ought to do.

Before Listening

👥 **Predicting Content.** Work with a partner. Look at the map and diagram. Discuss the questions.

1. Use your dictionary and look up these terms: *containment*, *radiation*, *radioactive*, *half-life*. How do you predict these words will be used in the lecture?
2. Locate the containment structure in the diagram. Why do you think this structure is important? Explain your ideas.

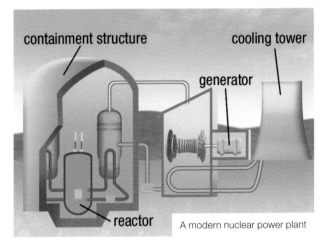

A modern nuclear power plant

Listening: A Guest Speaker

Critical Thinking Focus: Using an Outline to Take Notes

Using an outline can help you take organized and clear notes. In an outline, indicate main ideas with Roman numerals (I, II, III) and capital letters (A, B, C). Indicate details with numbers. As information becomes more specific, move it to the right.

🎧 track 2-3 **A** | Listen to the introduction to a lecture about the Chernobyl nuclear disaster. Read the outline as you listen.

I. Background
   A. 1970s & 1980s: Soviet Union developed nuclear technology
   B. 1986: 25 plants w/ safety probs.
II. Chernobyl disaster
   A. Causes
      1. Mistakes during safety test
      2. No containment building to limit fire and radiation
   B. Result: explosion→people dead

B | Discussion. With a partner, discuss the questions. Refer to the outline in exercise **A**.

1. What topics did the introduction cover?
2. Which items are main ideas? Which items are details?

track 2-4 **C | Listening for Main Ideas.** Listen to the entire lecture and answer the questions.

1. Check (✔) each effect of the explosion that the speaker mentions.
   ____ a. People were forced to leave their homes.
   ____ b. Animals died from exposure to radiation.
   ____ c. Young people became ill with thyroid cancer.
   ____ d. Billions of dollars were spent on health and cleanup costs.
   ____ e. Modern nuclear power plants are built with containment structures.
2. What happened to the town of Pripyat?
   a. It was abandoned.
   b. It burned to the ground.
   c. It was turned into a tourist attraction.
3. What is surprising about Chernobyl today?
   a. The residents of Pripyat have returned.
   b. Many animals have come back to the area.
   c. The radiation from the explosion has disappeared.

track 2-4 **D | Outlining.** Listen again. Continue the outline from exercise **A** on page 66. Complete the outline with details from the lecture. (*See page 206 of the Independent Student Handbook for more information on outlining.*)

C. The Chernobyl plant today
  1. Still extremely _____
  2. There are plans to build a _____
D. Radioactivity
  1. Many areas still contaminated with cesium _____
  2. Half-life of _____ years
E. The exclusion zone today
  1. _____ people live there
  2. Animals have returned, for ex., _____

After Listening

Discussion. With a partner, answer the questions. Use your notes as well as your own ideas.

1. Describe the town of Pripyat before and after the disaster.
2. These days, a small number of tourists travel to Chernobyl. Would you go there if you had the opportunity?

Language Function

Emphasizing Important Information

Here are some expressions used to emphasize important information.

Don't forget that . . .
Let me stress that . . .
I want to emphasize that . . .
I would like to stress that . . .

I would like to point out that . . .
You need to remember that . . .
It is important to note/remember that . . .

track 2-5

A | In the lecture about Chernobyl, the speaker used a number of useful expressions to emphasize her point. Listen to the excerpts and fill in the missing expressions.

1. _____ Chernobyl had no containment structure. This building would have limited the fire and contained the radioactivity.

2. Thyroid cancer can be cured, but _____ survivors must spend a lifetime taking medication.

3. _____, however, that it will be decades before large numbers of people are allowed to come back and live in the exclusion zone.

Wild horses, called Przewalski horses, walk through the Chernobyl exclusion zone. These horses are extinct in the wild and can only be found in a few nature reserves and in the Chernobyl exclusion zone.

B | Form a group with two other students. Choose one of the types of energy below and read the facts. Then tell the members of your group what you know about your energy source. Add your own ideas. Emphasize the fact that you think is the most interesting.

> Oil prices are rising. For example, it cost me almost $60 to put gas in my car yesterday. Last year, it would have cost me only $40. Still, it is important to remember that . . .

Oil

- The price of oil is rising.
- Oil spills pollute the environment.
- The top three oil-producing countries in the world are Saudi Arabia, Russia, and the United States.

Coal

- Coal deposits in the United States contain more energy than all the world's oil reserves combined.
- Coal is a relatively inexpensive energy source.
- Coal mining is dangerous. Between 1969 and 2000, more than 20,000 coal miners were killed.

Wind

- Wind power is clean, but is sometimes very noisy.
- The world will never run out of wind.
- Denmark gets 20 percent of its electricity from wind power.

Grammar

The Future Perfect

The future perfect describes a state or a completed action in the future. We use this tense when the state or action will be completed by a specified future time or event. The future perfect is formed with *will* + *have* + the past participle.

> *If you start saving your money now, in ten years you* **will have saved** *enough money to retire.*

With the future perfect, a time expression is often used with *by* or *by the time*.
> **By** *my 30th birthday, I* **will have graduated** *from college.*

A | With a partner, complete these predictions about energy use in the future. Fill in each blank with the future perfect form of the verb in parentheses. Then take turns saying each sentence.

2025 1. By 2025, the capacity of batteries _____ (increase) by 1000 percent.

2030 2. By 2030, oil production _____ (return) to the level it was in 1980.

2040 3. By 2040, we will still be using oil, but its role _____ (change) significantly.

2050 4. By 2050, electric cars _____ completely _____ (replace) gasoline-powered cars.

2060 5. By 2060, corporations _____ (build) wind farms along the coasts of most nations.

B | **Self-Reflection.** Form a group with two or three other students. Use *by* or *by the time* and the future perfect to make predictions about your future. Respond to your classmates' sentences. Use the topics listed below to help your discussion.

- graduate from college
- get a job
- buy my first house
- buy a car
- learn to drive
- learn a new language

> By next year my husband and I will have bought a house.

> That's nice. Where would you like to live?

Role-Playing a Town Meeting

A | Form a group with three other students. You will role-play a city council meeting about building a nuclear power plant. Read the situation and the role cards. Assign two students to each role.

Situation: The city council has approved a plan to build a nuclear power plant in your city. A small group of residents are against the plan. They are going to meet with city council members to discuss their concerns.

Role #1: Residents against the Nuclear Power Plant

1. Nuclear power plants aren't safe. We don't want a nuclear accident to happen here.

2. Nuclear power plants produce waste that is dangerous for many years.

3. People who live near a nuclear power plant might get cancer.

Role #2: City Council Members

1. Nuclear safety technology has greatly advanced in recent years.

2. France, Belgium, and Slovakia rely on nuclear power for more than 50 percent of their electricity. There have been no big nuclear accidents in those countries.

3. Nuclear power could help us stop using oil.

B | Work with the group member who shares your role. Think of more arguments to support your point. In addition, try to think of responses to the other side's arguments.

> I think they will say that . . .

> If they say that, we should emphasize that . . .

C | **Role-Playing.** Role-play the discussion in your group. Use expressions of emphasis when appropriate.

> Thank you for meeting with us. We have a few concerns about this nuclear power plant.

> I understand. First of all, let me stress that we will do everything possible to make this power plant safe.

Student to Student: Conceding a Point

In a debate or discussion, people often argue from different points of view. If an argument is very convincing to you, you can let the other person know that you agree with their point or that you accept that their point is true. Here are some expressions to concede a point.

Good point.
Fair enough.
I'll give you that.

Solar cells turn sunlight into electricity.

SOLAR POWER

Before Viewing

Understanding Visuals. Read the information. Use the words in blue to label the diagram.

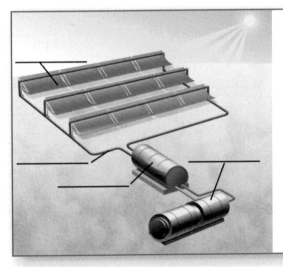

There are many different kinds of solar power systems. This diagram shows how parabolic trough solar power works.

1. Sunlight hits curved mirrors that direct all the light and heat to the middle of the mirror.

2. In the middle of the mirror, a tube filled with synthetic[1] oil is heated to about 700°F.

3. The oil runs into a boiler where it turns water into steam.

4. The steam spins an electric turbine, which turns and makes electricity.

[1]**Synthetic** products are made from chemicals or artificial substances rather than from natural sources.

While Viewing

A | Watch the video. Fill in the blanks with the word or words you hear.

The most powerful source of (1) _____ on the planet is actually out in space. It's (2) _____. More energy falls as sunlight on the United States in a single day than it uses in a (3) _____. But it's been difficult to turn that sunlight into (4) _____. Many people already use some (5) _____. But the world's need for power is great, and for solar power to be an alternative to other energy sources, it has to be both affordable and (6) _____.

B | Watch the video again. Check (✔) the five true statements.

1. ___ Sacramento doesn't use much solar power.
2. ___ Many new homes have solar cells.
3. ___ Many people drive solar-powered cars.
4. ___ Solar panels shade parking lots.
5. ___ Solar panels shade city buildings.
6. ___ Sacramento gets lower prices by buying a lot of solar panels at one time.
7. ___ Solar power is very expensive to residents of Sacramento.
8. ___ People can sell electricity back to the power company.

C | Viewing for Specific Information. Watch the video again. Circle the best answer to each question.

1. Where is the Kramer Solar Junction facility located?
   a. In the mountains
   b. In a desert
   c. By the sea
2. How many people can the facility provide power for?
   a. Half a million
   b. Five million
   c. Eight and a half million
3. What happens on days when there is no sun?
   a. The facility buys back power from customers.
   b. The facility uses power from batteries.
   c. The facility uses backup natural gas generators.
4. What does the facility produce a lot of?
   a. Power
   b. Carbon dioxide
   c. Smog

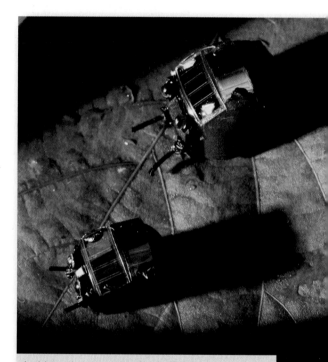

Ladybug robots crawl down a leaf. The robots are powered by solar power collectors attached to their backs.

After Viewing

Critical Thinking. With a partner, discuss the questions.

1. What are some problems that could occur when using solar power?
2. In general, do you think the government should be responsible for developing alternative energies? Or, should it be left to private corporations to develop alternative energies? Explain your answer.
3. Mirrors now cover 1000 acres of the Mojave Desert at the Kramer Solar Junction power facility. What impact could this have on the local environment there?

A | **Meaning from Context.** Read and listen to the information. Notice the words in blue. These are words you will hear and use in Lesson B.

track 2-6

People wait in line for gasoline.

When oil was inexpensive and abundant, people learned to depend on it for heat and fuel. More recently, oil has been more difficult to find, as it is hidden deep beneath the earth under many layers of solid rock. There have even been oil shortages, and we have had to wait in long lines and pay high prices for gasoline. A serious disadvantage of oil, coal, and similar fuels is the pollution they create around our cities.

Water is released at a hydroelectric dam.

Today, researchers are focusing on energy sources beyond oil. Countries and companies are pursuing alternative energy. They are looking for energy sources that are renewable and can never be used up. These alternative energies follow the principle that energy production should be sustainable, not temporary. People are showing a lot of enthusiasm for new energy technologies such as wind and hydroelectric power. Government incentives in the form of money or tax breaks have helped convince some companies to develop alternative energy technologies. Experts think that in the future the world will utilize alternative energy for a larger percentage of its total energy needs.

B | Write each word in blue from exercise **A** next to its definition.

1. _____ (adj.) present or existing in large quantities
2. _____ (n.) the feeling of being very interested in or excited about something
3. _____ (n.) things that encourage you to want to work hard or take action
4. _____ (n.) pieces of a material or substance that cover a surface or are between two other things
5. _____ (v.) making an effort to achieve a goal
6. _____ (n.) a factor which makes a person or a thing less useful or successful than other people or things
7. _____ (n.) a general belief about the way something should behave
8. _____ (v.) to use
9. _____ (adj.) resources that are natural and always available, such as wind and sunlight
10. _____ (n.) conditions in which there is not enough of something

A | What do you know about geothermal energy? Work with a partner and take the quiz. Circle **T** for *true* and **F** for *false*. Then check your answers at the bottom of the page. Which of these facts surprised you? Explain.

GEOTHERMAL ENERGY: What do you know?

1. Geothermal energy is a type of **renewable** energy.   **T**   **F**

2. Geothermal energy is found in the **layers** of rock beneath the earth's surface.   **T**   **F**

3. Geothermal energy is the most **abundant** energy source on earth.   **T**   **F**

4. The U.S. government offers **incentives** to homeowners to install geothermal systems in their homes.   **T**   **F**

5. Geothermal energy works on the same **principle** as the steam engine: when water is converted to steam, it produces force.   **T**   **F**

6. Geothermal energy has been **utilized** for cooking and heating only in the past 50 years.   **T**   **F**

Visitors swim in a hot spring created by geothermal energy. Geothermal energy is derived from the earth's internal heat.

B | **Self-Reflection.** With your partner, discuss the questions.

1. Do you plan to **pursue** more education sometime in the future? Explain.
2. What is a hobby or activity that you are **enthusiastic** about? Why do you enjoy it?
3. There is a **shortage** of nurses in the world. Would you ever consider becoming a nurse? Explain.
4. Do you have an **incentive** for learning English? What is it?
5. Do you think that people who avoid technology are at a **disadvantage** compared to people who use technology often? Explain.

ANSWERS: The false statements are #3 (Other sources such as coal are more abundant.); #4 (The government offers incentives to install solar systems, but not geothermal.); and #6 (Geothermal energy has been used for thousands of years.)

Before Listening

Understanding Visuals. Work with a partner. Look at the diagrams. How do wind and hydroelectric systems generate electricity? Share some ideas with your partner. (*See page 216 of the Independent Student Handbook for more information on understanding visuals.*)

Wind Power

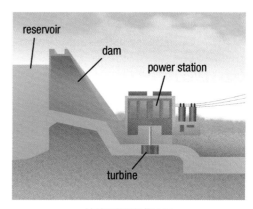

Hydroelectric Power

Listening: A Study Group Discussion

track 2-7 **A** | **Listening for Key Concepts.** Listen to a student speaking at the beginning of a study group meeting. Are these statements true or false? Circle **T** for *true* or **F** for *false*.

1. The group is meeting for the first time.	**T**	**F**
2. The group is preparing for a presentation.	**T**	**F**
3. The presentation is about renewable energies.	**T**	**F**
4. The first speaker will talk about fossil fuels.	**T**	**F**

track 2-8 **B** | **Using a Graphic Organizer.** Listen to students presenting their research on solar, wind, and hydroelectric power. Complete the notes in the T-charts below and on page 77.

Solar Power Advantages	Solar Power Disadvantages
1. No fire = no _____	1. Cost of _____
2. Free	2. _____ cut off energy supply
3. 100% _____	3. _____ technology isn't good enough yet

Wind Power Advantages	Wind Power Disadvantages
1. Clean, renewable	1. Look _____
2. No emissions = no _____	2. Turbines make _____
3. Costs _____	3. No wind = no _____
4. Many govs. offer _____	4. Tech. for _____ hasn't been developed yet

Hydroelectric Power Advantages	Hydroelectric Power Disadvantages
1. Water is _____	1. Damage to _____
2. Once built, doesn't need _____	2. Destroys _____
3. No _____	3. Forces people _____
4. Cost: _____	

After Listening

Critical Thinking. Using your notes from pages 76 and 77, discuss the questions with a partner.

1. Which advantages do all three forms of energy share?
2. Imagine that your community has decided to build a renewable energy facility. Which energy source is best for your area? Consider the advantages and disadvantages of solar, wind, and hydroelectric power. Also consider the environment and weather in your area.

Pronunciation

Stressing Two-Word Compounds

track 2-9

In many two-word compounds, the stress is on the first word.

book review   **foot**print   **green**house   **living** room   **moving** van

Stressing both words in these situations can sound strange or can change the meaning of the sentence.

The peas were grown in a **green**house. (a glass building for growing plants)
I saw you standing in front of a **green house**. (a house painted the color green)

track 2-10 **A** | Listen to each sentence and check (✔) the correct meaning of the underlined phrase.

1. I met an English teacher.
   - ❑ a teacher of the English language
   - ❑ a teacher who is English
2. I had a glass of orange juice.
   - ❑ juice made from oranges
   - ❑ orange-colored juice, maybe mango
3. The police spotted a moving van.
   - ❑ a van in motion
   - ❑ a large van for moving furniture
4. Where should I put this hot plate?
   - ❑ a plate that is hot
   - ❑ a small stove for keeping food warm
5. That's a beautiful yellow jacket.
   - ❑ a flying insect
   - ❑ a coat

B | With a partner, take turns saying the sentences from exercise **A**. Stress either the first underlined word or both of the underlined words. Your partner will tell you the meaning of the word or phrase he or she hears.

Language Function

Expressing Approval and Disapproval

Here are some expressions you can use to express approval or disapproval.

Approval

It's OK that . . .
I think it's fine to (verb) . . .
I (strongly) approve of (noun) . . .
It's OK (for someone) to (verb) . . .

Disapproval

It's wrong to (verb) . . .
It's not right that . . .
I (strongly) disapprove of (noun) . . .
It's not right (for someone) to (verb) . . .

A | In the study group discussion, there were a number of expressions for expressing approval and disapproval. Listen and fill in the missing expressions you hear.

track 2-11

1. On the downside, some people _____ wind turbines because they're ugly. They also complain about the noise the machines make, although most people think _____ put up wind turbines on farmlands.

2. A lot of people think _____ to destroy animal habitats this way. They also believe _____ that people are forced to leave their homes.

B | Read the statements. Use the ratings below to indicate your approval or disapproval of each topic.

1 = strongly approve   2 = approve   3 = neither approve nor disapprove   4 = disapprove   5 = strongly disapprove

Statements	My Rating
a. The city council has voted to raise taxes by one percent in order to put solar energy systems in all government buildings. Do you approve or disapprove of raising taxes?	
b. A dam will provide cheap hydroelectric power to millions of people. However, it will require hundreds of people to leave the valley where they have been living for many years. Do you approve or disapprove of building the dam?	
c. A proposed geothermal plant near your town will reduce your energy bills. However, the steam that is released contains a gas that smells like rotten eggs. Do you approve or disapprove of building the geothermal plant?	
d. Your neighbor wants to install a wind turbine in his backyard. Do you approve or disapprove?	

C | **Discussion.** Form a group with three other students and compare your ratings from exercise **B**. One student should read each statement. Then group members should take turns giving and explaining their ratings. Discuss whether you agree or disagree with your classmates' ratings.

Grammar

The Future Perfect Progressive

The future perfect progressive is used to talk about actions that will be in progress before a specific time in the future. This tense is formed with *will* + *have* + *been* + the present participle.

> By 2020, we **will have been drilling** oil wells for over 160 years.

The future perfect progressive emphasizes the duration of an action up to a specific future time. Often, this tense is used with a time expression and *for*.

> In just two weeks, we will have been meeting **for three months**.

A | Complete the sentences with the future perfect progressive form of the verb in parentheses.

1. In June of next year, my father _____ (living) in Brazil for 10 years.
2. In November, that company _____ (sell) wind turbines for six months.
3. On his next birthday, John _____ (drive) for 15 years.
4. In 2025, France _____ (produce) electricity with nuclear power for 60 years.
5. Next February, Sally _____ (work) as a nurse for 25 years.
6. In 2030, Iceland _____ (use) geothermal energy to heat homes for 100 years.
7. By next year, my book club _____ (meeting) for 5 years.

B | Fill in the blanks with the future perfect or the future perfect progressive form of the verb in parentheses.

I've been thinking about going to college for a while. In fact, by the end of June I (1) _____ (work) for two years. At that point, I'd like to quit my job and start studying. I have decided to get a degree in business at City University. By January 30, I (2) _____ (submit) my application. I hope that by May I (3) _____ (received) their answer. I hope to study with Professor Morse. He is very experienced. By next year, he (4) _____ (teach) business courses for more than 20 years. The local government wants people to study, so they began giving financial incentives to students last year. By the time I graduate, they (5) _____ (give) financial incentives for five years.

C | **Discussion.** With a partner, discuss the questions.

Which of these inventions and technologies do you use? When did you start using them? By 2025, how long will you have been using them? Talk about additional technologies that you use often.

- video games
- smart phone
- personal computer
- high-definition television

> I started using a cell phone in 2003. By 2025, I will have been using a cell phone for 22 years!

ENGAGE: Creating and Using Visuals in a Presentation

Your group is going to deliver a presentation to the class about an unusual source of energy. To support your presentation, your group will make a poster or a slide presentation with pictures, graphs, or other visual information. Your visual should include answers to these questions:

1. What is an unusual source of energy?
2. How does this energy source work?
3. What are the advantages and disadvantages of using this energy source?

A | Discussion. Form a group of two or three students. Examine the list of unusual energy sources and select one to research.

This biomass plant burns rice to generate electricity.

biodiesel	hydrogen fuel cells
biomass	methane from landfills
energy-generating floors	sugar
ethanol	tidal or ocean power

B | Researching. Outside of class, research your topic online or in the library. Use the outline below as a guide while you take notes about your topic. Find several images that relate to your energy source. (*See pages 211–212 of the Independent Student Handbook for more information on doing research.*)

  I. Type of energy
     A. Description
     B. Source
 II. Examples of how the energy is used
     A. Places
     B. Purposes
III. Advantages
 IV. Disadvantages
  V. Future of this form of energy

C | Planning a Presentation. As a group, use your notes from exercise **B** and your images to create a poster or slide presentation about your energy source. Be sure that your poster or slide presentation answers the three questions in the box at the top of the page.

D | Presentation. When you give your presentation, all group members should speak. Be sure to explain the images you present, and answer any questions from your audience.

Presentation Skills: Fighting Nervousness

It is normal to be a little nervous at the beginning of a presentation. However, the first impression you make on your audience is very important. Make an effort to speak slowly and calmly at the beginning of your presentation. Memorizing the first few sentences you plan to say can sometimes help. Soon you will begin to feel more comfortable and gain confidence.

Migration

ACADEMIC PATHWAYS

Lesson A: Listening to a Radio Show
Talking about Your Family History
Lesson B: Listening to a Conversation between Friends
Doing a Research-Based Presentation

Think and Discuss

1. Look at the photo. Where do you think these birds are going?

2. What are some of the reasons that people and animals move in large numbers?

3. Where on our planet do you believe the first human beings lived? Why do you think so?

Migrating snow geese and Canada geese fly as the sun sets.

Exploring the Theme: Migration

Look at the map and photos. Then answer the questions.

1. Look at the map. What do the arrows mean?
2. Who lived in Europe before the arrival of modern humans?
3. When did modern humans possibly arrive in Australia?
4. Think about your family and your ancestors. Where did they come from?

NORTH AMERICA
15,000 years ago

SOUTHERN EUROPE
20,000 years ago

WEST AFRICA
70,000 years ago

SOUTH AMERICA
15,000–12,000 years ago

Early Modern Humans

The earliest evidence of modern humans in Australia is at Lake Mungo. Items found there are around 50,000 years old. This and other facts from genetic research support the theory that modern humans migrated to Australia from Africa.

Generalized route

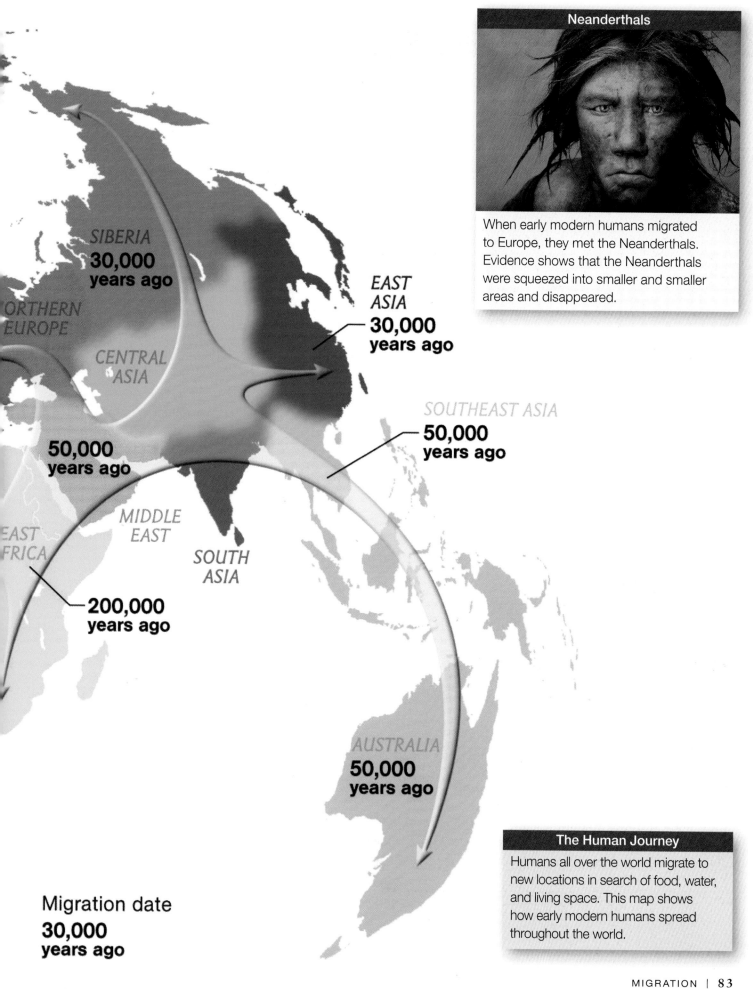

Neanderthals

When early modern humans migrated to Europe, they met the Neanderthals. Evidence shows that the Neanderthals were squeezed into smaller and smaller areas and disappeared.

SIBERIA
30,000 years ago

NORTHERN EUROPE

CENTRAL ASIA

EAST ASIA
30,000 years ago

SOUTHEAST ASIA
50,000 years ago

50,000 years ago

MIDDLE EAST

SOUTH ASIA

EAST AFRICA

200,000 years ago

AUSTRALIA
50,000 years ago

Migration date
30,000 years ago

The Human Journey

Humans all over the world migrate to new locations in search of food, water, and living space. This map shows how early modern humans spread throughout the world.

track 2-12 **A** | **Meaning from Context.** Read and listen to the information about migration. Notice the words in blue. These are words you will hear and use in Lesson A.

A scientist studies DNA and other genetic material.

The first migrations in human history were probably voluntary. People chose to leave their birthplace in search of food, water, or living space. Other migrations have been involuntary, which means that people were forced to travel. Between the 16th and 19th centuries, for instance, European slave traders kidnapped an immense number of African natives and transported them against their will to the Americas. There, the Africans encountered a world unlike anything they had ever seen in their native lands. They were forced to work in terrible conditions, and many died young.

The practice of slavery declined in the 18th and 19th centuries. Subsequently, it was made illegal, and the descendants[1] of those early African slaves became free. Africans were absorbed into the cultures of the Americas, and today they are described, for example, as African Americans, Afro-Caribbeans, or Afro-Latin Americans.

In recent years, DNA[2] researchers believe that they have linked the DNA of all humans on our planet with the DNA of African natives. Scientists assume that the entire world was populated as a result of a migration that began in Africa around 70,000 years ago. The implications of this idea would have shocked the European slave traders. They probably would have found it incredible to think that people all over the world were, in a sense, related to one another.

[1]Someone's **descendants** are the people in later generations who are related to them.
[2]**DNA** is a substance that carries information in the cells of the body. It is responsible for characteristics being passed on from parents to their children.

B | Write each word in blue from exercise **A** next to its definition.

1. _____ (n.) unstated conclusions based on given facts
2. _____ (adv.) later or afterwards
3. _____ (adj.) very unusual, surprising, or difficult to believe
4. _____ (v.) met someone unexpectedly
5. _____ (n.) large-scale movements of people or animals
6. _____ (adj.) extremely large or great amounts
7. _____ (v.) became less in quantity, importance, or strength
8. _____ (v.) take something into a larger group and make it part of the group
9. _____ (v.) connected physically or logically
10. _____ (v.) to believe something to be true, although it is not a proven fact

A | **Using a Dictionary.** Complete the paragraph with the correct form of a word from the box. Use your dictionary to help you.

absorb	assume	implication	migrate	subsequently

Early modern humans (1) _____ to Britain around 30,000 years ago. (2) _____, however, most left just 3000 years later. Britain became very cold when an ice age began, and early modern humans left to find warmer areas. Humans returned to Britain when temperatures became warm again. Until recently, scientists (3) _____ that people returned slowly and in small numbers. Now, however, scientists believe that humans actually returned very quickly and in large numbers. Scientists developed this theory by using *carbon dating*. Carbon dating is a process used to tell exactly how old an object is by measuring the amount of

Early modern humans hunt during the ice age.

carbon-14 it contains. Carbon-14 is a natural material that living things (4) _____ until they die. In Britain, scientists discovered the bones of a large number of animals such as horses and hares. The bones had marks on them showing that the animals had been killed and cut up by humans with tools. Scientists used carbon dating and found that the animals were killed very soon after the ice age ended. The (5) _____ was clear to the scientists: A large number of humans had followed the animals back to Britain soon after the temperature warmed.

B | **Discussion.** With a partner, answer the questions.

1. Early humans traveled **immense** distances to populate the world. Tell your partner about the longest trip you have ever taken.

2. Choose a time or a place in human history that you find **incredible**. Explain to your partner why you find this event interesting.

3. When old cultures **encounter** newer ones, both cultures change in positive and negative ways. What types of changes could happen when two cultures meet? Share your ideas with your partner.

4. In many developed countries, such as Italy and Japan, the population is **declining**. What effects might this have on these countries?

C | **Choosing the Right Definition.** Study the numbered definitions for **link**. Write the number of the definition next to the correct sentence below.

_____ a. Thousands of years ago there was a link between Asia and North America.

_____ b. Her necklace fell to the floor when one of the links broke.

_____ c. There is a link between exercise and good health.

link /lɪŋk/ **(links, linking, linked)**
[1] N-COUNT If there is a **link** between two things, there is a relationship between them; for example, one thing causes or affects the other. • *the link between cell phones and car accidents*　[2] N-COUNT A **link** between two things or places is a physical connection between them. • *A tunnel links between England and France.*　[3] N-COUNT A **link** is one of the rings in a chain. • *a broken link on a bicycle chain*

Before Listening

Predicting Content. With a partner, discuss the questions.

1. Look at the photos. Can you guess which of these people are related to each other? After you have guessed, look at the answer at the bottom of the page.

2. Sometimes, people who are genetically related look very different from one another. How does this happen?

3. Do you and your relatives look alike, or are there members of your family who look very different from everyone else? Explain.

Listening: A Radio Show

Critical Thinking Focus: Understanding Scientific Theories

In science, a *theory* is a general principle that is used to explain or predict events. Scientists look for *evidence* to prove that a theory is correct. For example, the evidence from carbon-14 dating supports the theory that humans returned to Britain shortly after the end of the ice age.

A | **Listening for Key Concepts**. Listen to the radio show and choose the best answer to each question. (*See page 202 of the Independent Student Handbook for more information on improving listening skills*.)

1. Which of these would be a good title for the radio show?
   a. Modern Humans—Not Neanderthal Descendants
   b. New Research Links Modern Humans to Africa
   c. Modern Humans Settled South America Last

2. What type of evidence does Dr. Corke mainly rely on?
   a. DNA research
   b. Ancient bones and tools
   c. Animal migration paths

3. Which statement about Neanderthals is true?
   a. They became modern humans.
   b. They crossed into the Americas.
   c. They no longer exist.

ANSWER: All of the people in the photos are related either closely or distantly to the woman on the far left.

B | Note-Taking. Listen again. As you listen, complete the time line about human migration. (*See page 206 of the Independent Student Handbook for more information on note-taking.*)

150,000 years ago	50–70,000 years ago	30,000 years ago	20,000 years ago
Ancestors of all people alive today lived in Africa	Group of ppl. left _____ & arrived in _____	2 grps. reached _____ & _____	_____ _____

C | Listening for Details. Listen again. Match each sentence beginning with the correct ending.

_____ 1. The group that followed the coast around the Arabian Peninsula and India . . .

_____ 2. The group that moved into Europe . . .

_____ 3. The group that migrated into Central Asia . . .

_____ 4. People who lived in southern Siberia . . .

a. probably encountered fewer Neanderthals.

b. eventually reached Australia if the DNA evidence is correct.

c. most likely migrated to North America between 15,000 and 20,000 years ago.

d. probably encountered a larger number of Neanderthals.

After Listening

Critical Thinking. Form a group with two or three other students. Discuss the questions.

1. According to the information in the radio show, what could cause people with the same genetic ancestor to look very different from one another?

2. Dr. Corke said that "there is no evidence of Neanderthal DNA in the DNA of modern humans." What does this imply about the relationship between modern humans and Neanderthals?

3. In what ways do you think humans have changed over time?

Language Function

> ### Expressing Surprise
>
> Here are some expressions you can use to show surprise.
>
> **Surprised**
> *No kidding.*
> *That's (really) surprising.*
> *I'm (really) surprised to hear that.*
> *I find that quite surprising.* (formal)
>
> **Very Surprised**
> *Wow!*
> *That's amazing/astonishing/incredible!*
> *Imagine that!* (formal)

 track 2-14 **A** | Read the information about expressing surprise. Then listen and repeat the expressions in the box.

track 2-15 **B** | In the radio show, the speakers used a number of useful phrases for expressing surprise. Listen and fill in the missing expressions.

1. **Dr. Corke:** This difference, called a mutation, is then passed down to all of that person's descendants, even 50,000 years in the future.
   Interviewer: _____!

2. **Dr. Corke:** If they're right, all people are linked to that woman through their mothers.
   Interviewer: _____.

3. **Dr. Corke:** We don't think they were absorbed into the modern human family. If they had been absorbed, DNA analysis would tell us that, you see. The evidence would be there in the DNA of Europeans today.
   Interviewer: _____! DNA certainly does tell us a lot!

C | Take turns telling a partner information about yourself. React to your partner's information, and use an expression of surprise if you are truly surprised.

> I have lived in 13 different countries in my life.

> That's incredible! What countries did you live in?

D | **Discussion.** Work with your partner. One student is Student A and the other is Student B. Read the animal facts to your partner. Respond to your partner with an expression of surprise from the box on page 88. Discuss any facts that are very surprising to you.

> Giraffes and humans have the same number of bones in their neck—seven.

> That's really surprising. I thought giraffes would have a lot more bones than humans have.

A giraffe

Student A

1. Giraffes and humans have the same number of bones in their necks—seven.
2. Cows cause more human deaths each year than sharks do.
3. Cockroaches can live as long as nine days without their heads, because the brain of the insect is located in its body.
4. It is estimated that there are nearly two billion cats in the world today.
5. The blue whale weighs 170 tons, which is about as much as 22 elephants.

A murder of crows

Student B

1. Any group of birds can be called a flock, but a group of crows is also called a murder of crows.
2. Deer are responsible for more human injuries and deaths than any other animal due to the many traffic accidents they cause.
3. Scientists have identified about 1.7 million species of animals, but there are many more species that have not been identified yet. There could be more unidentified species than identified ones.
4. The skin of a polar bear is actually black. Black skin helps the bears absorb as much of the sun's heat as possible.
5. Whiskers allow a cat to judge the width of a space, and whether it can fit into the space or not.

Grammar

Using Past Modals to Make Guesses about the Past

To make guesses about the past, use *could have*, *may have*, or *might have* and a past participle.

> Modern humans entering Central Asia **could have run** into Neanderthals.

In short responses that are guesses, do not use the past participle.

> A: *Did they come from Siberia?*
> B: *They* **may have**.

When the verb *be* is used, keep the past participle in the sentence.

> A: *Were there 1000 people in the group?*
> B: *There* **might have been**.

A | Form a group with two or three other students. Read the situations and make guesses about what happened for each situation. Use *could have*, *may have*, *might have*, and the past participle of a verb.

1. Samantha walked halfway to the bus stop this morning, then suddenly turned around and walked back to her house. Why did she turn around?

> She could have left the stove on.
>
> She may have left her wallet at home.
>
> She might have forgotten to lock the door.

2. Yesterday, Ali had to go to the hospital after playing basketball. What was wrong with him?
3. Dana got more exercise today than she has in years. What did she do?
4. In the 20th century, millions of people migrated to the United States. Why did they leave their own countries to go there?

B | **Discussion.** With a partner, discuss these questions about the early modern humans who left Africa. Make guesses using *could have*, *may have*, and *might have*. Give reasons for your guesses.

1. What did the early modern humans eat? How did they hunt?
2. What did they wear?
3. What were their families like?
4. What kinds of homes did they live in?
5. What tools did they use?
6. How did they spend their free time?

> They might have eaten vegetables that they planted.
>
> I don't know about that. You need to stay in one place to farm vegetables. These people may have moved around too much.

Talking about Your Family History

A | **Using a Graphic Organizer.** Where did your family members come from originally? If they left that place, where did they go? Fill in the chart with information about your family. If you are not sure about something, write a question mark. (*See page 214 of the Independent Student Handbook for more information on using graphic organizers.*)

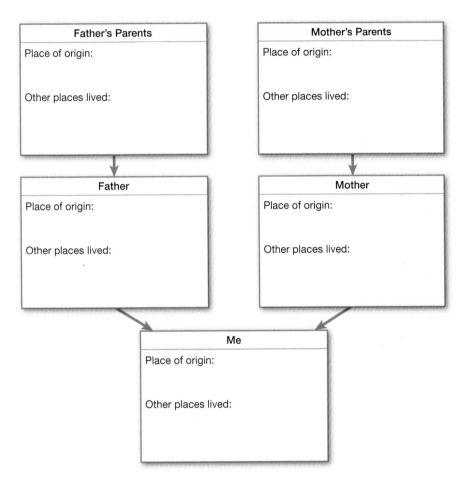

Father's Parents
Place of origin:

Other places lived:

Mother's Parents
Place of origin:

Other places lived:

Father
Place of origin:

Other places lived:

Mother
Place of origin:

Other places lived:

Me
Place of origin:

Other places lived:

B | **Discussion.** Form a group with two or three other students. Use the information from exercise **A** to talk about migration in your family. State the people's place of origin and other places where they lived. If you are not sure about where a family member came from, use *could have*, *may have*, or *might have* and make a guess. React to other members of your group and use expressions of surprise where appropriate.

> I was born in Chicago and my parents were born in Holland. They came to the United States in 1967. I'm not sure about my mother's parents. I think they may have migrated from Poland.

> No kidding! That's where my grandmother is from.

Student to Student:
Expressing Interest

Use these expressions when another person is talking to show you are interested in what they are saying:

That's (really) interesting.
How interesting/fascinating.
Really?
How about that!

WILDEBEEST MIGRATION

The Serengeti

Migrating wildebeest cross a river.

Before Viewing

A | **Understanding Visuals.** You are going to watch a video about a yearly migration of wildebeest. Look at the map on this page and answer the questions.

1. Which two countries does the wildebeest migration travel through?

   _____

   _____

2. Use the map key to follow the migration of the wildebeest throughout the year. Where are the wildebeest today?

B | **Using a Dictionary.** You will hear these words in the video. Match each word with its definition. Use your dictionary to help you.

1. calf (n.)   ____
2. carcass (n.)   ____
3. graze (v.)   ____
4. herd (n.)   ____
5. predator (n.)   ____

a. to eat grass or other growing plants
b. a large group of animals of one kind
c. an animal that kills and eats other animals
d. a young wildebeest
e. the body of a dead animal

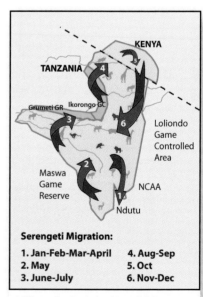

Serengeti Migration:

1. Jan-Feb-Mar-April   4. Aug-Sep
2. May   5. Oct
3. June-July   6. Nov-Dec

Millions of animals such as wildebeest and zebras migrate through the Serengeti National Park, shown here in green.

While Viewing

A | **Sequencing Events.** Watch the video. Number the events in order from 1 to 5. The first event has already been numbered for you.

_____ a. The wildebeest graze in the Masai Mara.

_1_ b. The wildebeest give birth.

_____ c. The wildebeest arrive at the Masai Mara.

_____ d. The migration begins.

_____ e. The wildebeest arrive back at the Serengeti.

B | **Note-Taking.** Watch the video again. Complete the student notes with information from the video.

An elephant crosses the road in the Serengeti National Park.

Wildebeest Migration

- 2 mil. animals travel _____ miles

- At beginning of yr., all wildebeest give _____ in same month

  - Calves can run _____ 2 days after birth

- Nobody knows what triggers _____

- 200,000 of the _____ wildebeest will die from starvation, disease, and overexertion

  - Others die from predators; cat tries to separate calf from _____

- Kenya's Masai Mara: _____ create huge area of _____

- In _____ , the wildebeest head south again to the
  _____ .

After Viewing

Critical Thinking. Discuss the questions with a partner.

1. In the video, you heard that "no one knows what triggers the migration." What are some possible explanations for why the wildebeest start their migration?

2. Recently, the government of Tanzania wanted to build a highway across the Serengeti National Park. The road would have cut across the migration routes of the wildebeest. What arguments could be made against building this highway? What arguments could be made in favor of building it?

A | Meaning from Context. Read and listen to the interview about butterfly migration. Notice the words in blue. These are words you will hear and use in Lesson B.

Interviewer: I'm talking with Maxine Felton, a butterfly expert. For more than 20 years she has **dedicated** herself to the study of butterflies. What kinds of butterflies do you study, Maxine?

Maxine: I study the monarch butterfly. It is an orange, black, and white butterfly that's **approximately** 10 centimeters across.

Interviewer: What is special about the monarch butterfly?

Maxine: Well, it is the only butterfly that migrates north to south with the seasons, the same way that many birds do.

A woman takes a photo of hundreds of butterflies.

Interviewer: How interesting! And how do you follow the monarch butterfly migration?

Maxine: Well, I glue little numbered labels on their wings. The labels help me follow their migration patterns. The labels are small, so they don't **interfere** with flying. Nighttime is the best time to glue on the labels, because monarchs stay on the ground at night. Their flying is **restricted** to the daylight hours.

Interviewer: And where do the monarchs go in the winter?

Maxine: Many go to the Mexican Monarch Butterfly Reserve. When the butterflies arrive there, they cover the trees in **overwhelming** numbers.

Interviewer: That must be a beautiful sight! It sounds like there are plenty of monarchs.

Maxine: Well, actually, there are fewer than there once were. There are various threats to monarchs. For example, in the Butterfly Reserve some **illegal** logging still takes place. In many places, plants such as corn and wheat have **displaced** many of the milkweed plants that monarchs need for food.

Interviewer: I see. Is there any good news for monarch butterflies?

Maxine: Yes, there is. Many new conservation agencies and areas have been **established** to protect monarchs. Recently, the World Wildlife Fund, the Mexican government, and Mexican billionaire Carlos Slim **invested** 100 million dollars in a fund to protect wildlife in Mexico. Part of the money will help to **ensure** the continued protection of monarch butterflies in Mexico.

B | Self-Reflection. With a partner, discuss the questions below.

1. If you had 100 million dollars to **invest**, what would you spend it on? Explain your choices.
2. Do you think it is OK for scientists to track animals as long as their efforts don't **interfere** with the animals' migration? Why, or why not?

USING VOCABULARY

A | Complete the paragraph with the correct form of a word from the box.

approximately	ensure	illegal	invest
displace	establish	interfere	overwhelming

Salmon fishing in the Pacific Ocean is a huge business. In a good year, (1) _____ 800,000 tons of salmon are caught, but today salmon populations are facing (2) _____ challenges. River dams are one problem. Salmon are migrating fish that must return far up rivers and streams to the spot where they were born in order to reproduce.[1] Dams built on rivers can (3) _____ with salmon

Salmon swim upstream.

migration and, as a result, with salmon reproduction. Drift nets in the ocean are another obstacle. These nets, which are 32 feet (10 meters) across and 30 miles (48 kilometers) long, are (4) _____ in many countries because they kill too much sea life. Still, certain countries continue to use them.

As competition for wild salmon increases, new ways of meeting the demand are being tested. Farmers have (5) _____ salmon farms where the fish are raised in saltwater cages. The farms have been very successful, and farm-raised salmon has (6) _____ wild salmon in many restaurants. Moreover, some countries have (7) _____ money to help raise and release young salmon in rivers and streams. These salmon make their way to the ocean, where they grow to adulthood. Many will be caught and eaten, but the ones that return upstream will produce millions of babies to (8) _____ that salmon will survive.

[1]When people, animals, or plants **reproduce**, they produce babies.

B | **Critical Thinking.** Work with a partner. Read the information and discuss the questions.

Salmon travel through the national waters of many countries without restrictions. The governments of the United States and Canada believe that every migrating salmon belongs to the country where it was born, no matter where it goes in the ocean. The fishermen of some countries believe that fish, a gift of nature, belong to everyone. These fishermen believe that they should be able to catch and keep the salmon.

1. Which position do you agree with? Explain your reasons.
2. If a fisherman catches a migrating salmon, how could he figure out if it is a migrating salmon from a different country?

Before Listening

Prior Knowledge. Form a group with two or three other students. Look at the photos and read the captions. Then discuss the questions.

Each year, tourists come in large numbers to visit the Serengeti Mara ecosystem.

Local residents of Robanda stand near the western border of the Serengeti National Park.

1. Where were these photos taken? Do you know anyone who has been to this place?
2. Why have tourists with cameras come to this place?
3. Do you think tourism helps or hurts the people of Robanda? Explain.

Listening: A Conversation between Friends

track 2-17 **A** | **Listening for Main Ideas.** Listen to Sandy and Larry talking about Larry's trip. Circle the correct answers.

1. The size of the Serengeti Mara ecosystem has _____.
   a. increased   b. decreased

2. The human populations in Kenya and Tanzania have been _____.
   a. increasing   b. decreasing

3. The Robandans _____ to accept money to move from their village.
   a. want   b. don't want

4. Animal populations in the Serengeti Mara ecosystem are _____.
   a. in trouble   b. doing all right

track 2-17 **B** | Read the statements. Then listen again. Circle **T** for *true* or **F** for *false*.

1. Sandy has been to Tanzania to see the wildebeest migration before.   **T**   **F**
2. Bush meat is an important source of food in northern Tanzania.   **T**   **F**
3. Wildebeest are the only animals in the Serengeti Mara ecosystem.   **T**   **F**
4. The Ikoma people did not want to leave the park in 1951.   **T**   **F**
5. The people of Robanda have agreed to accept money to move again.   **T**   **F**

After Listening

Critical Thinking. Discuss the questions with a partner.

1. In your own words, explain the conflict between the needs of the animals and the needs of people of the Serengeti Mara ecosystem.
2. If you were villagers from Robanda, would you accept the offer of money to move off the land? Why, or why not?
3. In Tanzania, successful ecotourism corporations can be extremely powerful. How can the government of Tanzania make sure that corporations do not abuse their power?

Pronunciation

Using Question Intonation

In most *yes/no* questions, the intonation rises at the last content word in the sentence. Content words are words that are important to the meaning of the sentence.

Do you have the time?

Can you show me the pictures you took?

In *wh-* questions, the intonation rises and then falls at the end of the sentence.

How was your trip?   *When did you get there?*

 A | Listen to the questions. Draw intonation lines like the ones in the box above.

1. Have you ever tried bush meat? Would you like to?

2. Why do animals migrate? What about humans?

3. Is migrating dangerous for animals? What are the risks?

4. How many tourists visit Tanzania each year?

5. Do you enjoy photography?

6. Should the people of Robanda be forced to move?

B | With a partner, take turns asking and answering the questions from exercise **A**. Be sure to use correct question intonation.

Language Function

> ### Expressing Hopes
>
> We use the following expressions to express hopes about the future.
>
> *I (really) hope (that) . . .*
> *I'm hoping (that) . . .*
> *It would be nice/great/wonderful/ideal if . . .*

 A | In the conversation, Larry and Sandy used a number of useful expressions for expressing hopes. Listen and fill in the missing expressions.

1. **Larry:** _____ there were enough land for people and for animals, but there isn't.

2. **Sandy:** Hmm. _____ that some compromise can be reached.

3. **Sandy:** What a wonderful trip you had! I'm really jealous! _____ to go on a trip like that.

B | **Role-Playing.** Form a group with two or three other students. As a group, choose one of the following scenarios and role-play the situation. Be sure to use phrases for expressing hopes.

1. Your city council has announced plans to build a new community center. Talk about your hopes for the new community center. For example, you can talk about the location, the cost, and the activities and classes that you want the community center to have.

> I hope that the community center isn't too far away.

> Yes, that's important. And it would be great if they offered language classes.

2. Your next-door neighbors moved out, and your apartment manager told you that new neighbors are going to move in next week. Express your hopes about the new neighbors. For example, you can talk about who the neighbors will be, what kind of neighbors they will be, or what kind of relationship you will have with them.

3. You and your group members are going on a camping vacation in a national park. You've never gone camping before. Express your hopes for the trip. For example, you can talk about the weather, the campground, the activities available, and animals you might encounter.

Grammar

Using Past Modals to Make Inferences

We use *must have* and *can't have* to make inferences from evidence. Use *must have* + past participle to infer that something was almost certainly true or almost certainly happened.

> It **must have been** incredibly difficult for the Ikoma people to leave the Serengeti.

Use *can't have* + past participle to infer that something was unbelievable or nearly impossible.

> Well, it's their land, so they **can't have felt** happy about being asked to move again.

Making Inferences. With a partner, read the scenarios. Then answer the questions by making inferences with *must have* and *can't have*.

1. Researchers have found that Native Americans' DNA links them to people living in southern Siberia. The DNA does not link them with Europeans. Where did the Native Americans originally migrate to the Americas from?
2. Researchers have been unable to find any Neanderthal DNA in studies of modern humans, although they know that Neanderthals lived in Europe and Asia when modern humans first came there. What happened to the Neanderthals?
3. The oyamel tree of Mexico is the favorite habitat of the monarch butterfly. Three trees were found on the ground in the Mexican Monarch Butterfly Reserve. Logging is illegal there, and logging companies are careful to obey the law. What happened to the oyamel trees?
4. A large group of wildebeest suddenly stopped grazing and began running as fast as possible. Why did the wildebeest suddenly start running?

These two Dutch artists created this sculpture of a Neanderthal woman.

Your group is going to do a research project about a migrating animal. Then you will give a presentation to the class with the information you found.

A | Getting Background Information. Form a group with two or three other students. Discuss the answers to the following general questions about migration:

- Why do animals migrate?
- What are some types of migration?
- How do animals know when to migrate?
- How do animals know where to go?

B | Researching. Select a migrating animal that you will present to the class. Find a photo of the animal and print it out. Do not choose an animal that you learned about in this unit. On your own, research the animal. When you research the animal, follow these steps:

1. Look for information on the Internet, or in newspapers, books, and encyclopedias.
2. Choose relevant key words to help you narrow down your search.
3. Make sure the information is accurate and reliable. (*See pages 211–212 of the Independent Student Handbook for more information on researching.*)

C | Organizing Information. Use the chart to take notes about the animal you selected. Then discuss your notes with your group members. Did you all find similar information?

Name of Animal	
Size of Animal	
Habitat	
Lifespan (Length of Life)	
Geographic Range	
Distance Traveled	
Time of Migration	
Reason for Migration	
Description of the Migration	
Other Interesting Points	

D | Presentation. Organize your notes and practice your presentation. Then present the information to the class. Answer any questions from your audience.

Presentation Skills: Preparing for Audience Questions

Questions from the audience are part of most presentations, so it's a good idea to be prepared for them. As part of your preparation, spend some time thinking about the kinds of questions that your audience might ask you. Then think about how you will answer.

Tradition and Progress

ACADEMIC PATHWAYS

Lesson A: Listening to a Student Presentation
          Interviewing a Classmate
Lesson B: Listening to a Study Group Discussion
          Evaluating Web Sources

Think and Discuss

1. What is interesting or surprising about this photo?
2. What does the word *progress* mean to you?
3. What traditions are important to you? What would happen if these traditions disappeared?

A man in Alaska uses a laptop computer while sitting on a snowbank.

Exploring the Theme:
Tradition and Progress

Look at the photos and read the captions. Then discuss the questions.

1. Which of these photos do you find the most interesting? Explain.
2. Why would people want to keep their traditions?
3. How do you think life has changed for these people over the last 10 years?

Female weavers work in Chinceros, **Peru**. The weavers keep their traditional weaving skills alive by using them in a modern way—to earn money to support their families and their town.

Peru

A woman in Kyoto, **Japan** shops for food along with her helper, a talking robot.

A teenager learns to play a new sport—basketball—near his home in Batsumber, **Mongolia**.

Japan

Mongolia

India

Tanzania

A monk talks on a cell phone at a monastery in **India**.

The Hadza people of **Tanzania** are one of the last hunter-gatherer groups on earth. Today, their traditional way of life is changing.

A | **Meaning from Context.** Read and listen to the article. Notice the words in blue.
These are words you will hear and use in Lesson A.

track 2-21

Long ago, people lived as hunters and gatherers. Over time people learned how to grow plants and raise domestic animals. Once this happened, there was a transition to agriculture in many societies. However, even today there are groups who reject farming and continue to hunt animals and gather their own food.

The Hadza people are a group of hunter-gatherers who live in an isolated part of northern Tanzania. They have lived in the Great Rift Valley for a period of 10,000 years. The Hadza communicate in their own special language, called Hadzane.

A Hadza hunter climbs a tree to see animals in the distance.

The Hadza are not part of the modern economic system of Tanzania. When they are hungry, they can hunt or gather what they need for free. Hadza men can make a little money by displaying their hunting skills for tourists. It is an interesting contradiction that although the Hadza have very little, they share a lot. In fact, they share everything they have with others.

Tanzania

In the Great Rift Valley, modern farming has spread in recent years, and this development has had serious consequences for the Hadza. Their homeland is now only 25 percent of the size it was in the 1950s. Hunting is now more difficult for them, as there are fewer animals than before. The Hadza people anticipate that their way of life will disappear in the near future.

B | Write each word in blue from exercise **A** next to its definition.

1. _____Anticipate_____ (v.) to realize in advance that an event may happen
2. _____Domestic_____ (adj.) not wild; kept on farms or as pets
3. _____Consequences_____ (n.) the results or effects of an action
4. _____Contradiction_____ (n.) a situation in which two opposite facts are true at the same time
5. _____Display_____ (v.) showing
6. _____Agriculture_____ (n.) farming and the processes used to take care of crops and animals
7. _____Isolated_____ (adj.) far away from large cities and difficult to reach
8. _____Period_____ (n.) a length of time
9. _____Reject_____ (v.) to turn down or not accept
10. _____Transition_____ (n.) a change

A | Discussion. With a partner, discuss the questions.

1. In many ways, the Hadza people reject the modern world. Do you know other people or groups that reject things about the modern world? Why do they reject those things?
2. Many societies transitioned from hunting and gathering to agriculture. In what ways did people's lives probably change as a result?
3. How might people such as the Hadza, who speak their own language, communicate with the outside world?

B | Using a Dictionary. Work with your partner. Find the form and definition of each vocabulary word to complete the information below. Use your dictionary to help you.

Vocabulary Word	Related Words	Related Definitions
1. anticipate (v.)	(n.) anticipation	looking forward to something
2. agriculture (n.)	(adj.) agricultural	related to science of farming
3. consequences (n.)	(adv.) consequently	As a result of something.
4. contradiction (n.)	(v.) contradict	to deny the truth of a statement
	(adj.) contradictory	Opposite.
5. displaying (v.)	(n.) Display	show, exhibit.
6. domestic (adj.)	(adj.) Domesticated	to become/be bred to different environment
7. isolated (adj.)	(v.) isolate	
	(n.) isolation	Separation / lonely
8. period (n.)	(adj.) Periodic	Repeated cycles.
9. reject (v.)	(n.) Rejection	not accepted or refuse.

C | Self-Reflection. Form a group with two or three other students. Discuss the questions.

1. Do you think it is rude to **contradict** your parents, teachers, or other people who have authority? What do you say if you disagree with their ideas?
2. Have you ever experienced a **rejection** such as not getting a job you wanted? Explain what happened.
3. Have you ever done something that had **consequences** you did not expect? Explain the situation.

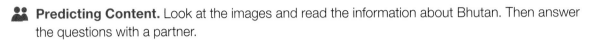

Before Listening

  Predicting Content. Look at the images and read the information about Bhutan. Then answer the questions with a partner.

1. Where is Bhutan located? Is it a large or a small country?
2. What image do you see on Bhutan's flag? What do you think it means?
3. Do you think Bhutan is a modern country?
4. Bhutan is trying to measure its *Gross National Happiness*. What do you think this phrase means?

The flag of Bhutan

Bhutan Fast Facts

Population: 708,427
Capital: Thimphu
Area: 14,824 square miles
(38,394 square kilometers)

Listening: A Student Presentation

🎧 **A** | **Listening for Main Ideas.** Listen to a student's presentation about the country of
track 2-22   Bhutan. Then choose the correct answers.

1. Why did Bhutan reject the modern world?
   a. Using technology was against the law.
   b. The government wanted to avoid negative influences.
   c. The people believed they didn't need any technology.
2. What government change is happening in Bhutan?
   a. It is moving toward democracy.
   b. It is becoming an absolute monarchy.
   c. The king is taking away many of the people's powers.
3. Sompel says that cultural preservation is a challenge for Bhutan because _____.
   a. half of the population is under the age of 30
   b. many people can't read or write
   c. Bhutan produces movies about cultural issues
4. What is Sompel's attitude about Bhutan's future?
   a. It is confusing to him.
   b. It makes him feel sad.
   c. He is hopeful.

B | **Completing an Idea Map.** Listen again to part of the presentation. Complete the idea map with information from the presentation. *(See page 214 of the Independent Student Handbook for more information on using graphic organizers.)*

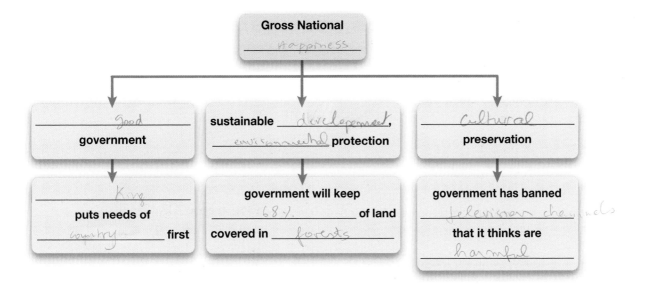

Gross National

Happiness

good government

sustainable _development_, _environmental_ protection

Cultural preservation

King puts needs of _country_ first

government will keep _68%_ of land covered in _forests_

government has banned _television channels_ that it thinks are _harmful_

After Listening

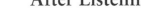 **Critical Thinking.** Form a group with two or three other students. Discuss the questions.

1. Do you think that the decision to open up Bhutan to the modern world was the correct decision? Explain.

2. Bhutanese people were allowed to watch TV for the first time in 1999. If it had been your decision to make, which television programs would have been shown first? Which ones would have been shown later or not at all? Give reasons for your decisions.

3. What does a government have to do to make sure its citizens are happy? Brainstorm some ideas with your group.

Children play video games in a Thimphu café.

Student to Student:
Congratulating the Group

If you feel your group has done a good job on a task, use these expressions to congratulate everyone.

Nice job, everybody!
We make a great team!
Great going, gang!
Way to go, guys!

Language Function

> **Using Fillers**
>
> When we speak, we sometimes forget a word or need a moment to think about what we want to say next. In these situations, we use fillers to fill the gaps in the conversation.
>
> **Informal**
> . . . *umm* . . .
> . . . *oh, you know* . . .
> . . . *hang on* . . .
> . . . *it's on the tip of my tongue* . . .
>
> **More Formal**
> . . . *let me think* . . .
> . . . *just a moment* . . .
> . . . *how should I put it* . . .
> . . . *oh, what's the word* . . .

track 2-24   **A** | In the student presentation, the speaker uses a number of fillers. Listen to the sentences and fill in the missing expressions.

1. He wants our country's development to be guided by . . . _Let me think_
   . . . oh yes, *Gross National Happiness*.
2. There are four parts . . . ___umm___ . . . four "pillars" to this approach: good government, sustainable development, environmental protection, and cultural preservation.

B | Work with a partner. Take turns saying the sentences from exercise **A**, using different fillers to fill the pauses.

C | **Self-Reflection.** With your partner, take turns answering the questions below. Use fillers to allow yourself extra time to answer.

Where did you go on your last vacation?

Oh, let me think . . . I went to Buenos Aires.

1. Where did you go on your last vacation?
2. What was your favorite TV show when you were a child?
3. What did you have for dinner last night?
4. Who was your favorite teacher?
5. Who was the last person you danced with?
6. What was the title of the last book you read?

D | With your partner, read the definition of *buzzword* and the four buzzwords in the box. Then practice the conversations below. When you see a blank, use a buzzword. Continue each conversation and use fillers as needed.

A **buzzword** is a word or expression that has become common in a particular field and is being used often by the media. For example:

- **the blogosphere:** all blogs on the Internet, the bloggers, and their opinions
- **brick-and-mortar:** a company operating in a building or a store, not on the Internet
- **climate change:** changes in weather and temperature over a long period of time
- **go green:** take steps to reduce one's negative impact on the environment

(See page 208 of the Independent Student Handbook for more information on building your vocabulary.)

A *brick-and-mortar* store operates in a building, and not on the Internet.

Planting a tree is one way to *go green*.

1. **A:** Wow, another hot day! This must be the tenth in a row!
   B: I know! If you ask me, it's probably due to ___climate change___...
2. **A:** Have you finished setting up your environmentalism blog yet?
   B: No, but I will soon. I'm really excited to enter ___the blogosphere___...
3. **A:** I sold my car and I'm only using a bicycle now. I'm also being careful to recycle everything that I can.
   B: Really? I can't believe it! You're the last person I thought would ever ___go green___...
4. **A:** Did you know that a new bookstore is opening downtown?
   B: Who cares? I buy all my books online. I have no use for ___brick-and-mortar___ bookstores anymore.

Grammar

Verb + Gerund

Certain verbs can be followed by a *gerund* but not by an infinitive. A *gerund* is a word ending in *-ing*. Here are some verbs that can be followed by a *gerund*.

admit	appreciate	defend	enjoy	quit
avoid	be used to	deny	look forward to	risk

*The king will not open up Bhutan all at once and **risk ruining** it.*
*We **are looking forward to visiting** the islands off Cornwall this summer.*

A | Read this article about the Amish people. <u>Underline</u> the verbs that are followed by a gerund.

An Amish man takes his horse-drawn carriage down a busy road.

The Amish people of the United States enjoy living simply. They stop attending school around the eighth grade, and they live without modern conveniences. The Amish resist using technologies such as electricity, automobiles, and computers. Many do not even like having their picture taken. Amish people are accustomed to riding in horse-drawn carriages. Most Amish people live in the states of Pennsylvania, Indiana, or Ohio. The average Amish family has five children.

The population of Amish people in the United States keeps growing. A recent survey counted 230,000 Amish people. Sixteen years ago, there were only about 115,000 Amish people. Older Amish communities no longer have enough land for their people. Although the Amish recommend separating oneself from the modern world, many can no longer avoid going out into the modern world to find a place to live. Rather than risk living near people who are not Amish, some Amish have moved far from their traditional homes to isolated areas of the United States and Canada.

B | **Collaboration.** Work with a partner. Use five of the verbs you found in exercise **A** to write sentences about your own feelings or experiences. Underline the verb + gerund in each sentence. Then share your sentences with a partner.

> I <u>enjoy giving</u> chocolate to my friends on Valentine's Day, but I hate chocolate myself.

Interviewing a Classmate

 A | Work with a partner. Your partner will choose a country or a city where he or she has lived. Interview your partner to determine the *Gross National Happiness* of the country or city. Read each question to your partner. Mark your partner's answer with a check (✔). Then switch roles.

Gross National Happiness	Yes	No
Pillar 1: Good Government		
1. Does the government respond to the needs of the people?		
2. Does the government treat people fairly and with equality?		
3. Is the government's use of money, property, and other resources efficient?		
Pillar 2: Sustainable Development		
1. Do most people enjoy their jobs?		
2. Do most jobs provide enough money to live on?		
3. Do most companies protect workers from dangerous working conditions?		
Pillar 3: Environmental Protection		
1. Are levels of pollution, noise, and traffic acceptable?		
2. Are there parks or natural areas available to the public?		
3. Are there areas set aside for nature?		
Pillar 4: Cultural Preservation		
1. Do people try to maintain traditions along with new practices?		
2. Are old buildings restored and valued?		
3. Do young people value and respect the older generations?		

 B | **Discussion.** With your partner, discuss the questions from exercise **A**. Take notes on your partner's responses. If you answered *no* for any question, explain why you chose that answer.

C | Share your *Gross National Happiness* interviews with the class. Who in the class said *yes* to most questions? Who in the class said *no* to most questions? Talk about the answers with your class.

Farm Restoration

The *Reinvest in Minnesota* project helps farmers return their farmlands to a natural state.

Okabena Creek, Minnesota

Before Viewing

A | Meaning from Context. Read the sentences. Notice the words in blue. You will hear these words in the video.

1. I had an epiphany—it's more important to be happy than to be successful.
2. The area around Tintagel Castle in the United Kingdom experiences erosion as the sea takes more rock and soil each year.
3. When the actress died, she left 1000 acres of land for a wildlife reserve—a legacy for nature lovers to enjoy for many years in the future.
4. Marginal farmland is difficult to farm and does not produce a lot of crops.
5. During long, dry summers, many forests in California become susceptible to fire.
6. The flooding of the Mississippi River took its toll on riverside towns and washed away houses and farms.

B | Using a Dictionary. Match each word in blue from exercise **A** with its definition.

1. epiphany (n.)   _____   a. land or money given to future generations
2. erosion (n.)   _____   b. to have a bad effect or do a lot of damage
3. legacy (n.)   _____   c. likely to be affected by
4. marginal (adj.)   _____   d. a moment of sudden understanding
5. susceptible to (adj.) _____   e. not very useful; on the edge of usefulness
6. took its toll (v.)   _____   f. the removal of soil or rock by wind or water

While Viewing

A | Watch the video. Then circle the correct answers.

1. What problem did Okabena Creek cause for farmer Dale Aden?
   a. There wasn't enough water in it for farming.
   b. It sometimes flooded part of his farmland.
   c. He couldn't use the water because it was polluted.
2. What was Dale Aden's epiphany about his marginal farmland?
   a. He realized that he could farm more corn and soybeans on it.
   b. He realized he could stop farming it if someone would buy it.
   c. He realized that he could return the land to wildlife.
3. What does the organization *Reinvest in Minnesota* do?
   a. It buys marginal farmland from farmers for wildlife.
   b. It helps farmers flood their land so people can't live there.
   c. It buys corn and soybeans to help farmers buy land.
4. What is Aden's marginal farmland used for today?
   a. It is used for farming only during dry years.
   b. It is returned to a natural state for wildlife to live on.
   c. Aden collects bird eggs from the farm to sell in markets.

B | Watch the video again. Complete the sentences with no more than three words from the video.

1. Aden said that he was a third _____ on this land.
2. For many years, Aden watched helplessly as _____ flooded its banks and soaked his crops.
3. Aden said that it takes _____ to pay for the lost crop.
4. Aden's friend planted prairie grass that will soon provide _____.
5. Aden calls the sound of birds singing "_____."
6. Aden couldn't be _____ for the way the project has turned out.

After Viewing

Critical Thinking. Form a group with two or three other students. Discuss the questions.

1. The government program *Reinvest in Minnesota* pays farmers such as Dale Aden for their farmland. Do you think this program is a good idea? Why, or why not?
2. In this video, Dale Aden returned his land to a natural state. What are some possible positive and negative effects that this could have? Brainstorm these effects with your group.

Birds returned to the farmland once the land had been converted into a wildlife area.

A | Using a Dictionary. Check (✔) the words you already know. These are words you will hear and use in Lesson B. Then write each word from the box next to its definition. Use your dictionary to help you.

❏ enable ❏ found ❏ highlight ❏ perspective ❏ regain
❏ federal ❏ grant ❏ objective ❏ portion ❏ undertake

1. _____Grant_____ (v.) to give
2. _____Found_____ (v.) to establish or start
3. _____Enable_____ (v.) to make possible
4. _____Objective_____ (n.) a goal you are trying to achieve
5. _____Perspective_____ (n.) a way of thinking that is usually influenced by your own experiences
6. _____Regain_____ (v.) to get something back that you had lost
7. _____highlight_____ (v.) to emphasize or focus attention on
8. _____Federal_____ (adj.) related to the central government of a country
9. _____Portion_____ (n.) a part
10. _____Undertake_____ (v.) to start doing a task and accept responsibility for it

not appreciate - take for graded

B | Read the interview and fill in each blank with the correct word from exercise **A**. Then listen and check your answers.

track 2-25

Saving the World's Languages

A: What's happening to the world's languages?

B: Well, most people don't know that a language dies every 14 days. When a language dies, no one can speak the language anymore. National Geographic helped (1) _____found_____ a project to save the world's most unique languages.

A: How many languages are dying?

A Huilliche man plays a musical instrument he built.

B: Scientists think that over half of the languages spoken today may no longer exist in 2100. In Chile, for example, the Huilliche language may die soon. Only a small (2) _____Portion_____ of people can speak the language, and most of the speakers are over 70 years old.

A: Why does a language disappear?

B: There are many reasons. Governments sometimes create (3) _____federal_____ policies that tell citizens to speak only one language. Also, people may forget a language if they don't speak it often.

A: What made you (4) _____undertake_____ the task of trying to save these languages?

B: Language is key to understanding how speakers think and communicate. Our (5) _____objective_____ is to help people keep their cultures alive. From my (6) _____perspective_____ as a scientist, I think our work is very important.

A: What do you do to help groups (7) _____Regain_____ dying languages?

B: We (8) _____enable_____ people to study their language by giving them recording devices. We make dictionaries, and we (9) _____highlight_____ how people can teach their language to others. In the future, we can (10) _____grant_____ access to the recordings, so people can learn the language and keep it alive.

the s's with vowel
a, o, u, i

A | Complete the paragraph with the correct form of a word from the box.

| enable | federal | found | grant | portion | regain | undertake |

For many years, Native Americans in the United States have lived on reservations. Reservations are areas of land that were (1) _____granted_____ to the Native Americans by the (2) _____federal_____ government of the United States. The first reservations were (3) _____founded_____ as early as 1786. In its early history, the United States fought with many Native American groups, or tribes, and took away much of their land. Putting people on reservations (4) _____enabled_____ the government to control the Native American groups more easily. On these reservations, Native Americans have often lived in poor economic conditions. In recent years, however, the situation has improved, and there are many successful Native American businesses on these reservations. Some Native American groups give a (5) _____portion_____ of the profits from the businesses to everyone in their group. The money has allowed them to (6) _____undertake_____ projects to improve their reservations. Some groups are using their money to buy back some of their original lands. Government records show that Native Americans have (7) _____regained_____ nearly a million acres of land in this way.

Native American groups wear traditional clothing at a celebration.

B | **Choosing the Right Definition.** Study the numbered definitions for **objective**. Write the number of the definition next to the correct sentence below.

objective /əbdʒɛktɪv/ **(objectives)** [1] N-COUNT Your **objective** is what you are trying to achieve. • *Their objective was to preserve Native American traditions.* [2] ADJ **Objective** information is based on facts. • *A scientist is concerned with objective facts, not opinions.* [3] ADJ If a person is **objective**, they base their opinions on facts rather than on their personal feelings. • *He loves his children so much that he can't be objective when he talks about them.*

_3_ a. Try not to take sides in the argument and maybe you can remain objective.
_1_ b. His objective was to learn as many Native American languages as possible.
_2_ c. It's an objective truth that humans lived in Yellowstone 11,000 years ago.

C | **Discussion.** Form a group with two or three other students. Read the statements. Do you agree or disagree with each statement? Share your opinions with your group.

1. Schools should **highlight** the role of the U.S. government in taking away Native American lands.

2. From my **perspective**, Native Americans should not live separated on reservations. Instead, they should live with the general American population.

Before Listening

Prior Knowledge. With a partner, look at the map and answer the questions.

1. Read the names of the Native American groups. Have you heard of any of these Native American groups on the map? If so, what do you know about them?
2. What are some other Native American groups that you have heard about?

Listening: A Study Group Discussion

track 2-26 **A** | **Listening for Main Ideas.** Listen to a group of classmates reviewing for an exam. Then choose the correct answers.

1. What is the main topic of the conversation?
   a. The poor condition of Native American reservation land
   b. How Native Americans are restoring their lands to their original condition
   c. Conflicts over land ownership between Native Americans and European Americans

2. Originally, what was the attitude of the United States government toward Native American culture and traditions?
   a. The government wanted to change them.
   b. The government was sorry for damaging them.
   c. The government supported them.

3. According to the conversation, what is an important source of revenue for the Native Americans?
   a. Donations from people who support their cause
   b. Money provided by the United States government
   c. Revenue from businesses on their reservations

Critical Thinking Focus: Evaluating Numbers and Statistics

When you hear a speaker say a number or statistic, try to evaluate the number by asking yourself questions. For example:

Is this a large or a small number?   *What percentage of the total is it?*
Is it larger or smaller than I expected?   *Does this number seem accurate?*

B | Note-Taking. Listen again and complete the notes.

Background

> 300 Native American ___Reservations___ in the U.S.

U.S. forced them to adopt ___their language and traditions___

Most reservations located ___west___ of Miss.
Land not suitable for ___agriculture___

1970: U.S. granted right to run various ___businesses___
Used money to ___improve land / buy land___

InterTribal Sinkyone Wilderness Area

Founded on the ___coast___, north of San Francisco

Access very ___limited___

Gather food, have religious ___ceremonies___ here

Big Cypress Swamp

Owned by the Seminole group in ___Florida___

Bringing back ___animals___ that used to live there

Removing ___plants___ that weren't there originally

The InterTribal Sinkyone Wilderness Area

After Listening

 Discussion. With a partner, discuss the questions.

1. Describe the Native American relationship with nature. Does your culture have any traditions or beliefs related to nature? Explain.
2. The Native Americans are removing animals from the Big Cypress Swamp that were not there originally. How did these animals get into the swamp? Share your ideas with your partner.

Pronunciation

Linking Consonants to Vowels

When a word ends in a consonant sound and the next word begins with a vowel sound, the two words are linked so that they sound like one word. Linking can occur in strings of two or more words.

turn off   *deer and other animals*

A | Listen to the six words and linked phrases. Then listen again and repeat.

 B | Practice saying the sentences with a partner. Mark the linked words as in the example. Then listen and check your pronunciation.

1. Click on the file to open it.
2. You should speak out again.
3. He doesn't have an opinion.
4. The car dealer made an offer.
5. This car is new and improved.
6. Land conservation isn't easy.

Language Function

Expressing a Lack of Knowledge

In conversation, you often hear things that you didn't know about before. You can use the following expressions to explain that a certain fact is new to you.

I had no idea (that) . . .   *I didn't realize (that) . . .*
I never knew (that) . . .   *I wasn't aware (that) . . .*

track 2-30 **A** | In the study group discussion, the speakers expressed a lack of knowledge. Listen to the sentences and fill in the expressions.

1. **Amina:** _I have no idea that_ there are more than 300 Native American reservations in the United States, did you?
   Jose: No, I definitely didn't. And _I wasn't aware that_ the reservations only make up two percent of the total land area of the United States.

2. **Lauren:** For a long time the people who lived there lived in bad economic conditions.
   Jose: _I didn't realize that_. So, when did things begin to get better?

B | Read the beginnings of these newspaper articles. Use the expressions from the Language Function box to tell a partner about the information that is new to you. Discuss other things you know or would like to know about each topic.

Olmec Stone Carvings Discovered

A giant stone carving of three cats was recently discovered in Mexico. The carvings are believed to be the work of the Olmec people. The Olmec people lived in Mexico and Central America between 1200 and 400 BC.

New Theories about Machu Picchu

Machu Picchu is a unique place high in the mountains of Peru. It has ruins[1] of structures built by the Inca people. It is one of the most popular tourist destinations in the world. There are various theories about Machu Picchu's purpose, but nobody knows for sure why it was built. Some theories say it was a religious place, but some scientists now believe that it was the home of the Incan king.

[1] **Ruins** of a building are parts that remain after the building has fallen down.

> I had no idea that the Olmec people carved cats in stone.

> Neither did I. I wonder what else they carved.

Grammar

Verb + Object + Infinitive

Some verbs can be followed by an object and an *infinitive*. An *infinitive* consists of *to* + verb.
> *Their prosperity **is allowing them to save** a part of the Big Cypress Swamp.*

The verbs in this list are usually followed by an infinitive. Some of them are followed by an object and an infinitive.

advise	ask	forbid	invite	permit	remind	warn
allow	encourage	force	order	persuade	tell	

> *She **asked me to invite** her brother to the party.*

> *I **will encourage him to open** his own business.*

To form the negative, insert *not* before the infinitive:
> *The guide **reminded us not to enter** the reservation without permission.*

A | Collaboration. With a partner, write four statements using the verb + object + infinitive pattern. Use the verbs from the list in the box above.

1. <u>Victor persuaded his friend to move to the city.</u>
2. My parents forced me to enter the medical school.
3. This sign allowed the students to pay half price tickets to the museum.
4. The instructor asked the students to submit their assignment on time.
5. Our neighbor invited us tonight to have a drink.

B | Self-Reflection. Work with your partner. Talk about people or events that have influenced your life. Use the verbs from the grammar box and the verb + object + infinitive pattern while speaking.

> My parents always encouraged me to go to college.

> That's great. Did you follow their advice?

Presentation Skills: Varying your Voice Volume

Volume means the loudness or softness of your voice. When speaking to a partner or a small group, you can use your regular, everyday volume level. However, for larger groups and class presentations, your everyday voice can sound too quiet. For presentations, you will need to increase your volume. You can also introduce excitement into your voice by varying the volume. Emphasize some words by saying them more loudly than others. Create drama by lowering your voice as well. Varying your volume will help keep your audience interested during conversations and presentations.

You may have to do research on the Internet for class or work. However, information found on the Internet isn't always reliable. Anyone can create a Web site, and while some Web sites are created by experts, most are not. When you want to use information from a Web site in a presentation or paper, it is necessary to evaluate the Web site. Web sites should contain accurate and objective information and be free of *bias*. Bias is an unfair opinion about a group or idea.

A | Do an Internet search about a popular tradition in a country of your choice. Select a Web site from the search results. Evaluate the Web site and complete the form below.

Web Site Evaluation Form

Search Topic: _Van gujjar_   Name of Site: _Himalayan Immigration_

Web Address: _____

1. Who is the author of the Web site?

   ☑ Author unknown

   ❑ Author's name _____

   ❑ Author's qualifications (if available) _College educative_

2. Is there contact information for the author or the Web site owner on the site?

   ❑ Yes   ❑ No

3. What is the suffix on the Web site address?

   ❑ .gov   ☑ .com   ❑ .edu   ❑ Other: _____

4. What is the general purpose of the Web site?

   ❑ scholarly   ☑ educational   ❑ entertainment

   ❑ to give an opinion   ❑ to sell something

5. When was information posted or last updated? _____

6. How does the site look?

   ☑ well-maintained   ❑ out-of-date

7. Is the site easy to use?

   ☑ Yes   ❑ No

8. Does the Web site include advertisements?

   ❑ Yes   ❑ No   ❑ If yes, what kind? _Food_

B | Imagine that you had to write a paper about the topic you selected. With a partner, discuss your Web site. Decide if each Web site is an appropriate and reliable source to use in your paper. Explain what makes your Web site a good source or a poor source.

C | With your partner, join another pair of students. Each group member will present his or her Web site to the group. Use your form to explain your Web site. As a group, rank the Web sites from the most reliable to the least reliable.

Money in Our Lives

ACADEMIC PATHWAYS

Lesson A: Listening to a Radio Interview
          Discussing Values
Lesson B: Listening to a Conversation between Friends
          Preparing a Budget

Think and Discuss

1. What is happening in this photo? Read the caption. Does this activity surprise you?

2. An old saying goes, "Love of money is the root of all evil." Does this saying seem true to you? Explain.

Friends pin money to a man's suit during his birthday party in New Orleans, Louisiana.

121

Exploring the Theme:
Money in Our Lives

Look at the photos and the chart and read the captions. Then discuss the questions.

1. Which country in the chart has the largest public debt per person? Which country has the smallest? Does any of the information in this chart surprise you?
2. What are some of the ways that money can affect people's happiness?
3. Twenty years from now, how do you imagine you will pay for most things?

Electronic Money

Today, electronic money such as credit and debit cards is replacing paper money. Many experts predict that the world will one day have a cashless economy.

Money and Happiness

As part of a yearly tradition, a girl gives a child money in a red envelope. Scientists are studying money to see how it affects our lives and our happiness.

Public Debt Per Person

Brazil, $5668
China, $922
United States, $37,953
Kenya, $394
Japan, $87,600
Russia, $1253
Spain $17,539
Singapore, $43,191
Italy, $38,026
Turkey, $4498
United Kingdom $32,208

Source: The Economist

Many governments spend more money than they have. *Public debt* is money that is owed by a government. Unfortunately, public debt is growing. When debt gets too high, it can threaten the economy of a country.

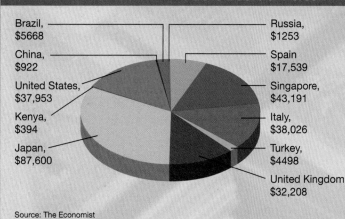

In Hong Kong, stacks of money are on display. People buy and use this decorative money as part of a tradition to honor their ancestors.

A | **Meaning from Context.** Read and listen to the paragraphs. Notice the words in blue. These are the words you will hear and use in Lesson A.

Credit card debt is a major problem in the United States, as these statistics show:

- The average debt per household is reported to be about $15,799.

- Unpaid credit card bills in a recent year totaled around 69 billion dollars.

Kelly Jones got herself in debt by using 10 credit cards, but she recently ceased using them completely. To pay off her $15,000 debt, Jones works 64 hours a week at two jobs. She started a debt-management plan, and hopes to pay off her bills in seven years. She will no longer purchase unnecessary items. "I have no idea what I bought. I have nothing to show for it," she says. Now, Jones warns young people not to repeat her errors, and tells them about what can happen if they rely on credit cards too much.

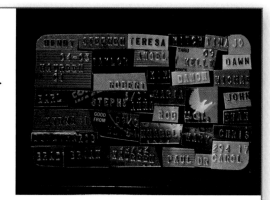

A financial counselor[1] sorts through thousands of pieces of cut-up credit cards. Obviously, these cards won't be used again. Counselors ask people who are in debt to cut up all of their credit cards. This is just one component of a process to help clients[2] pay their bills. Counselors display the cut-up cards to demonstrate that people are not alone. Cutting up credit cards shows the commitment that hundreds of people have made to control their spending. Each year millions of people seek help to get out of debt. Many of these people receive counseling and education to promote better money management.

[1]A **counselor** gives information and support to people who need help.
[2]A **client** is a person who receives a service from a company or professional.

B | Write each word in blue from exercise **A** next to its definition.

1. _____ (v.) stopped
2. _____ (v.) to show
3. _____ (v.) to buy
4. _____ (n.) one part, which together with other parts makes a whole
5. _____ (v.) to advance, encourage, or improve
6. _____ (adv.) clearly; used when something is said that is already understood
7. _____ (n.) mistakes
8. _____ (adj.) extremely important
9. _____ (n.) a promise to complete a task
10. _____ (n.) information in the form of numbers

A | Complete each sentence with the correct form of a word from the box.

cease	error	obviously	promote	purchase	statistics

1. _____ things you want can make you happy for a short time, but the feeling doesn't last very long.

2. One common _____ people make is spending money on items they don't need.

3. Spending money on others _____ happiness more than spending money on oneself.

4. My car is still being repaired, so _____ I will need to take the bus to work.

5. According to government _____, people making over $100,000 a year spend almost 20 percent of their time on relaxing activities such as watching TV and visiting friends.

6. British philosopher John Stuart Mill said, "Ask yourself whether you are happy and you _____ to be so."

B | **Discussion.** With a partner, discuss the questions.

1. "Happiness requires your emotional **commitment** to your career." What do you think this statement means? Do you agree or disagree with it? Explain.

2. Can you think of a movie, play, or story that **demonstrates** the theme that money doesn't buy happiness? Explain how it demonstrates that theme.

3. Most people would agree that having money is a **component** of happiness. What are some of the other components of a happy life? Give examples.

C | **Choosing the Right Definition.** Study the numbered definitions for the word **major**. Write the number of the definition next to the correct sentence below.

> **major** /meɪdʒər/ **(majors, majoring, majored)** [1] ADJ You use **major** when you want to describe something that is more important, serious, or significant than other things in a group or situation. • *Unemployment is a major problem for workers and the economy.* [2] N-COUNT At a university or college, a student's **major** is the main subject that he or she is studying. • *I need to choose a major by the end of my second year.* [3] V-I If a student at a university or college **majors** in a particular subject, that subject is the main one he or she studies. • *I'm majoring in biology at Northwestern University.*

_____ a. Why don't you choose a major that will be useful to your career?

_____ b. They made some major changes to their spending habits to get out of debt.

_____ c. I want to make a lot of money, so I'm planning to major in business.

Before Listening

A | Read the statements about money. How happy does each situation make you? Rank them from 1 (the happiest) to 5 (the least happy).

_____ Having money in the bank

_____ Spending money on items you want

_____ Giving money to other people

_____ Earning money

_____ Receiving money as a gift

B | **Discussion.** Form a group with two or three other students. Compare and discuss your rankings from exercise **A**. Then come up with a new ranking list for your group. Take a group vote on which item should be ranked number 1 and so on.

Listening: A Radio Interview

track 3-3 **A** | **Listening for Main Ideas.** Listen to a radio interview about money and happiness. Then choose the correct answer for each question.

1. What does a recent study by psychologist Elizabeth Dunn show?
   a. Spending money brings us more happiness than saving money.
   b. Spending money on others brings us more happiness than spending it on ourselves.
   c. Possessions bring us more happiness than experiences.

2. What caused Dunn to research the relationship between money and happiness?
   a. She had more money and wanted to know how to use it.
   b. She lost her job as a professor and needed to live on less money.
   c. Her university asked her to study student happiness levels.

3. What common error do people make when they try to buy happiness with money?
   a. They are afraid to buy the things that will really make them happy.
   b. They think major purchases such as houses will make them happy.
   c. They use scientific research instead of their own feelings when spending money.

4. In their study, what question did Leaf Van Boven and Tom Gilovich want to answer?
   a. Does having money in the bank make people happier than spending it?
   b. Does spending money on things help people think of themselves differently?
   c. Does money spent on experiences make people happier than money spent on items?

5. What did Angus Deaton and Daniel Kahneman's study reveal?
   a. Making more than a certain amount of money causes unhappiness.
   b. Making more than a certain amount of money doesn't affect happiness much.
   c. Making more than a certain amount of money causes greater happiness.

B | **Note-Taking.** Listen again and complete the outline with information from the radio interview. (*See page 206 of the Independent Student Handbook for more information on note-taking.*)

Happiness Studies

I. Elizabeth Dunn

  A. Research question: Do people get more happiness from spending money on themselves or _____?

  B. Experiment:

    1. Gave people _____

    2. Asked some people to spend it _____, others _____

    3. At end of day, _____

  C. Result: _____

II. Leaf van Boven & Tom Gilovich

  A. Research question: What is the value of spending money on _____ versus _____?

  B. Experiment: _____

  C. Result: _____

III. Angus Deaton & Daniel Kahneman

  A. Research question: Does more money = _____?

  B. Experiment: _____

  C. Result: _____

After Listening

Critical Thinking Focus: Summarizing

A summary is a shortened version of a text or listening passage that contains all of the main ideas and a few important details. A summary usually includes (1) a general opening statement, (2) the main ideas, and (3) a concluding statement. The parts of the summary should be connected with transitions. A summary can be written or oral, and it should not include your opinion.

A | **Summarizing.** Work with two other students. Use your notes from exercise **B** above to summarize the studies on money and happiness. Each student should summarize one study. (*See page 206 of the Independent Student Handbook for more information on summarizing*).

B | **Discussion.** With your group, discuss the questions.

1. Elizabeth Dunn's study shows that giving money away makes people happier than spending it on themselves. Why do you think this is true?

2. Compare a time when you spent money on an experience with a time when you bought an item you wanted. Which purchase made you happier? Explain.

Language Function

Showing That You Are Following a Conversation

There are a number of useful expressions for showing that you are following or understanding someone while they are speaking to you.

I see.
Oh!
Uh-huh. (Use with rising intonation.)
Really? (Use with falling intonation.)
Is that so? (Use with falling intonation.)
Is it? Are you? Did they? (These are tag questions with falling intonation.)

🎧 track 3-4 **A** | In the radio interview, the interviewer used a number of expressions to show that he was following the conversation. Listen and fill in the missing expressions.

1. **Dr. Simmons:** That's what Dunn said in a recent interview with National Geographic.

   Dave Martin: _____? How did she discover that?

2. **Dr. Simmons:** So, Dr. Dunn decided to do some scientific research to see if people might get more happiness from using their money to help other people, rather than themselves.

   Dave Martin: _____. And how did she research this topic?

3. **Dr. Simmons:** Since then, Dr. Dunn has completed a lot of other research on money and happiness.

   Dave Martin: _____?

4. **Dr. Simmons:** Actually, there are no statistics to prove that owning a home makes people happy.

   Dave Martin: _____. Are there other studies relating money and happiness?

B | Read the questions and complete the survey.

How worried are you about . . .

	Very	Somewhat	Slightly	Not at all
the world economy?	❏	❏	❏	❏
getting a job?	❏	❏	❏	❏
keeping your job?	❏	❏	❏	❏
personal debt?	❏	❏	❏	❏
national debt?	❏	❏	❏	❏
increasing food prices?	❏	❏	❏	❏
increasing fuel prices?	❏	❏	❏	❏
crime?	❏	❏	❏	❏

C | Discussion. Work with a partner. Choose three of your responses to the survey on page 128 and explain them to your partner. Give reasons why you chose each answer.

> I'm worried about getting a job. I've been looking for one for a while now.

> Have you? What kind of job are you looking for?

D | Critical Thinking. Form a group with two or three other students. Recently, the Nielsen Company gave the survey on page 128 to hundreds of people around the world. Look at the photo below and read the caption. How do you think people in other parts of the world answered this survey? Use the expressions from the Language Function box on page 128 in your discussion.

In the Asia-Pacific area, people are the most worried about rising food prices.

Grammar

Using Connectors to Add and Emphasize Information

Connectors are words and phrases to add or emphasize information while we speak.

To join similar ideas, use *and*, *also*, *as well as*, or *both . . . and . . . .*
> Some people spend money on other people, **and** some spend it on themselves.
> I have a checking account. I **also** have a savings account.
> I have **both** a checking account **and** a savings account.

To add information and emphasize it, use *not only . . . but also . . . .*
> We've **not only** cut out any short trips, **but also** cancelled our yearly vacation.

To emphasize a sentence, use *furthermore*, *what's more*, *in fact*, or *actually*.
> Buying a home is too expensive for me right now. **In fact**, I'll probably rent forever.
> I love my job because the work is fun. **What's more**, my office is near my house.

👥 **Understanding Visuals.** Work with a partner. Study the graphs. With your partner, answer the questions about the graphs. Use connectors from page 129 when possible.

1. What do these graphs show? Explain one of the graphs to your partner.

Around 23 percent of people in Latin America are cutting down on take-out meals. Also, 14 percent are using their cars less often.

2. How do you spend your extra money? How does your spending compare with the world average?

3. How will you save your money in the future? Talk about the habits from the graphs that you think are useful.

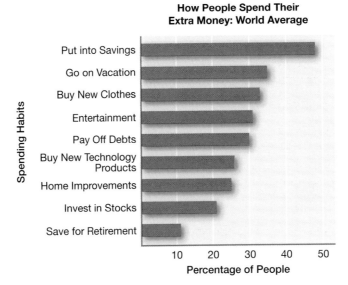

How People Spend Their Extra Money: World Average

Spending Habits:
- Put into Savings
- Go on Vacation
- Buy New Clothes
- Entertainment
- Pay Off Debts
- Buy New Technology Products
- Home Improvements
- Invest in Stocks
- Save for Retirement

Percentage of People: 10 20 30 40 50

Source: The Nielsen Company, Global Online Survey, 2010

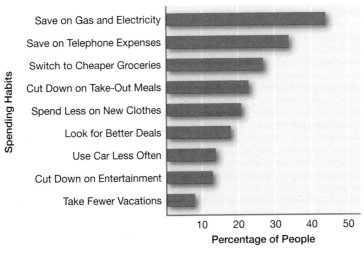

Spending Habits People Will Continue After the Economy Improves: Latin America

Spending Habits:
- Save on Gas and Electricity
- Save on Telephone Expenses
- Switch to Cheaper Groceries
- Cut Down on Take-Out Meals
- Spend Less on New Clothes
- Look for Better Deals
- Use Car Less Often
- Cut Down on Entertainment
- Take Fewer Vacations

Percentage of People: 10 20 30 40 50

Source: The Nielsen Company, Global Online Survey, 2010

Discussing Values

The *values* of a person or group are the beliefs that they think are important. Your personal experiences, family and friends, and education can help you choose your values. Some examples of values are respect for others, honesty, friendliness, and kindness.

A | List the most expensive items, services, or experiences that you have ever purchased. Then list the items, services, or experiences that gave the most happiness. Circle the items that are on both lists.

Expensive List	Happiness List
1. _____	1. _____
2. _____	2. _____
3. _____	3. _____
4. _____	4. _____
5. _____	5. _____
6. _____	6. _____
7. _____	7. _____
8. _____	8. _____

B | Work with a partner and compare your lists. Explain why the items on your Happiness list made you happy. Take turns asking and answering questions about interesting items on your partner's lists.

> Tell me about your watch. Why does it make you happy?

> I love it because it was a gift from my grandfather.

C | **Critical Thinking.** With your partner, discuss the questions.

1. What are some of your personal values? How does money relate to your personal values? Explain.
2. Scientists believe that spending money on experiences makes us happier than spending money on items. Based on your lists from exercise **A**, do you agree with this? Explain.
3. What conclusions can you make about what makes you happy from the information in your lists? Explain this to your partner.

**Student to Student:
Asking Sensitive
Questions**

Some people are uncomfortable talking about sensitive topics such as money, death, or family issues. If you must ask a question about a sensitive topic, use one of these expressions to make your partner feel more comfortable.

Do you mind if I ask you . . . ?
Excuse me for asking, but . . . ?
If you don't mind my asking . . . ?

The Black Diamonds of Provence

The village of Richerenches in Provence, France

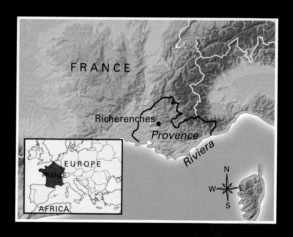

Before Viewing

A | **Using the Dictionary.** You will hear these words in the video. Match each word with its definition. Use your dictionary to help you.

1. discreetly (adj.) _____
2. lucrative (adj.) _____
3. broker (n.) _____
4. export (v.) _____
5. sensitive (adj.) _____

a. a businessman who sets up purchases and sales
b. easily affected by small amounts of something
c. to sell products and materials to another country
d. profitable; making a lot of money
e. carefully; quietly

B | **Predicting Content.** You are going to watch a video about finding, buying, and selling truffles. Why do you think truffles are expensive? Share your ideas with a partner.

While Viewing

A | Watch the video. Then circle the correct answer to each question.

1. What do many truffle hunters do in winter?
   a. Take a vacation
   b. Work on their farms
   c. Sell truffles

2. Why do truffle brokers sell and buy truffles for cash?
   a. To avoid taxes
   b. To do business faster
   c. To control the price of truffles

Black truffles are an expensive delicacy.

3. What are truffles used for?
    a. Simple family meals
    b. Expensive gourmet dishes
    c. A few traditional French dishes
4. What problem do truffle hunters and brokers have today?
    a. The price of truffles is falling rapidly.
    b. The demand for truffles is declining.
    c. There aren't as many truffles as there used to be.

💻 **B | Note-Taking.** Watch the video again. Complete the notes with information from the video.

Richerenches:

• a town in _____, in southern France

• has one of the largest _____ in France

Truffles:

• are black with _____ veins

• are used a lot in France, _____, and _____

Possible reasons for decline:

• _____

• _____

Dogs:

• have sensitive _____

• can _____ truffles

After Viewing

👥 **Critical Thinking.** Form a group with two or three other students. Discuss the questions.

1. Why do you think truffles are called "black diamonds"? Give evidence to support your answer.
2. Look again at the possible reasons for decline that you wrote in While Viewing, exercise **B**. What other possible reasons could there be for fewer truffles?
3. In Before Viewing, exercise **B**, you discussed why truffles are expensive. Was your answer correct? Now that you have watched the video, write a new answer to the question that includes more information. Share your answer with the group.

The black truffle is a type of *fungus*—a plant that has no flowers, leaves, or green coloring.

track 3-5 **A** | **Meaning from Context.** Read and listen to the interview. Notice the words in blue. These are the words you will hear and use in Lesson B.

Q: The world's financial crisis shows that the way individuals manage their money can affect the whole world. Still, many people are unsure of how the crisis began. I'm speaking with economist Ken Lonoff. Mr. Lonoff, where did the crisis begin?

A: It began in the United States. As you know, most people want to buy their own home, but very few people can pay in paper currency—cash, that is. Banks have to help these consumers by loaning them money to buy things. People need to meet certain criteria to get a loan. For example, they need to have a job and be able to pay their bills.

A man reacts to sudden changes in the stock market.

Q: So, how exactly did this crisis begin?

A: Well, in the years that preceded the crisis, the economy was good. Financial professionals made as many loans as they could and earned a fee for each one. They were happy to assist anyone who wanted a loan. Even people without jobs were capable of getting loans. A huge number of these loans were made.

Q: When did things start to go wrong?

A: Things started to go wrong in 2007, when many people could not pay back their loans. These loans were the foundation for many businesses in the United States and all over the world. Huge sums were lost, and many companies went out of business. Loans became very difficult to get, and as a result, economies of countries around the world were affected.

B | Write the correct word in blue from exercise **A** to complete each definition.

1. _____ are people with special training in a job or career.

2. The money and coins used in a country are its _____.

3. _____ of money are amounts of money.

4. A group of people is made up of many _____.

5. _____ are people who buy things or pay for services.

6. An event that happened before another _____ it.

7. _____ are the factors used to judge or decide something.

8. A _____ is the money paid to a person or organization for a service.

9. If you are _____ of completing a task, you are able to do it.

10. When you help a person, you _____ them.

A | Read the personal finance tips below. Complete each sentence with the correct form of a word from the box.

assist	capable	consumer	fee	precede	professional	sum

Personal Finance Tips

- Pay the most important bills first. Payment of overdue bills should (1) _____ payment of bills that are not late yet.

- Always pay your bills on time. That way, you will avoid unnecessary late (2) _____.

- Set up your bank account so that a certain (3) _____ is automatically moved to a savings account each month. It's a good way to force yourself to save money.

- For questions about investing money, insurance, or taxes, be sure to hire a financial (4) _____. They have the knowledge and training to (5) _____ you with your questions. Do not rely solely on the advice of family and friends.

- Always keep some money available for emergencies. You should be (6) _____ of living on your savings for at least three months if you lose your job.

- Smart (7) _____ compare prices before buying an item. Before you pay a price that is too high, check the prices at other stores and on the Internet.

B | **Discussion.** With a partner, discuss the questions.

1. Which of the above Personal Financial Tips have you followed in your life? If you were a financial **professional**, what suggestions would you give to a person who wanted to save money?

2. Think of a major purchase you made in the past year. What **criteria** did you use to choose that item?

3. How much money do you think an **individual** spends during his or her life? Explain why you chose the number you did.

4. Do you think that the entire world should use one **currency**? Why, or why not?

Before Listening

 Read about these three types of payment cards. With a partner, discuss the questions that follow.

Three Types of Payment Cards

Debit Cards: Debit cards are directly connected to the money in your bank account. When you use your debit card, money is immediately taken out of your account.

Credit Cards: When you use a credit card, you are borrowing money. The credit card company makes the payment for you and you must pay the money back. If you don't make your payments on time, you can be charged late fees. A *charge card* is a specific type of credit card. The main difference is that you must always pay your balance in full each month.

Stored-Value Cards: Stored-value cards have electronic money stored right on the card. Anyone can use these cards, not just the person who originally bought the card. Examples are prepaid phone cards and gift cards.

---

1. Which of these payment cards do you use? How often do you use them?
2. What other methods of payment do you regularly use?

Listening: A Conversation between Friends

 track 3-6 **A | Listening for Main Ideas.** Listen to three people talking about money. Then circle the correct answer to each question.

1. Where are the people?
   a. At a restaurant
   b. At an ATM
   c. At work
2. What payment cards do the speakers use the most?
   a. Credit cards
   b. Debit and stored-value cards
   c. Debit and credit cards
3. According to Tina, why are credit cards dangerous?
   a. They're easy to steal or copy.
   b. They contain the owner's personal information.
   c. It's easy to get into debt if you have a credit card.
4. What is the problem with stored-value cards?
   a. There is a limit on how much value they can have.
   b. If they're lost, their value cannot be replaced.
   c. They are very expensive to buy.
5. Which statement about peer-to-peer lending is correct?
   a. It allows people to borrow from banks more easily.
   b. It is used mostly for large international loans.
   c. It allows individuals to loan money directly to other individuals.

Walter Cavanagh is known as "Mr. Plastic Fantastic." He holds the world record for the largest credit card collection—over 1400 working cards.

B | Listening for Details. Listen again. According to the speakers, are these statements true or false? Circle **T** for *true* or **F** for *false*.

1.	Debit cards preceded credit cards.	**T**	**F**
2.	Peer-to-peer lending services are managed by banks.	**T**	**F**
3.	Peer-to-peer lending services allow international loans.	**T**	**F**
4.	James is going to pay for lunch.	**T**	**F**

After Listening

Discussion. With a partner, discuss the questions.

1. Would you like to get involved in borrowing or lending through peer-to-peer loans? Explain.
2. How often do you visit a bank? What is a typical experience at a bank like for you?

Pronunciation

> ### Vowel-to-Vowel Linking
>
> When one word ends in a vowel and the next word starts with a vowel, English speakers often link the words together. To link a vowel to a vowel, you insert a /y/ or /w/ sound between the words. There are two rules for linking vowels.
>
>
>
> 1. When the first word ends in the sound /iy/, /ey/, /ay/, or /oy/, insert /y/:
>   *happy ending* → **happy /y/ ending**
>   *hardly ever*　　　*nearly everything*　　　*see it*　　　*the end*
>
> 2. When the first word ends in the sound /uw/, /ow/, or /aw/, insert /w/:
>   *do over* → **do /w/ over**
>   *Do you ever*　　　*go online*　　　*do it*　　　*so easy*

A | Work with a partner. Practice saying the phrases below. Insert a /y/ or /w/ into the phrases, according to the rules from the Pronunciation box. Then listen to check your pronunciation.

1. be __/y/__ able
2. the value _____ of
3. Do _____ it again.
4. Say _____ it in English.

5. nearly _____ all
6. the _____ answer
7. Who _____ ate it?
8. want to _____ understand

B | **Self-Reflection.** With your partner, answer the questions. Focus on vowel-to-vowel linking.

1. Do you ever buy things you don't need? Give an example.
2. What was the last movie you watched in a movie theater? Did you stay until the end?
3. How many times do you go online every day?
4. Why are you studying English?

Language Function

Digressing from the Topic

Sometimes, in the middle of a conversation, we suddenly want to talk about a new topic. *Digressing* means talking about a new or different topic. Here are some expressions we can use to signal that we are bringing up a new topic.

If something the other person said made you think of the new topic, say:

Speaking of . . .   *That reminds me . . .*

If a new topic enters your head suddenly, but is not being discussed, say:

Incidentally . . .   *By the way . . .*

 A | In the conversation on page 136, you heard two useful expressions for digressing from the topic. Listen to the sentences and fill in the missing expressions.

track 3-9

1. **Tina:** _____, here's a trivia question for you. Which came first: the credit card or the debit card?

2. **James:** _____, I read about an interesting way of borrowing and lending money. It's called peer-to-peer lending.

B | **Discussion.** With a partner, discuss one of the topics below. Look at the possible digressions from the topic. As you talk about the topic, digress from the topic when you have an idea that you would like to talk about.

Topic #1: Taking out a loan

Possible Digressions:
You discovered an interesting new store.
You want to find a higher-paying job.

Topic #2: Giving money to charity

Possible Digressions:
You donated old clothes to charity.
You bought a new smart phone.

I've been thinking about taking out a loan to buy a new car.

Really?

Yes, I'm tired of driving such an old car.

That reminds me, I heard that there's a new way to get loans over the Internet.

Grammar

Using Connectors of Concession

We use connectors to show a relationship between two statements. *Concession* is a special type of contrast. We use concession to show the differences between two statements, or to explain information that is surprising or unexpected.

To connect clauses, use *yet*.
> Money is only paper, **yet** most people spend their entire lives trying to get more of it.

Within a sentence, use *although*, *even*, or *though*.
> **Although** Loretta worked for ten hours, she didn't finish her project.

Between sentences, use *even so*, *nonetheless*, or *nevertheless*.
> The loan I received was small. **Even so,** it made a huge difference in my life.

A | **Collaboration.** Read the sentences. With a partner, match the sentences that go together. Then use connectors and combine each pair of sentences. Write as many different sentences as you can.

1. My boss knows I need a raise. _____f_____
2. The government is printing a lot of money. _____
3. I'm trying to find a job. _____
4. Almost everyone wants to be a millionaire. _____
5. Mary donates a lot of money to charity. _____
6. I bought a small house to save money. _____

a. Money can't buy happiness.
b. She doesn't make much money herself.
c. I could have bought a bigger one.
d. It isn't creating any jobs.
e. I'm not having any luck.
f. She refuses to give me one.

A man works on a money-printing machine in Germany.

B | **Discussion.** With your partner, look at the sentences you wrote in exercise **A**. Have a conversation about each topic.

> I just bought a house a few months ago.

> That's great. What does it look like?

You will role-play a meeting between a financial professional and a client to discuss ways that the client can save money. With your partner, you will prepare a budget and present it to your classmates.

A | Work with a partner. Read the role cards and choose your role.

Role #1: Financial Professional

You are a financial professional. Discuss the client's budget with him or her, ask questions, and offer suggestions for reducing expenses and increasing savings.

Role #2: Client

You recently moved into a new home and now your expenses are more than your income. Explain the problem and ask about ways to reduce your expenses.

B | **Role-Playing.** Study the client's monthly budget and discuss the questions with your partner. Work with your partner and write a budget plan so that the client's income is more than his or her expenses. Also include a plan for how to repay the client's debt.

1. What is the difference between income and expenses? Use your dictionary to help you.
2. Which expenses cannot be changed?
3. On which items do you think the client needs to spend more money?
4. On which items do you think the client should spend less money?
5. Which loan should the client pay back first? Explain.

Income:	$3200	Expenses:		Debts:	
Savings:	$ 0	Rent:	$1040	Student loan: (2% interest for 15 years)	$10,500
		Food:	$ 300		
		Heat and Electricity:	$ 200		
		Gas for Car:	$ 120		
		Entertainment:	$ 425	Car loan balance: (4% interest for 4 years)	$ 4600
		Health insurance:	$ 450		
		Charity donation:	$ 100		
		Credit card payment:	$ 400	Credit card balance: (18% interest per year)	$ 1290
		Student loan payment:	$ 100		
		Car loan payment:	$ 140		
Total Income: $3200		**Total Expenses:**	**$3275**	**Total Debt:**	**$16,390**

C | **Presentation.** With your partner from exercise **B**, present your budget plan to another pair of students. Then compare the plans. How were they similar? How were they different?

Presentation Skills: Dealing with Difficult Questions

Sometimes during a role-play, presentation, or conversation, someone might ask you a question that you don't know how to answer. One way to answer is to say, "I don't know." A better way to answer is to say, "That's a very interesting question. I'll have to get back to you on that." Then, research the answer on your own and share the information with the person who asked you the question.

Health and Fitness

ACADEMIC PATHWAYS

Lesson A: Listening to a Question-and-Answer Session
          Discussing Environmental Health Concerns
Lesson B: Listening to a Conversation between Friends
          Sharing Advice about Health and Fitness

Think and Discuss

1. Think of activities such as rock climbing that require extreme fitness.
   How do people prepare to do these activities?
2. What can you do to cheer yourself up when you feel sad or are
   facing a stressful situation?

Without a rope, a rock climber climbs up a wall in Yosemite National Park in the United States.

Exploring the Theme:
Health and Fitness

Look at the photos and read the captions. Then discuss the questions.

1. What is the steel room used for?
2. How can chemicals such as DDT affect your health?
3. Where is it possible to go rock climbing? What kinds of equipment would you need?
4. Have you ever tried yoga? What are the health benefits of practicing yoga regularly?

Health Dangers

This steel room at Georgia Tech Research Institute is used to measure indoor air pollution that can affect our health. Small amounts of dangerous chemicals can be released from surprising sources including desks, electronics, and clothing.

A warning sign tells people to stay away from a building in Zambia where the government stores DDT. The chemical can be deadly if mishandled, but it can also be used to kill dangerous bugs.

Rock Climbing

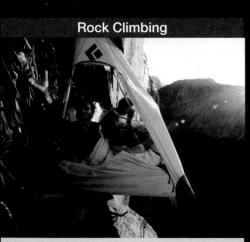

Rock climbing is more popular than ever before. These rock climbers stop on the side of a mountain as they take a break from their climbing.

A man is doing yoga on Wharaiki Beach in New Zealand.

track 3-10 **A** | **Meaning from Context.** Read and listen to the article about pesticides. Notice the words in blue. These are words you will hear and use in Lesson A.

Professor Steve McLaskey of the Maharishi University of Management carries organic vegetables from the university greenhouse to the cafeteria.

Before scientists discovered it was dangerous, DDT was used as a pesticide.

In the well-known song *Big Yellow Taxi*, the singer asks a farmer to "put away the DDT." DDT is a **pesticide**—a chemical compound[1] used to kill insects. Farmers throughout the world spray pesticides on their growing crops to keep bugs and other insects away. In the past, DDT was considered a safe pesticide. It was sprayed directly on children to kill insects and was even used to help make wallpaper for bedrooms. Since then, DDT has been **assessed** by scientists. After years of testing, scientists concluded that DDT was harmful to humans, birds, insects, and even some other kinds of animals. Farmers in many countries stopped using DDT after they learned it could be harmful. However, DDT was not **eliminated** from the environment. According to scientists, DDT **persists** in the environment for many years. **Traces** of the pesticide have been found in soil, animals, and in humans all over the world.

In the past several decades, more and more markets have been offering shoppers the **option** of fruits and vegetables grown without pesticides or other chemicals. There is a growing number of people who **appreciate** these **organic** fruits and vegetables. People who buy organic food fear that the **constant** consumption of food grown with pesticides could be dangerous to their health. They worry that, little by little, small amounts of dangerous chemicals will **accumulate** in their bodies until the amount is large enough to cause health problems. Scientists are still researching the effects of pesticides on humans, but it is clear that the amount of organic food available is growing. According to the Research Institute of Organic Agriculture, people around the world spent over $50 billion on organic products and food in 2010.

[1]In chemistry, a **compound** is a substance that consists of two or more elements.

B | Write each word in blue from exercise **A** to complete each definition.

1. The word _____constant_____ describes an event that is always happening.
2. If a chemical _____persists_____ in the environment, it continues to exist.
3. Foods and plants grown without the use of pesticides and harmful chemicals are _____organic_____ foods.
4. When things _____accumulate_____, they collect or are gathered together over time.
5. If you have _____assessed (it)_____ something, you have considered it in order to make a judgment about it (for example, how good or how bad it is).
6. Chemicals that farms use to kill insects or to keep insects off of their crops are called _____pesticides_____.
7. If you _____appreciate_____ a person, you are grateful for the person because you recognize his or her good qualities.
8. _____Traces_____ of a substance are very small amounts of it.
9. An _____option_____ is a choice between two or more things.
10. When an item is _____eliminated_____, it has been removed completely.

A | **Understanding Collocations.** *Collocations* are groups of two words that are often used together. Complete the collocations by matching each word from the box on the left with the correct word from the box on the right. Then use the collocations to complete the sentences. *(See page 208 of the Independent Student Handbook for more information on building your vocabulary.)*

constant _____	without _____	evidence	a trace
show _____	accumulate _____	exposure	appreciation

1. In the past, people complained that many natural sweeteners had a bitter taste. Today, however, manufacturers produce sweeteners _____ *without a trace* of bitterness.

2. J. Gordon Edwards believed that DDT wasn't a danger to human health. He pointed out that workers at Montrose Chemical Company in California wore no masks or goggles, but were never harmed by their _____ *constant exposure* to DDT.

3. Scientists need decades to _____ *accumulate* enough _____ *evidence* to declare that a new food is safe for humans to eat.

4. A gift basket of organic fruits is a nice way to _____ *show appreciation* to your friends, family, or coworkers.

Critical Thinking Focus: Asking Questions for Further Research

When you read or hear about a new topic, you may want more information or want to learn about another point of view. When you want to do further research on a topic, ask these questions.

What additional information would I like to know?
What other sources might have information about this topic?

Later, you can do research to answer your own questions.

B | **Collaboration.** Read the information in exercise **A** on page 144. Then read the statements below. In your notebook, write questions for further research for each statement. Do research to answer your questions. Take notes and be sure to list the source where you found your information. Then form a group with two or three other students. Discuss your questions and research findings with your group.

1. DDT was once considered safe for humans.
2. DDT doesn't disappear quickly.
3. The amount of organic food available in markets is growing.

Before Listening

 Predicting Content. With a partner, look at the photo and read the information. Then answer the questions.

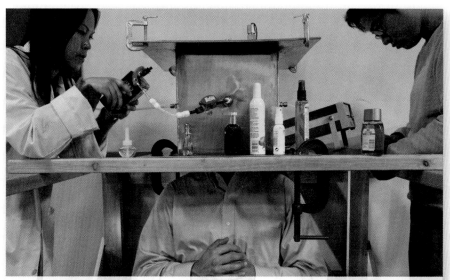

Household products such as detergents and perfumes can contain dangerous chemicals. Scientists test this man's reactions to different chemicals by spraying them into the box around his head.

1. How do you think chemicals in household products affect a person's health?
2. What dangers in food or the environment could affect a person's health?

Listening: A Question-and-Answer Session

A | **Listening for Main Ideas.** Listen to the question-and-answer session that followed a lecture on health. Then choose the correct answers.

track 3-11

1. How dangerous are PBDEs to human health?
   a. Small amounts cause health problems mostly in children.
   b. Small amounts probably do not cause any serious health problems.
   c. Small amounts are linked to several serious diseases in adults.

2. How dangerous is lead paint to human health?
   a. It is a threat to the health of children.
   b. It is not a serious health risk for humans.
   c. It is mainly a problem for people who are sick.

3. How much swordfish and tuna does Dr. Wallace think is OK to eat?
   a. He recommends eating no swordfish or tuna at all.
   b. He recommends eating swordfish and tuna in moderation only.
   c. He recommends eating as much swordfish and tuna as you want.

4. Which statement is true about the danger of cell phone radiation?
   a. Cell phone radiation has caused cancer in people and rats.
   b. Cell phone radiation is not a threat to human health.
   c. Different studies have come to different conclusions about cell phone radiation.

B | **Note-Taking.** Listen again. Complete the notes with information from the question-and-answer session.

PBDEs

 Impact on health: High amounts can cause cancer in ___lab animals___

 Dr. W. suggests: For small amounts in humans, ___aren't worth worrying about___

Lead paint

 Impact on health: Small amounts of it can cause ___brain damage in children.___

 Dr. W. suggests: ___make sure the paint not chipping or move to a new house___

Mercury

 Impact on health: Permanent damage to ___memory and ability to learn.___

 Dr. W. suggests: Eat fish ___in moderation___

Cell phones

 Impact on health: Driving and using a cell phone can lead to ___accidents___

  Radiation from cell phones ___can cause brain cancer___

 Dr. W. suggests: ___Turn off your cellphone and use head sets___

After Listening

Discussion. Form a group with two or three other students. Read the photo and caption below. Then discuss the questions.

1. If you had a chance to talk to Dr. Wallace, what health-related question would you ask him?
2. Would you like to be tested for chemicals? Explain. What types of chemicals do you think scientists would find?
3. What are some lifestyle changes you could make to allow fewer chemicals inside your body?

David Ewing Duncan had tests to find out what chemicals were in his body. He found out that he was carrying many compounds, including 16 types of pesticides. The compounds come from foods, drinks, and even frying pans.

Language Function

> ### Expressing Uncertainty
>
> Sometimes we want to talk about a particular topic, but we may not be certain that the information we have is correct. Here are some expressions to show listeners that we are not sure about what we are saying.
>
> *It appears/seems to me (that) . . .*
> *I'm not quite/altogether sure (that) . . .*
> *It appears/looks/seems as though . . .*
> *. . . appears/looks/seems (to be) . . .*
> *I could be wrong, but it appears/doesn't appear (that) . . .*
> *I'm not quite/altogether sure, but it appears/looks/seems (that) . . .*

track 3-12 **A** | In the question-and-answer session, Dr. Wallace used a number of expressions to talk about information he wasn't sure about. Listen and fill in the missing expressions.

1. In high amounts, they have caused health problems in laboratory animals. However,

   _____it looks although_____ the small amounts of PBDEs that normally

   accumulate in the human body aren't worth worrying about.

2. Large fish at the top of the food chain, such as tuna and swordfish, accumulate

   high amounts of mercury and pass it on to people who eat seafood. Now,

   _____It doesn't appear that_____ traces of mercury in the blood are a serious problem,

   but I could be wrong.

3. _____I am not all together sure that_____ you can eliminate radiation exposure from cell phones,

   but people who are concerned about it can reduce the risk by using a headset.

B | **Discussion.** Look at the photos. What is happening in each photo? Discuss what you see with a partner. Use expressions from the Language Function box above.

> I'm not quite sure, but it appears that two women are helping an actress put on her makeup.

1.

3.

2.

4.
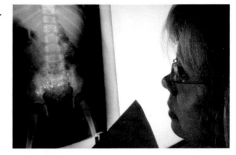

C | With your partner, read the captions that correspond to the four photos from exercise **B** on page 148. Write the number of the correct photo next to each caption. Did you and your partner correctly guess what was happening in each photo?

_____ a. In Mexico, a brick-maker faces exposure to the smoke from his kiln, an oven used for making bricks.

_____ b. A doctor looks at an X-ray showing lead paint inside the body of a two-year-old girl from Ohio. Even today, lead paint is still harming children who swallow it.

_____ c. People cover their mouths and faces to protect themselves from chemicals as they ride on motorbikes in Vietnam.

_____ d. At the Campaign for Safe Cosmetics in California, makeup artists exhibit chemical-free makeup.

Grammar

Phrasal Verbs

Phrasal verbs consist of two words: the first word is a verb, and the second is called a particle. (Particles are often prepositions.) Examples of phrasal verbs are *grow up*, *turn off*, *turn up*, and *throw out*.

    phrasal verb
    ┌─────┐
I **grew up** in the country, so I got plenty of fresh air and exercise.
    ↓   ↓
  verb particle

> Some companies **get around** laws by illegally disposing of dangerous chemicals.

Phrasal verbs are more common in spoken English than in written English. The meaning of a phrasal verb often has little or nothing to do with the words that make up the phrasal verb. For example, *blow up* means *explode*, *let down* means *disappoint*, and *put off* means *postpone*.

For some phrasal verbs, the particle can come after the object. For some phrasal verbs, the particle must come before the object.

> The solution to that problem is simple: **turn** your cell phone **off** while driving.
> The solution to that problem is simple: **turn off** your cell phone while driving.

EPA: environmental protection Agency.

👥 **A** | **Using a Dictionary.** Work with a partner. Read the book summary of *A Civil Action*. Use the correct phrasal verb from the box to replace each verb in parentheses. Use your dictionary to help you.

finding out	got together	keeping back	thrown out
gave in	hold out	put back	turned down

Book Summary: *A Civil Action*

Author: Johnathan Harr, Genre: Non-Fiction

During a court case, a lawyer gives evidence to defend a certain point of view.

After (1) _____finding out_____ (discovering) that her child had leukemia,[1] Anne Anderson began to notice many other cases of leukemia near her home in Woburn, Massachusetts. It was surprising, because leukemia is a rare disease. Soon, Anne realized that something in the town might have caused the cancer. Eventually, she (2) __got together__ (gathered) with other families and hired a lawyer.

Lawyer Jan Schlichtmann (3) __turned down__ ~~an invitation~~ (refused) the case at first, but later he accepted the case. Schlichtmann soon found evidence that the town's water had been contaminated by a chemical called trichloroethylene (TCE). Schlichtmann filed a lawsuit against the companies responsible: Unifirst, W.R. Grace & Co., and Beatrice Foods, Inc. The lawsuit was a long and expensive one, and he had to hire other lawyers to assist him.

Unifirst settled[2] for a little over a million dollars. The money was immediately (4) __put back__ (reinvested) into the cases against the other two companies. The case against Beatrice Foods was (5) __thrown out__ (dismissed) because of a lack of evidence. Schlichtmann found a former employee of W.R. Grace who knew that the company had dumped dangerous chemicals in the water. Though Schlichtmann wanted a high settlement, a difficult financial situation meant that he couldn't (6) __hold out__ (wait) any longer. He accepted a settlement for $8 million from W.R. Grace.

Schlichtmann paid the money to the families, (7) __keeping back__ (withholding) expenses and fees. Some of the families thought that Schlichtmann charged too much, so he (8) __gave in__ (yielded) and gave away more of the money. Schlichtmann would later lose his house and car and he even lived in his office for a time.

[1]**Leukemia** is a type of cancer that affects the blood.
[2]In law, **to settle** means to agree to end a lawsuit, usually for a payment.

👥 **B** | **Critical Thinking.** With your partner, discuss the questions.

1. Do you think that the result of the lawsuit was fair for the companies, the families, and the lawyers that were involved? Explain.
2. How could the city of Woburn prevent this situation from happening again in the future? Brainstorm some ideas.

Discussing Environmental Health Concerns

A | Work with a partner. How concerned is your partner about things in the environment that affect his or her health? Use the survey form to interview your partner. Check (✔) your partner's answer to each question.

How concerned are you about . . .	Not at All Concerned	Somewhat Concerned	Very Concerned
chemicals used to grow food?			
chemical compounds in paints and materials around your home?			
chemicals in medicines?			
chemical compounds added to food such as preservatives,[1] colors, and flavors?			
chemicals such as mercury produced by industries?			
radiation from cell phones or X-ray machines?			
chemicals produced by plants and insects?			

[1]**Preservatives** are chemicals that help keep food fresh for a long period of time.

B | **Self-Reflection.** With your partner, discuss your answers to the survey. Give reasons for your answers, and give examples from your daily life.

> I'm concerned about chemicals used to grow food. I eat a lot of vegetables, and I'm not sure how they are grown.

C | **Collaboration.** With your partner, think of three possible actions to take to protect yourselves from some of the environmental health concerns mentioned in the chart. Write your suggestions below. Then share your ideas with the class.

> We decided that buying organic foods would be good for our health.

Actions:

1. _____

2. _____

3. _____

Student to Student: Going First

Before making short presentations or talking with your group, use these phrases to ask the members of your group who will be the first to speak:

In Pairs
Should I go first?
Do you want to go first?

In Groups
So, who wants to go first?
Will anyone/anybody volunteer to go first?
Does anyone/anybody want to go first?

Paraguay Shaman

Victoriano is a shaman in Cuyabeno, Ecuador.

Paraguay

Before Viewing

A | Prior Knowledge. The video you are going to watch is about a scientific expedition to collect plants from a rainforest in Paraguay. Many medical scientists are studying rainforest plants. Form a group with two or three other students. Why do you think scientists are interested in studying these plants? Write down a few ideas.

1. _____
2. _____

B | Using a Dictionary. You will hear these words in the video. Match each word with its definition. Use your dictionary to help you.

1. potential (adj.) ____
2. renowned (n.) ____
3. extensive (adj.) ____
4. shaman (n.) ____
5. urgent (adj.) ____

a. a person who is believed to have spiritual powers
b. the ability to become useful in the future
c. needing immediate action
d. a large area
e. well-known

While Viewing

A | Watch the video. Then circle the correct answers.

Deforestation is destroying many of the useful plants in the reserve.

1. Why are the scientists interested in rainforest plants?
   a. The plants could help cure some diseases.
   b. Many of them are dangerous to eat.
   c. The plants could be a new source of food for the world.
2. What is Gervasio's part in the video?
   a. He wants to stop the scientists from collecting rainforest plants.
   b. He teaches the scientists how to survive in the rainforest.
   c. He leads the scientists to plants he knows about.
3. Why are the scientists in a hurry to find these plants?
   a. The plants are disappearing very quickly.
   b. There is little money available for collecting plants.
   c. Every scientist wants to be the first one to study an important new plant.

B | **Viewing for Specific Details.** Read the statements. Then watch the video again. Circle **T** for *true* or **F** for *false*.

1.	People in Paraguay are just beginning to understand that some plants can cure diseases.	T	F
2.	The rainforest is disappearing more quickly in Paraguay than in most other countries.	T	F
3.	Gervasio is looking for a leafy green plant.	T	F
4.	Gervasio's wife uses the plant to prepare tea.	T	F
5.	The book will help Gervasio learn more about plants.	T	F

After Viewing

Critical Thinking. Form a group with two or three other students and discuss the questions.

1. How did Gervasio know which plants were useful and which ones were not?
2. Had Gervasio ever worked with scientists before? How do you know?

The Mbaracayú Forest Nature Reserve is home to thousands of different species of plants.

A | **Meaning from Context.** Read and listen to the information about yoga. Notice the words in **blue**. These are the words you will hear and use in Lesson B.

track 3-13

Swami Vivekananda

Yoga was **initially** practiced over 5000 years ago in India. In India, yoga is a tradition that is related to both religion and culture. **Prior to** the 19th century, yoga was not well understood and was rarely practiced in other parts of the world. The introduction of yoga to other countries is **attributed** to the Indian yoga master Swami Vivekananda, who toured Europe and the United States in the 1890s.

A woman does yoga on the railing of a bridge.

Many different **versions** of yoga are practiced, from traditional styles such as hatha and Sivananda yoga to modern versions such as chair yoga and laughter yoga. For fans of yoga, it is the **ultimate** workout because it involves not only the body but the mind as well. There are many health benefits associated with yoga. It helps you be more flexible, stronger, and it relieves stress. Yoga-style meditation[1] called yoga nidra can be very relaxing. Some yoga teachers claim that just a half an hour of yoga nidra is **equivalent** to two or three hours of sleep.

A yoga class in India

As yoga grows in popularity, more people are teaching yoga and more yoga schools and centers are opening. Since the 1960s the **expansion** of yoga has been remarkable, and today yoga is taught and practiced everywhere. It has become a truly **global** business with yoga retreats[2] in the United States, Mexico, Thailand, New Zealand, France, Egypt, and many other countries. According to **data** in the *Yoga Journal*, 14.3 million people in the United States alone practiced yoga in 2010. Scientists and researchers are now completing the first World Yoga Survey to count how many people around the world practice yoga. It is estimated that more than 30 million people practice yoga around the world and that there are over 70,000 yoga teachers. In many places, there are no laws controlling the quality of schools and teachers. Some people are asking for **legislation** to make sure the quality of yoga education remains high.

[1]In yoga, **meditation** is sitting quietly for a long time with a calm and clear mind.
[2]In a yoga **retreat**, groups of people go away for several days to practice yoga in a nice, peaceful place.

B | Write each word in **blue** from exercise **A** to complete each definition.

India

1. _____Expansion_____ is the act or process of becoming larger.
2. If B is the cause of A, then we can say that A is _____attributed_____ to B.
3. The _____ultimate_____ form of something is the very best form of it.
4. Information, especially in the form of facts or numbers, is known as _____data_____.
5. _____Initially_____ means at the beginning of a process or situation.
6. If one thing is _____equivalent_____ to another, they are the same.
7. _____Versions_____ of an item are forms of the item with some differences.
8. _____Global_____ means concerning or including the whole world.
9. If an event happens _____Prior to_____ a particular time, it happens before that time.
10. When a government passes _____Legislation_____, it makes a new law or laws.

A | Read the information and fill in each blank with the correct form of a word from the box.

attribute	equivalent	initially	legislation	prior to

A recent report stated that most illnesses can be (1) _attribute_ to lifestyle-related causes such as stress at work or not being physically active. Joining a health club or gym can be a great way to get in shape and stay healthy. It's important to get as much information as you can about a health club (2) _prior to_ joining one and starting to pay membership fees. Here are some things to do when you (3) _initially_ visit a health club:

- Take a tour of the club and inspect every part of it.
- Ask if members have to pay a fee if they cancel the membership. Some clubs charge members a high fee if they decide to leave.
- Ask about the qualifications of the instructors. All instructors should be certified in fitness instruction and life-saving skills or have (4) _equivalent_ qualifications.

It's also important to know your rights as a health club member. Most areas have laws protecting health club customers. Visit the government's consumer affairs Web site to find out about new (5) _legislation_ about health clubs that has been passed.

B | **Using a Dictionary.** A *synonym* is a word or expression that means the same thing as another word or expression. Each word in the box is a synonym for a vocabulary word. Write each synonym in the box next to the correct vocabulary word.

best	figures	international	maximum	overall	statistics

1. data: _statistics_ , _figures_
2. global: _international_ , _overall_
3. ultimate: _best_ , _maximum_

C | Use a synonym from exercise **B** to complete each sentence. (See page 208 of the Independent Student Handbook for more information on building your vocabulary.)

1. The World Health Organization is an _international_ organization of 193 countries.
2. Going to college was the _best_ decision I ever made.
3. I always set the exercise machine on the _maximum_ level.
4. I added up these _figures_ , and they are incorrect. Check your addition again.
5. The world has a lot of health issues, but _overall_ , people are living longer.
6. The hospital input the _statistics_ about your health history into the computer.

D | With a partner, discuss the questions.

1. Would you like to try yoga? If you have tried it, what version did you try?
2. What are the most important things for you in choosing a health club? What rules should health clubs enforce?

Before Listening

👥 **Prior Knowledge.** With a partner, discuss the questions.

1. Would you like to try rock climbing? Why, or why not? If you have gone rock climbing before, describe your experience.
2. What are some of the dangers of rock climbing?
3. What kind of equipment do rock climbers use?

A rock climber uses a thin rope to cross over Yosemite Falls.

Listening: A Conversation between Friends

🎧 track 3-14 **A** | **Listening for Main Ideas.** Listen to the conversation about rock climbing.

1. What is the woman's attitude toward rock climbing?
   a. She wishes she had learned how to do it.
   b. She's concerned that it's dangerous.
   c. She thinks she'd be good at it.

2. Why did the man start rock climbing?
   a. For exercise
   b. For excitement
   c. To meet people

3. Which of these versions of rock climbing is the most difficult?
   a. Bouldering
   b. Traditional rock climbing
   c. Free solo climbing

4. Which statement about rock climbing accidents would the man agree with?
   a. Fewer people should go rock climbing.
   b. Taking some risks is part of rock climbing.
   c. Climbing should be done in climbing gyms.

🎧 track 3-14 **B** | **Listening for Details.** Listen again. Match each version of rock climbing with the correct description below.

a. indoor climbing   b. bouldering   c. traditional rock climbing   d. free solo climbing

___b___ 1. People climb on large rocks as high as 16 feet.

___a___ 2. It takes place in climbing gyms.

___d___ 3. People don't use ropes at all.

___c___ 4. It requires lots of equipment.

C | Listen again. Then read the statements. Circle **T** for *true* or **F** for *false*.

track 3-14

1. A half an hour of jogging is equivalent to about an hour of rock climbing.   **T**   **F**

2. There are thousands of climbing gyms around the world.   **T**   **F**

3. There was a rock climbing accident in Yosemite last year.   **T**   **F**

4. Free solo climbing is no longer allowed in Yosemite.   **T**   **F**

5. There is one death in every 320,000 climbs.   **T**   **F**

6. Between 1990 and 2007, 40,000 people died in rock climbing accidents.   **T**   **F**

7. Stan tries to be very careful when he is climbing.   **T**   **F**

8. Stan has decided to give up rock climbing.   **T**   **F**

D | **Discussion.** Form a group with two or three other students and discuss the questions.

1. An *extreme sport* is a sport or activity that is exciting but dangerous. What other extreme sports are you familiar with? Do you participate in any extreme sports? What do you like about them?

2. Stan said, "If you don't take any risks, you'll never have any fun!" Do you agree with this statement? Explain.

Pronunciation

Dropped Syllables
In some words, unstressed vowels sometimes can be omitted or dropped, especially in casual speech.

track 3-15

every   mystery

ev~~e~~ry   myst~~e~~ry

Listen to the words and cross out the dropped syllable in each word. Then practice saying the words with a partner.

track 3-16

1. int~~e~~resting
2. veg~~e~~table
3. diff~~e~~rent
4. fav~~o~~rite
5. choc~~o~~late
6. asp~~i~~rin
7. hist~~o~~ry
8. ev~~e~~ning
9. gen~~e~~rally
10. bev~~e~~rage
11. cam~~e~~ra
12. rest~~au~~rant

Language Function

Showing Understanding

In a conversation, you sometimes want to show the other person that you understand or sympathize with him or her. Here are some expressions to show that you understand someone's feelings or situation.

You must be (tired).   *You must have been (glad).*
That must be (fun).   *That must have been (difficult).*

A | In the conversation, there were a number of useful expressions for showing understanding. Listen and fill in the missing expressions.

track 3-17

1. **Stan:** I spent today at Yosemite National Park. I was rock climbing.
   Jennifer: _That must have been fun_.

2. **Stan:** A half hour of rock climbing is equivalent to about an hour of jogging, and I was climbing for three hours today.
   Jennifer: _You must be exausted_.

3. **Stan:** The walls are pretty easy to climb—not too high—and the floor is usually pretty soft, so it doesn't hurt much if you do fall.
   Jennifer: _It must be pretty safe_ (somewhat), then, huh?

B | **Role-Playing.** Form a group with three other students. Each person will take one of the roles below. Take turns role-playing each situation. Your group members will respond and use expressions for showing understanding when appropriate.

Role #1: You just got back from a two-week vacation in Europe. You visited London, Paris, Madrid, Rome, and many other major cities. You made some new friends, and you bought some wonderful gifts and souvenirs.

Role #3: You have an important job interview tomorrow. The company offers an excellent salary and benefits, including health insurance and a retirement plan. If you get the job, you have to move to another city.

Role #2: You just moved into an apartment that is brand new. It's in a really nice part of town, and the rent isn't too high. You have a lot of space, and the Internet connection is really fast.

Role #4: You are a photographer. You have your own photography studio, and you often take pictures of famous people. There is going to be an exhibition of your work at a local museum.

It's nice to be home. I just spent two weeks traveling around Europe.

You must be exhausted! What did you do there?

C | Self-Reflection. Work with a partner. Talk about events that are going on in your life right now. Use the expressions for showing understanding.

> I have two jobs right now.

> You must be really busy. What kind of work do you do?

Grammar

Three-Word Phrasal Verbs

Some phrasal verbs consist of three words. The last word of a three-word phrasal verb is a preposition. Examples of three-word phrasal verbs are *look forward to* and *get rid of*.
> I'm **looking forward to** going camping next weekend!

The object of a three-word phrasal verb follows the preposition.
> Are you going to **get rid of** your rock climbing equipment?

A | Work with a partner. Match each three-word phrasal verb with its meaning.

1. stand up for   _f_
2. pick up on   _c_
3. come up with   _h_
4. put up with   _a_
5. get down to   _d_
6. get rid of   _g_
7. come down with   _b_
8. drop in on   _e_

a. to endure or bear *put up with the noise at night.*
b. to begin to suffer from (an illness)
c. to become aware of; perceive
d. to start doing something seriously or with effort
e. to visit
f. to speak or act in defense or support of
g. to throw away; dispose of
h. to produce or figure out

B | Use the correct form of each three-word phrasal verb from exercise **A** to complete the conversation. Then listen and check your answers. *(track 3-18)*

Tonya: Hi, Marc, how are you?

Marc: Tonya! What are you doing here? Isn't today your day off?

Tonya: I'm doing my grocery shopping and I wanted to (1) _drop in on_ you to say hello. Are you feeling OK? I thought maybe you had a headache.

Marc: Yes, I do. Maybe I'm (2) _coming down with_ a cold or something.

Tonya: Really? Why don't you just take some cold medicine? That usually (3) _gets rid of_ my colds right away.

Marc: No, I can't. I'm working, remember?

Tonya: Well, why don't you ask if you can take the afternoon off? Just (4) _come up with_ an excuse to tell the boss.

Marc: That's OK! I'm fine, really. I've got a lot to do and I have to (5) _get down to_ work. Thanks for coming to check on me.

Tonya: No problem. See you later!

C | Collaboration. Write sentences using each of the three-word phrasal verbs from exercise **A**. Share your sentences with a partner.

Sharing Advice

People often ask for advice on what to do in a situation. We use these expressions to share advice with others.

Suggestions
You may/might want to . . .
You should . . .
You could . . .

Strong Advice
Always/Never . . .
Don't forget to . . .
Make sure (not) to . . .

A | What advice about health and fitness can you share with your classmates? For each category in the chart, write two pieces of advice.

Categories	Advice
Daily Health	1. _____
	2. _____
Physical Fitness	1. *You should go hiking once a week.*
	2. *You may try to do exercise every day.*
Mental Health	1. *Don't forget to take a vacation if you are under stress at work.*
	2. *You could share your feeling with friends and families when you are stressed at*
Medicine	1. *take vitamins to feel energetic*
	2. *Make sure to take proteins to built up your muscles*
Food and Drink	1. *Always eat fresh food instead of process foods.*
	2. *Make sure not to drink lot of alcohol.*

Presentation Skills: Relating to Your Audience

Don't expect that your audience is automatically interested in what you have to say. It's important to grab the audience's attention. Here are some ways to relate to your audience.

- Tell them how what you are saying could affect them personally.
- Use words like *you, we, us,* and *our.*
- Encourage the audience to participate. Start some questions with "Raise your hands if you know . . ."
- Use real life stories to illustrate your points.

B | Work in groups of five. Divide up the categories among the members of your group. In the chart, circle the category you are responsible for.

C | **Discussion.** With your group, share and discuss each person's advice. Take notes on advice ideas for your category and prepare to present those ideas to the class.

D | **Presentation.** Take turns presenting advice ideas for each category to the class.

> You may want to brush your teeth after every meal, and don't forget to use dental floss.

Mind and Memory

ACADEMIC PATHWAYS

Lesson A: Listening to a TV Show
Giving a Short Persuasive Speech
Lesson B: Listening to a Conversation between Classmates
Using Memory Skills to Recall Information

Think and Discuss

1. How do animals show intelligence? Give examples.
2. What are some ways that humans show intelligence?
3. Do you think you have a good memory? Explain.

In Thailand, an elephant uses a paint brush and his trunk to paint a picture.

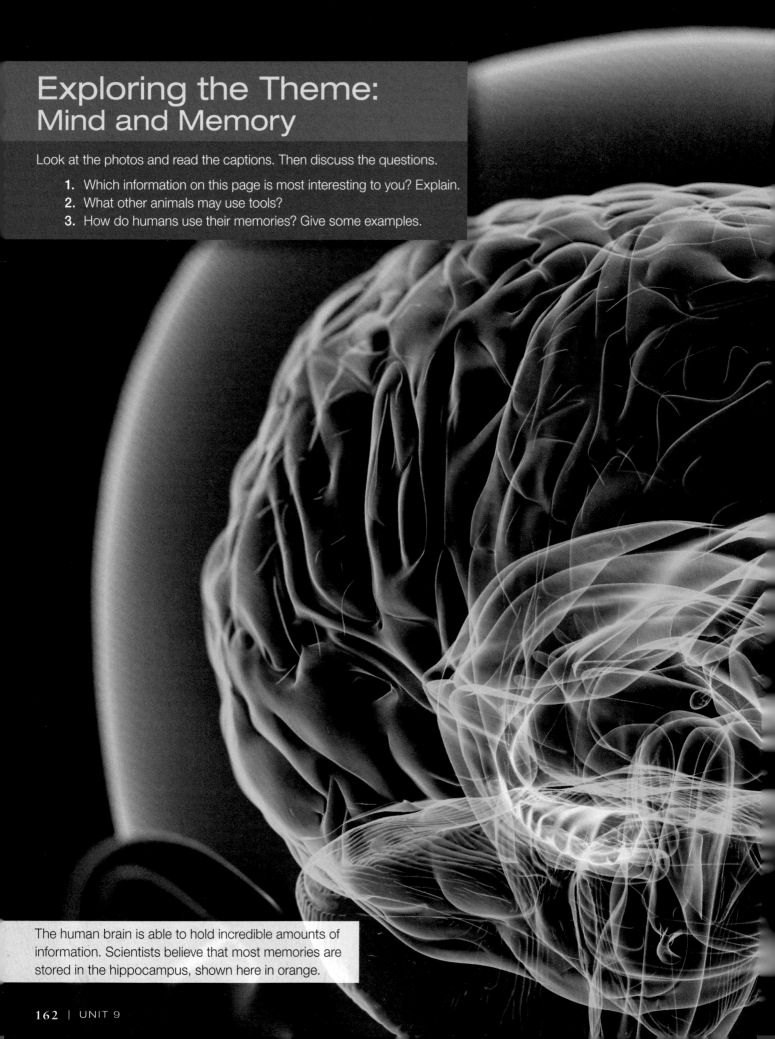

Exploring the Theme:
Mind and Memory

Look at the photos and read the captions. Then discuss the questions.

1. Which information on this page is most interesting to you? Explain.
2. What other animals may use tools?
3. How do humans use their memories? Give some examples.

The human brain is able to hold incredible amounts of information. Scientists believe that most memories are stored in the hippocampus, shown here in orange.

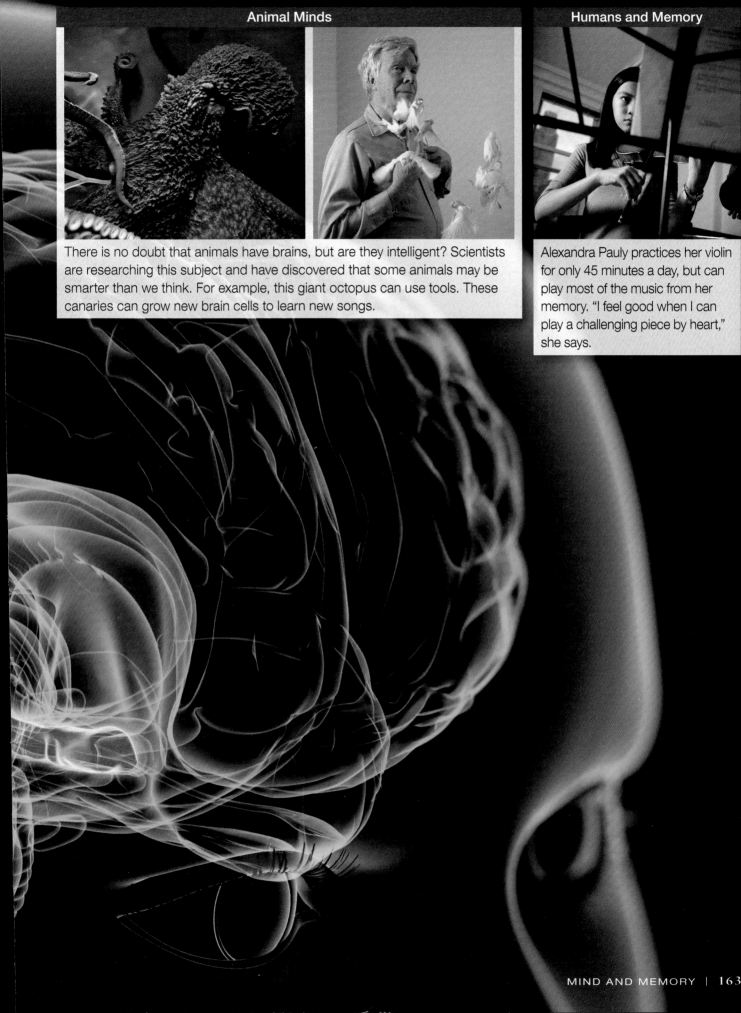

Animal Minds

There is no doubt that animals have brains, but are they intelligent? Scientists are researching this subject and have discovered that some animals may be smarter than we think. For example, this giant octopus can use tools. These canaries can grow new brain cells to learn new songs.

Humans and Memory

Alexandra Pauly practices her violin for only 45 minutes a day, but can play most of the music from her memory. "I feel good when I can play a challenging piece by heart," she says.

👥 **A** | **Using a Dictionary.** Work with a partner. Match each word with its definition. Use your dictionary to help you. These are words you will hear and use in Lesson A.

1. interpret (v.) _____
2. adjacent (adj.) _____
3. correspond (v.) _____
4. flexible (adj.) _____
5. illustrate (v.) _____
6. abstract (adj.) _____
7. motive (n.) _____
8. philosophies (n.) _____
9. capacity (n.) _____
10. underestimate (v.) _____

a. to show an example of an idea
b. the ability to do something
c. next to each other
d. based on general ideas rather than on real things
e. belief systems for explaining existence, knowledge, and thought
f. able to change easily
g. to think that something is smaller or less important than it really is
h. to have a close similarity or connection
i. a reason for a person's actions
j. to decide on the meaning of something when it is not very clear

🎧 track 3-19 **B** | Read the paragraphs and fill in each blank with the correct word from exercise **A**. Then listen and check your answers.

Are animals capable of showing concern for members of another species? According to the (1) _____ of many great thinkers such as Aristotle and Descartes, the answer is *no*. Recently, however, there has been a shift in the way many scientists think about this subject. The question is difficult because it is so (2) _____. Let's look at one specific case.

A video filmed at a small pond in Africa shows an antelope trying to cross the pond. A crocodile grabbed the antelope and tried to pull it under the water. Just then, a hippo resting in an (3) _____ pond ran over and scared the crocodile away. The crocodile released the injured antelope. Then the hippo, trying to help, gently nuzzled[1] the antelope.

An antelope crossing a pond tries to escape the jaws of a crocodile.

How should we (4) _____ the hippo's actions? It seems that the hippo's (5) _____ was to help the antelope, although the hippo didn't gain anything from it. The actions of the hippo (6) _____ to what we in the human world would call altruism.[2] This video raises the question of whether we humans (7) _____ an animal's (8) _____ to help other animals. This case can also (9) _____ how complex animal society can be. We should remain (10) _____ and open to the possibility that animals can be altruistic, too.

[1]Animals **nuzzle** by touching each other gently with their noses.
[2]**Altruism** is concern for the happiness and safety of others instead of yourself.

USING VOCABULARY

A | Complete the paragraph with the correct form of each word from the box.

| abstract | capacity | correspond | illustrate | interpret | underestimate |

In the 19th century, Charles Darwin developed his theory of evolution. This theory claims that all living things evolved from other living things by small changes, little by little, over millions of years. If that theory is true, then it shouldn't be surprising to find that animals have the (1) _____ for intelligence. In the first half of the 20th century, there was a shift away from Darwin's theory. Instead, *behaviorism* affected the way animals were seen. *Behaviorism* was a theory that ignored the possibility[1] of animals having intelligent minds. Today, many scientists agree that behaviorists (2) _____ the animal mind. Here are two examples of animals that (3) _____ intelligence:

Azy the orangutan communicates by touching (4) _____ symbols on a computer screen. There are about 70 symbols that he uses. When Azy wants to say a certain word, he presses the (5) _____ symbol. Using this system, Azy is able to identify objects, ask questions, and even give commands.

Koko the gorilla is able to use American Sign Language to communicate. In sign language, you speak by making words with your hands. Dr. Penny Patterson, who takes care of Koko, (6) _____ the signs that Koko makes with her hands. Dr. Patterson can communicate her own ideas to Koko using sign language as well.

Koko the gorilla uses American Sign Language to talk with Dr. Penny Patterson. Here, Koko is telling Dr. Patterson that she would like a pet cat.

[1]A **possibility** is a chance that something might happen or might be true.

B | **Discussion.** Form a group with two or three other students and discuss the questions.

1. What are some of the **motives** of people who work with and study animals? What do they hope to learn or gain from their work with animals?
2. A **flexible** mind is one that can easily adapt and make changes. Would you say that you are flexible? Explain.
3. What is your memory **capacity**? For example, how well are you able to remember names, dates, and telephone numbers after hearing them just one time?

Before Listening

 Predicting Content. Work with a partner and answer the questions.

1. You are going to hear about the two animals in the photos. In what ways do you think these animals demonstrate their intelligence?
2. You are also going to hear about an intelligent animal that has a brain larger than a human's brain. What animal do you think it is?

Alex, the African Gray Parrot

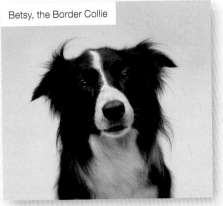

Betsy, the Border Collie

Listening: A TV Show

A | **Listening for Main Ideas.** Listen to the TV show about intelligent animals. Choose the best answer to each question.

track 3-20

1. Which statement best describes recent ideas regarding animal intelligence?
   a. Scientists are comparing intelligent animals to machines.
   b. Scientists no longer want to study animal intelligence.
   c. Scientists are no longer underestimating animal intelligence.

2. According to Diane Willberg, how do parrots and crows demonstrate intelligence?
   a. Parrots speak, and crows understand abstract concepts.
   b. Crows can make tools, and parrots understand abstract concepts.
   c. Parrots can see colors, and crows can recognize tools.

3. According to Samantha Bean, how does her dog Betsy demonstrate intelligence?
   a. Betsy is able to recognize objects in pictures.
   b. Betsy is able to recognize herself in pictures.
   c. Betsy is able to recognize objects adjacent to their pictures.

4. According to Matthew Leonard, what animals have self-awareness?
   a. Humans, elephants, apes, dolphins
   b. Humans, apes, dolphins, dogs
   c. Humans, elephants, birds, dogs

B | Note-Taking. Listen again and complete the notes with information from the TV show.

Beliefs about animal intelligence:

- Descartes: Animals are _____
- Scientists today believe _____
- Ex. of mental skills of animals: Good memory, _____
  _____

Diane Willberg:

- Parrots: _____
  - Shows parrot 2 green objects. Parrot says _____
  - Shows parrot 2 balls. Parrot says _____
- Crows Lab experiment: D.W. puts a _____ in a bottle
  - The crow _____

Samantha Bean:

- In one room _____ In another room _____
  S.B. shows Betsy _____ Betsy _____
- S.B. believes this shows _____.

Matthew Leonard:

- Self-awareness is _____
- Exs. of self-awareness: humans, _____

After Listening

Critical Thinking Focus: Questioning Results

At times, you may hear information that you think is not believable or reliable. In these situations, you should question the results or conclusions of the speaker. Ask yourself these questions:

Who completed this research? Could this person be biased?
Are the researcher's conclusions logical? Do the results make sense?
Did the experiment follow proper scientific procedure?

Critical Thinking. Form a group with two or three other students. Discuss the questions.

1. Who do you think funds studies about animal intelligence? Do you think these studies are useful? Explain.
2. Do you believe that the animals described in the TV show are truly intelligent? Explain.

Language Function

Enumerating

Listing reasons, facts, examples, or steps in a process is called *enumerating*. Here are some groups of expressions to help list information clearly.

To enumerate reasons and examples, use:
> *First, Second, Third*
> *For one thing, For another, And for another*
> *In the first place, In the second place, And in the third place*

To enumerate commands or steps in a process, use:
> *First, Next, After that*
> *First, Then, And then*
> *First, Second, Third*

A | In the TV program, there were a number of expressions for enumerating. Listen and fill in the missing expressions. *track 3-21*

1. **Diane:** Well, _____, I've found that crows are able to use tools and they can actually make the tools themselves. _____, my research shows that parrots understand abstract concepts such as shapes and colors.

2. **Samantha:** _____, I show Besty a picture, _____ she goes into the next room, chooses the corresponding object, _____ brings it back to me.

B | With a partner, look at the expressions for enumerating. Were the speakers in exercise **A** enumerating reasons, examples, commands, or steps in a process? Explain your answer.

C | **Collaboration.** Work with your partner. One student is Student A and the other is Student B. Read the statements. Write three reasons or examples to support your statement.

Student A: I am against using animals in circuses.
Student B: I am in support of using animals in circuses.

Reasons/Examples:

1. _____
2. _____
3. _____

D | **Discussion.** With your partner, discuss the ideas you wrote in exercise **C** on page 168. Use expressions for enumerating.

> Animals shouldn't be used in circuses. For one thing, they're forced to travel on trains and trucks all the time.

A horse performs at a circus in Barcelona, Spain.

E | **Enumerating.** Work with your partner. One student is Student A and the other is Student B. Read the instructions about how to do one of the tasks below. Then, without reading, tell your partner how to do the task. Use the expressions for enumerating.

Student A

Memorizing Information

You want to memorize the spelling of a difficult word or a long number such as a phone number. Repeat the word or number aloud. Break the word or number down into chunks or pieces. Put only two or three letters or numbers in each chunk. Repeat the chunks several times while looking at the word or number. After a few minutes, try to spell the whole word or repeat the whole number without looking at it.

Student B

Changing a Flat Tire

Your car has a flat tire and you want to put a new tire on the car. Stop your car in a safe place. Use a wrench to loosen the lugnuts on the wheel. Use a car jack to lift the car off of the ground. Remove the lugnuts and pull the flat tire off of the car. Put the new tire on the car. Place the lugnuts back on the tire, but only tighten them a little. Lower the car back to the ground. Tighten all of the lugnuts on the new tire.

Grammar

Subject-Verb Agreement with Quantifiers

Quantifiers such as *none, a few, some, each, a lot, all, most,* and *every one* are used to talk about quantity. Quantifiers can be followed by plural count nouns or by non-count nouns: *some of the animals, some of the food*

When followed by a plural count noun, the quantifiers *all, a lot, some, a few, both,* and *most* take a plural verb.

> **All** of our dolphins **are** very intelligent.
> **Some** of the puppies **were** white.
> Chimpanzees are smaller than gorillas, but **both** (animals) **are** primates.

The quantifiers *one, none, each, neither,* and *every one,* on the other hand, are followed by a plural count noun and a singular verb.

> **Each** of my parrots **is** very special.

A | Self-Reflection. Complete each sentence with a quantifier. Make the sentences true for yourself. Try to use as many different quantifiers from the box above as you can. Then circle the correct verb form.

1. _____ of my parents (like / likes) to drink coffee.

2. _____ of my neighbors (has / have) a pet.

3. _____ of my classmates (think / thinks) animals are intelligent.

4. _____ of the scientists in the TV show (work / works) with animals.

5. _____ of my friends (own / owns) a car.

6. _____ of my co-workers (use / uses) a computer.

B | Discussion. Form a group with two or three other students. Talk about the sentences from exercise **A** with your group.

> Both of my parents like to drink coffee. What about your parents?

> Only one of my parents likes to drink coffee.

C | Collaboration. Work with your group. Talk about your likes and dislikes. Then write five new sentences with quantifiers about your group. Try to use as many different quantifiers from the box above as you can.

Giving a Short Persuasive Speech

A | **Brainstorming.** Form a group with two or three other students. The chart below lists six roles that animals have in culture and society. Discuss these roles and fill in the chart with examples of animals that perform each role.

Roles	Examples
Work	*dogs rescue people*
Entertainment	
Pets	
Research	
Food	

B | Choose one of the roles from exercise **A**. Do you agree that animals should be used for this role? Write a sentence that shows your position. For example: *Animals should not be used for entertainment.* Share the sentence you wrote with your group.

C | **Presentation.** Now, each group member will give a two-minute persuasive speech to support his or her sentence. *(See page 211 of the Independent Student Handbook for more information on presentation skills.)* During your speech, you should:

1. State your position
2. Give examples and reasons to support your position
3. Restate your position in conclusion

D | After each member of your group has spoken, ask the group to vote on whether they agree or disagree with your position.

Student to Student: Joining a Group

If you need to join a group for a group work activity, you can say:

Do you mind if I join your group?
Do you want to work together?
Do you need another person?

Presentation Skills: Using Gestures

Even if you do not normally use your hands when you speak with friends, you should use hand gestures when you are giving a presentation. Gestures add emphasis to what you are saying and get your audience's attention. Practice your gestures in front of a mirror and make sure they look natural. Make sure to use various gestures, not just one over and over again.

Animal Minds

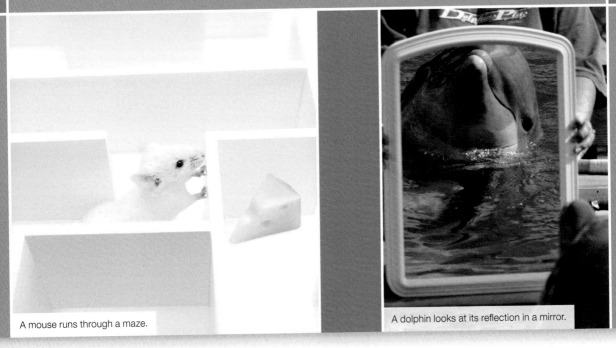

A mouse runs through a maze.

A dolphin looks at its reflection in a mirror.

Before Viewing

A | **Using a Dictionary.** You will hear the words in blue in the video. Read the sentences. Then match each word with its definition below. Use your dictionary to help you.

1. Dreams show that our minds are working even **unconsciously**.
2. Don't use **coercion** to train an animal. Rather, reward good behavior.
3. Computers have large memories but no other **cognitive** abilities.
4. In 1859, Charles Darwin's theory of evolution came as a **revelation** to the world.
5. Whale songs are very **sophisticated** and could contain a lot of information.
6. I locked the dog in the room, but it **outsmarted** me by unlocking the door.
7. Seeing claw marks and brown fur, we **deduced** that a bear had gotten into our car.

a. _____ (n.) surprising knowledge that is made known to people

b. _____ (adv.) without being fully aware

c. _____ (v.) to reach a conclusion based on things that are true

d. _____ (v.) to gain an advantage by thinking effectively

e. _____ (adj.) relating to the mental process involved in knowing, learning, and understanding

f. _____ (n.) the act of forcing a person or animal to do something that they don't want to do

g. _____ (adj.) complex or advanced

B | **Predicting Content.** With a partner, look at the animals in the photos on pages 172 and 173. Scientists have found certain cognitive abilities in each animal. What cognitive abilities do you think these animals have shown? Discuss each animal with your partner.

While Viewing

A | Watch the video. Then circle the correct answers.

1. What did a rat do that surprised scientists in the early 1900s?
   a. It followed a maze correctly from end to end and found the food.
   b. It got on top of a maze and used its memory to find the food.
   c. It completed a maze backwards as easily as it did forwards.

2. How do the trainers in the video shape dolphin behavior?
   a. They use coercion.
   b. They use a whistle and food.
   c. They use speaking and touching.

3. How did Karen Pryor cause dolphins to show creativity?
   a. By rewarding all behavior
   b. By rewarding only repeated behavior
   c. By rewarding only new behavior

A bird uses a stick as a tool to find food in a tree branch.

B | **Sequencing Events.** Watch the video again. Read the steps below. These are steps in the experiment Karen Pryor did to show creativity in dolphins. Number the steps in the correct order. The first step has been numbered for you.

_____ a. After two weeks, the dolphin had run through all the normal behaviors.

_____ b. The dolphin would start off with the behavior from the day before.

_____ c. The dolphin offered all kinds of new behaviors, for which the trainers gave the dolphin a bucket of fish.

_____ d. The dolphin and the trainers became very upset, and the trainers wondered if it was going to be the end of the experiment.

__1__ e. Karen picked a new behavior each day and rewarded the dolphin for it.

_____ f. In session 16, the dolphin offered a new flip followed by a new tail swipe, both of which were reinforced by the trainers.

After Viewing

Critical Thinking. Form a group with two or three other students and discuss the questions.

1. Are you convinced by what you saw and heard that dolphins can use imagination and show creativity? Explain.

2. Do you think the rat in the video displayed more or less intelligence than the dolphin in Karen Pryor's experiment? Explain your answer.

track 3-22 **A** | **Meaning from Context.** Read and listen to the information about memory. Notice the words in blue. These are the words you will hear and use in Lesson B.

The amount of information that the human brain can hold is virtually limitless. Most people do not have an aptitude for remembering complex lists or numbers. Some people, however, use their memory much more than the average person. A person who is able to remember long lists of data such as names and numbers is called a *mnemonist*. This word is derived from the word *mnemonic*, which originated from an ancient Greek word meaning "of memory."

Each year, mnemonists participate in the World Memory Championships. This championship is a series of games that test a person's memory. Contestants are expected to behave in an ethical way at all times: there must be no cheating, no help from others, and no use of drugs that enhance the memory. Some of the events include memorizing numbers, words, faces, or images. There is also a "Speed Cards" event in which individuals must memorize the exact order of 54 cards as quickly as possible. The world record is 21.90 seconds.

One of the most successful mnemonists in the world is a British man named Dominic O'Brien. He has won the World Memory Championship an unprecedented eight times. O'Brien uses his own memorization method. He uses information he already knows as a framework, and adds new facts to this information. He says that practicing memorization techniques can result in a dramatic increase in almost everyone's memory.

Memorizing the order of playing cards helps high school students in New York's South Bronx prepare for tougher academic challenges.

B | Write each word in blue from exercise **A** to complete its definition below.

1. To _____ means to improve in some way.
2. A person's _____ is a special ability to learn a task quickly and do it well.
3. A _____ is a structure that supports something else.
4. You can use _____ to mean "very nearly."
5. If an event is _____, it has never happened before.
6. A _____ is a particular way of doing or completing a task.
7. If a word _____ from another word, it got its meaning from that word.
8. If something is _____, it means that every detail is correct.
9. A _____ change happens suddenly and is very noticeable and surprising.
10. An _____ person is morally right or correct.

A | **Understanding Collocations.** The article below contains six collocations. Read the article and complete each collocation in blue using a vocabulary word from the box. *(See page 208 of the Independent Student Handbook for more information on building your vocabulary.)*

dramatic	ethical	exact	method	unprecedented	virtually

Who has a better memory: a chimpanzee (chimp) or a college student? The answer may surprise you. During a recent science experiment, Japanese researchers tested the short-term memory[1] of young chimpanzees against the short-term memory of college students. The (1) _____ result surprised everyone: the chimpanzees won. Many of the researchers believed that this result was (2) _____ impossible, because the human mind is superior to the chimpanzee mind.

This chimp, named Ayumu, did the best on the memory test.

Chimpanzees beating humans in a memory test had never happened before—it was completely (3) _____. "No one can imagine that chimpanzees—young chimpanzees at the age of five—have a better performance in a memory task than humans," said researcher Tetsuro Matsuzawa of Kyoto University.

The participants of the experiment were five-year-old chimpanzees and 12 college students. The chimps were taught the numbers 1 through 9 and their order. The testing (4) _____ was as follows: Both humans and chimps saw nine numbers displayed on a computer screen. When they touched the first number, the other eight numbers turned into white squares. The test was to touch the squares in the order of the numbers that used to be there.

Japan

Often, neither humans nor chimps were able to remember the (5) _____ location of the numbers. However, to everyone's surprise, the results showed that the chimps could do the task faster. People who support animal rights feel that this type of experiment raises (6) _____ questions. They do not believe that scientists should do research on the chimps at all.

[1]**Short-term memory** is information that we remember only for a short period of time.

B | **Discussion.** With a partner, discuss the questions.

1. The word *orangutan* originated from the Malay words *orang hutan*, which mean "man of the forest." Do you know where the word *gorilla* originated from? Suggest some ideas. Then research this information on the Internet to see if you were correct.

2. Imagine that you could take a medicine to enhance your brain in any way you wanted. Which part of your brain would you choose, and why? How would you use the extra power?

3. Do you have a great aptitude for a particular skill or talent such as mathematics or art? Explain.

Before Listening

Self-Reflection. Form a group with two or three other students and discuss the questions.

1. What are some of your earliest childhood memories? Do the memories seem clear to you or not?
2. When was the last time you had something to eat? What did you eat? What about the time before that? Continue and see how far back you can remember.
3. Do you have any tricks to help you remember things? What are they?

Listening: A Conversation between Classmates

track 3-23 **A** | **Listening for Main Ideas.** Listen to two people talking about memory. Circle the correct answers.

1. What is "superior autobiographical memory"?
    a. It is the ability to remember many numbers exactly.
    b. It is the ability to remember details about one's life.
    c. It is the ability to remember new words and phrases.

2. What is the *hippocampus*?
    a. A part of the brain that controls memory
    b. A type of memory that cannot be lost
    c. An operation to remove part of the brain

3. How did Dr. Scoville's patient lose his memory?
    a. His brain was damaged in an accident.
    b. His brain was damaged by a disease.
    c. Dr. Scoville removed part of the patient's brain.

4. What is the location method?
    a. It is a way of remembering things.
    b. It is a method for operating on the brain.
    c. It is a way of living without a memory.

This artist helps solve crimes by drawing pictures of criminals. She bases her drawings on memories of people who saw the crime happen.

track 3-23 **B** | Listen again. Complete the notes with information from the conversation.

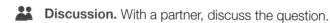

I. Superior Autobiographical Memory (SAM)
  A. Definition: _person has great ability to remember own life_
  B. How SAM works: _some parts of brain bigger than normal_
II. The Hippocampus (originated from words meaning _horse / sea monster_
  A. Dr. S Experiment: _removed hippocampus trying to cure epilepsy_
  B. Result: _patient lost memory_
    1. Contribution to science: _gained understanding of brain_
III. Method of Loci/The Location Method
  A. Use: _to remember lists of words_
  B. Steps
    1. Picture pathway that you know well
    2. _create an image for each word_
    3. Later, _put images on path, can move a long path to remember things._

After Listening

👥 **Discussion.** With a partner, discuss the question.

Trying to help, Dr. Scoville permanently damaged his patient's memory. However, scientists learned a lot of information about the brain because of Dr. Scoville and his patient. Do you think Dr. Scoville's actions were ethical? Explain.

Pronunciation

> **Using Word Stress to Clarify Information**
>
> To get more details from a speaker, listeners often ask a question by repeating what someone has said and adding another word for emphasis. The new word is stressed and said with a higher pitch.
>
> **Heather:** *So anyway, after he removed most of the hippocampus, he found that the patient had lost his memory.*
> **Maria:** *His **entire** memory?*

track 3-24

👥 Take turns saying these sentences to a partner. Your partner will ask you a question using the word in parentheses or his or her own idea. Be sure your partner uses word stress to clarify. Use your imagination to continue the conversations.

1. I bought a book of puzzles. (crossword)
2. I took an interesting test. (memory)
3. My mother bought me a car. (new)
4. He is a memory champion. (world)

Language Function

Checking Background Knowledge

Sometimes in a conversation, we need to ask how much our listener knows about a topic. Use these expressions to ask someone about his or her knowledge of a topic.

Asking about familiarity with a topic:
Do you know (about) . . . ?
Have you (ever) heard of . . . ?
You know (about) . . . , right?
You know (about) . . . , don't you?

Asking for details about a topic:
What do you know about . . . ?
How much do you know about . . . ?
What can you tell me about . . . ?

track 3-25   **A** | In Heather and Maria's conversation, there were a number of useful expressions for checking background knowledge. Listen to the sentences and fill in the missing expressions.

1. **Heather:** Well, we're having a memory contest in my psychology class.

   Maria: Why?

   Heather: Because we're learning about memory and the professor thought it would be a good experiment. _____ "superior autobiographical memory"?

2. **Maria:** Oh! I saw a TV show about that. _____ that show *Amazing Science*, _____?

3. **Heather:** Well, the scientists found that some parts of these people's brains are bigger than normal, including the part called the hippo—um, the *hippocampus*.

   Maria: I'm not sure I know what that is. _____ it?

4. **Maria:** I see. Memory is so important. I have a really bad memory. I'd love to learn how to improve it.

   Heather: Oh, there are lots of ways to enhance your ability to remember things. For example, _____ the method of loci?

B | **Checking Background Knowledge.** Work with a partner. Look at the list of topics that were introduced in Units 1 through 9. Choose two of these topics and find out if your partner is familiar with them. If so, ask for details about what he or she knows. Use expressions from the Language Function box.

Unit 1: Tourism in Venice
Unit 2: The Dusky Seaside Sparrow
Unit 3: Eco-fashion
Unit 4: Solar Power
Unit 5: Wildebeest Migration

Unit 6: Gross National Happiness
Unit 7: Types of Payment Cards
Unit 8: Types of Rock Climbing
Unit 9: Superior Autobiographical Memory

> Have you ever heard of the dusky seaside sparrow?

> Yes, I have.

> What do you know about it?

> Well, it was a bird that is now extinct.

Grammar

Present Participle Phrases

Adverb clauses can sometimes be reduced to present participle phrases. These phrases show reason or time.

Reason clause	***Because I have a poor memory myself***, *I'd be very interested in information on how to improve it.*
Participial phrase	***Having a poor memory myself***, *I'd be very interested in information on how to improve it.*
Time clause	***While he was trying to cure his patient***, *a doctor named William Scoville removed most of the patient's hippocampus.*
Participial phrase	***Trying to cure his patient***, *a doctor named William Scoville removed most of the patient's hippocampus.*

Be careful that the subject of the main clause is the same as the implied subject of the present participle phrase:

Incorrect: *Jumping from the top of the bookshelf, **I** caught the cat safely in my arms.*
(This means that I jumped from the top of the bookshelf.)
Correct: *Jumping from the top of the bookshelf, **the cat** landed safely in my arms.*
(This means that the cat jumped from the top of the bookshelf.)

A | **Collaboration.** Match each sentence in the first column with a sentence in the second column. Compare your answers with a partner. In your notebooks, combine each pair of sentences into a new sentence using a present participle phrase.

Researcher Jane Goodall has studied chimps for nearly 50 years.

1. He heard his master's whistle. __b__
2. It recognized itself in the mirror. _____
3. It saw another bird. _____
4. It took the fish from the trainer's hand. _____
5. It uses a touch screen. _____
6. She lived with chimps. _____

a. The ape displayed self-awareness.
b. The Border collie turned to the right.
c. The dolphin made a happy noise.
d. The blue jay waited to hide its food.
e. The orangutan communicates with people.
f. Jane Goodall made many discoveries about chimp society.

B | **Self-Reflection.** Complete each sentence below. Then change the sentence beginnings below to a present participle phrase and write a new sentence. Use your imagination. Share your sentences with your partner.

1. Because I am a responsible neighbor, . . .
2. While going to class (or work) each morning, . . .
3. When I see a puppy or a kitten in a pet shop window, . . .

> Being a responsible neighbor, I don't play loud music after 10 P.M.

ENGAGE: Using Memory Skills to Recall Information

You learned about the method of location, or the method of loci, in this unit. You can use this memory skill to help you prepare for presentations or remember information for school or work. To use the method, you put information along an imaginary pathway in your mind. When you wish to remember the information, you imagine yourself walking along the pathway.

A | Fill in the shopping list with items that you regularly buy at the supermarket or local stores. You will use the items in a test of memory.

Shopping List

1. _____	4. _____	7. _____
2. _____	5. _____	8. _____
3. _____	6. _____	9. _____

B | Work with a partner. Look at your partner's list for 30 seconds. Then without looking at the list, try to say as many of the items in order as you can. Your partner will write down how many you got right.

Number correct: _____

C | Think of a path through a place you know very well, such as your home or neighborhood. Take about five minutes to think of images for each item on your partner's list. Place the images along the path in your mind. For example, if the path is your home and the first item on the list is eggs, imagine eggs smashed on your front door. The more creative the images, the better you will remember them.

D | Give the shopping list back to your partner. Then visualize your path and say as many of the items in order as you can. Record how many you got right.

Number correct: _____

E | **Critical Thinking.** Form a group with two or three other students and discuss the questions.

1. Look back at exercises **B** and **D**. Did your score improve after you used the location method? Do you think this method is effective for helping you to remember information?

2. How can you use the method of location to prepare for a presentation? How can you use it to help you study or take effective notes? How can you use the method to help you learn new vocabulary? With your group, brainstorm and write a list of ideas. Share your ideas with the class.

Food Concerns

ACADEMIC PATHWAYS

Lesson A: Listening to a Powerpoint Lecture
                Role-Playing a Debate
Lesson B: Listening to an Informal Conversation
                Creating a PowerPoint Presentation

Think and Discuss

1. Has eating food ever made you or someone you know sick?
   What type of food caused the problem?

2. Who makes sure the food you eat is safe? How do you think
   food safety could be improved?

Thousands of red peppers from Mongolia dry in the sun.

Exploring the Theme: Food Concerns

Look at the photos and read the captions. Then discuss the questions.

1. How can scientists improve the way we grow plants and the way we raise animals for food?
2. What are some reasons for rising food prices around the globe?
3. Would you eat food that has been altered to include a medicine or a vitamin? Why, or why not?

Our Changing Food Supply

Around the world, disease-resistant foods have improved the quality of life for many people. Some experts believe that genetically-modified foods could transform agriculture throughout the world.

Eric Anderson checks on the chickens at his farm in Arkansas. He uses antibiotics—drugs that kill bacteria—to keep his birds healthy. Consumers are worried that the use of antibiotics and chemicals in their food could cause health problems in the future.

Our Food Future

Workers shovel tons of soybeans on a ship in Victoria, Brazil. With food prices rising sharply, the world is struggling to feed its citizens. Scientists and governments are trying to find new ways to grow the world's food supply.

Student chefs prepare vegetables during a cooking class in China.

A | **Meaning from Context.** Read and listen to the information about the world's food supply. Notice the words in blue. These are the words you will hear and use in Lesson A.

track 3-26

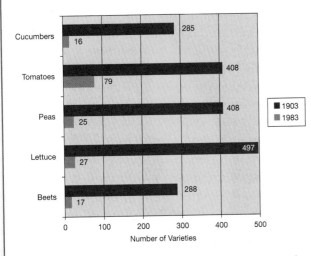

Number of Varieties

■ 1903
■ 1983

A man holds two jars of peas at a seed bank in Norway.

The world population is now over seven billion people. As a result, there is an intense need for additional food. Instead of using conventional farming methods, many large farms now only plant one crop such as corn, wheat, or rice. Farmers plant this crop over very large areas. This type of agriculture is known as *monoculture.* The benefit of monoculture is to maximize the harvest,[1] but there are experts who say that the benefit is offset by its negative effects.

One serious problem of monoculture is the effect it has had on the number of vegetable varieties grown by farmers. The number of vegetable varieties has greatly diminished since 1903, and many crop species no longer exist. In the future, if one of the plants farmers rely on is destroyed via disease or climate change, this could cause major problems in the world's food supply. Therefore, some scientists are now trying to modify the genes of other vegetables to recreate the lost vegetable varieties.

It's important to monitor and save the vegetable varieties that remain. Many experts advocate setting up "seed banks" to collect and keep the seeds of plants that are no longer planted by farmers. Many farmers and scientists devote themselves to the important work of setting up these seed banks. Today there are about 1400 of them around the world. The vegetable seeds inside these seed banks could be extremely important to the welfare of the people on earth.

[1]The **harvest** is the gathering of the crop or food that is grown on a farm.

B | Write each word in blue from exercise **A** next to its definition.

1. _offset_ _____ (v.) to balance or compensate
2. _devote_ _____ (v.) to spend your time or energy on a task
3. _via_ _____ (prep.) with the help of another means or person
4. _modify_ _____ (v.) to change something slightly, usually to improve it
5. _advocate_ _____ (v.) to support a plan or action and recommend it publicly
6. _welfare_ _____ (n.) the health, comfort, and happiness of a group or a person
7. _conventional_ _____ (adj.) ordinary and traditional
8. _intense_ _____ (adj.) very great or extreme in strength or degree
9. _monitor_ _____ (v.) to watch or keep track of; to check regularly
10. _diminished_ _____ (v.) became smaller in size, number, or importance

A | Complete the sentences with the correct form of a word from the box.

advocate	devote	intense	monitor	via
conventional	diminish	modify	offset	welfare

1. Scientists recently _____modify_____ the genes of an apple tree to grow bigger apples. They did this _____via_____ a technology called genetic modification.

2. The new type of apples are three times the size of _____conventional_____ ones.

3. The scientists don't _____advocate_____ selling the new type of apple tree yet because more tests need to be done.

4. The scientists have _____devoted_____ themselves to testing the apples for the next few months.

5. Representatives from agricultural companies are closely _____monitor_____ the tests.

6. Several food safety groups expressed _____intense_____ opposition to the trees, saying that they were dangerous. Scientists hope that the test results will _____diminish_____ these worries.

7. The agricultural companies and their scientists insisted that there was no danger, and that they always keep the _____welfare_____ of the public in mind.

8. The companies offered a large sum of money to _____offset_____ the costs of any health-related damage their new apple trees might cause.

Critical Thinking Focus: Remaining Objective

When studying a new subject, particularly an emotional or controversial one, it's important to remain *objective*. Being objective means that you should be willing to listen to arguments on both sides of an issue. You should form an opinion based on facts, and should not let your emotions and personal feelings change your opinion about a topic.

B | **Brainstorming.** Form a group with two or three other students. On page 184 you read about *monoculture*. Make two lists: one with arguments in favor of monoculture and another with arguments against it. Then rank your arguments from most convincing to least convincing. Share your rankings and arguments with another group or with the class.

Student to Student: Expressing Opinions

Here are some expressions you can use to express your opinion about a situation.

In my opinion, . . .   *(Personally,) I think . . .*
If you ask me, . . .   *As far as I'm concerned, . . .*
As I see it, . . .

Before Listening

 Brainstorming. By genetically modifying plants and animals, scientists improve them for consumers. Brainstorm some ideas for improvements scientists could make to the plants and animals listed in the chart. Add two or three more of your own ideas to the chart.

	Ideas for Improvement
Rice	*They could create rice with vitamins in it.*
Apples	
Salmon	
Cattle	

Listening: A PowerPoint Lecture

🎧 **A** | Listen to a PowerPoint lecture about genetically-modified (GM) foods. Choose the best
track 3-27 answer to each question.

1. In which order does the lecturer address these subjects? Number them 1 to 4.

___3___ a. possible negative effects of "gene flow"

___4___ b. a type of GM rice called "golden rice"

___1___ c. an explanation of GM animals and plants

___2___ d. where GM foods are being used

2. Which of these would be the best title for the lecture?
   a. GM Foods: The World Can Do Without Them
   b. GM Foods: Promising but Proceed with Caution
   c. GM Foods: Better and Safer than Conventional Foods

3. Which statement reflects the lecturer's opinion about the future of GM foods?
   a. More and more people will probably eat GM foods.
   b. They will remain illegal in most countries.
   c. Because they are too dangerous, few people will buy them.

These two Coho salmon are 18 months old, but one was genetically modified to be larger than the other.

🎧 **B | Note-Taking.** Listen again and complete the notes for each slide.

track 3-27

GM animals and plants grow _____ *faster*, *bigger*, produce _____ *pesticides*
   Exs. of GM experiments:
   - Rat genes into lettuce to produce _____ *Vitamin C*
   - _____ *Moth* _____ genes into apple plants to help them resist diseases
   - Modify salmon to make it grow _____ *twice* _____ as fast
   - GM cattle and sheep produce _____ *medicines* _____ in their milk
GM foods could be key to advances in _____ *agriculture and health*

Critics think GM foods are being _____ *rushed to market before* *they're fully understood.*
   Exs. of critics' fears:
   - Weeds with modified genes called _____ *superweeds*
   - Harmful effects on _____ *GM plants on insects and animals*
U.S. has been eating GM foods since _____ *1990s*
   Exs: Pizza, *ice cream*, *salad dressing*, *and baking powder*
   Countries with GM foods: _____ *China*, *Germany*, *S. Africa*, etc.
   Corps. offset risks through _____ *testing*; Government monitors _____ *the production and sale of GM foods*

Gene flow definition: _____ *is the movement of genes via flowers/seeds from one population to another*
   Mixing GM plants with _____ *conventional* plants could have long-term impact
   GM crops resist insects, insects could _____ *used to such crops*
   - Result: _____ *No weapons against insect.* _____ *(superpests)*

Golden Rice contains beta-carotene to help with _____ *Vit. A* deficiency
Critics don't like that _____ *the fact that big companies* control GM technology
Benefits of GM foods:
   - _____ *Genetic modification can increase* the amount of food produced
   - offer crops that _____ *resist disease*

After Listening

👥 **Critical Thinking.** With a partner, discuss the questions.

1. Do you think that the government should require companies to label foods that contain GM products? If so, what information should the labels have? Draw a sketch of what the label should look like.

2. In the lecture, the professor says that big companies control most GM foods. Why do you think some people are upset about this? What are some of the problems that could occur if only big companies control this technology?

Language Function

Confirming Understanding

When you are giving a presentation, having a conversation, or explaining something, you need to make sure everyone understands the topic. Here are some expressions you can use to confirm that the audience understands the topic.

OK so far?   Have you got that?
Any questions?   Are you following me?
Are you with me?   Does that make sense?

🎧 **A** | In the lecture, there were a number of useful expressions for confirming understanding.
track 3-28   Listen and fill in the missing expressions.

1. Many scientists feel that GM foods could be the key to the next advances in agriculture and health . . . ___OK so far___?

2. In North America and Europe, the value and impact of GM foods has become the subject of intense debate . . . ___Are you following me___?

3. However, in the U.S. at least, food companies don't have to specially label their GM products, because government agencies haven't found any GM foods to be significantly different from conventional foods. . . ___Does that make sense___?

In Shaanxi Province, China, farmers toss millet into the air. The wind separates the grains from their husks, or shell. These farmers still produce most of the world's food, but genetically modified foods could change that in the future.

B | Summarizing. Each student will read one of the stories about GM foods below. Explain the information to your partner. Use expressions from the Language Function box on page 188.

Student A Edible Medicine

Scientists at the University of Agricultural Sciences in Bangalore, India, have created a new melon. The melon has been genetically modified to contain a rabies vaccine. Rabies vaccine is a medicine that can prevent the deadly rabies disease. Rabies kills thousands of people every year and infects many animals such as dogs. The genetically-modified melon is a cheap and easy way to provide the vaccine to millions of people. Additionally, a powder derived from the melon could be added to dog food to give dogs the vaccine. The fruit has successfully prevented rabies in mice. Scientists are now testing the fruit on dogs.

Student B Building a Better Tomato

Mark D'Ascenzo is a researcher at Boyce Thompson Institute for Plant Research in Ithaca, New York. He is showing a slide representing 20,000 tomato genes. Scientists are trying to identify the genes that make certain tomatoes resistant to diseases. "We've isolated hundreds of genes that are interesting candidates," D'Ascenzo says, "but we're still years away from understanding the whole picture." Once scientists do understand how to make tomatoes disease-resistant, the genes can be inserted into new tomato plants.

Grammar

Causative Verbs

Causative verbs show that one action causes another action to happen. Causative verbs can follow two patterns.

The first pattern is **causative verb + object + infinitive** (*without* to). This pattern is often used with the causative verbs *have, let, make,* and *help*.

> The modified genes of GM salmon **make them grow** twice as fast.

The second pattern is **causative verb + object + infinitive** (*with* to). Most causative verbs follow this pattern. Verbs that follow this pattern are *allow, assist, convince, encourage, force, hire, inspire, motivate, require,* and *permit*.

> The government should **require companies to label** their GM products.

A | Read the story about the use of GM corn in the Philippines. Underline the causative verb + object + infinitive structures.

Philippine Farmers Adopt GM Corn

In 1991, the eruption of the volcano Mount Pinatubo ruined large areas of Philippine farmland. The hard soil and insect pests forced many farmers to give up on the land. Then in 2003, the Philippine government allowed farmers to plant GM corn. Although there were some fears about the dangers of GM corn, results of safety tests convinced the government to approve it.

A woman works on her farm on Samar Island in the eastern Philippines.

Global agriculture companies helped farmers get started and taught them to plant GM corn. Farmers used insect-resistant varieties that grow well in hard soil. Since then, the government has encouraged farmers to plant more crops. GM corn has enabled the farmers to produce more corn per acre (hectare) than ever before. In fact, GM corn has allowed farmers to produce three to four times as much corn per acre (hectare) as was possible before.

The success story of GM corn in the Philippines has motivated farmers to try other varieties of GM crops. Recently, Philippine farmers were winners of an international prize for outstanding agricultural projects. The prize is designed to inspire farmers to reach for excellence in agriculture.

B | **Discussion.** Work with a partner and read each situation. Use causative verbs to make suggestions.

1. The workers at a small restaurant are unhappy with their boss. The workers think that there aren't enough workers to help out during busy times. Also, the boss won't give the workers any time off.

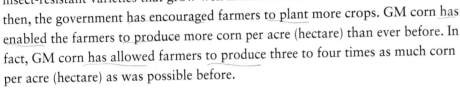

> The boss should allow the workers to take a day off.

> That's a good suggestion. And maybe the boss should . . .

2. A grocery store owner is having trouble controlling teenagers who hang around the store. They seem to do whatever they want. They eat food in the store, drop it on the floor, and even steal some food. The teens don't seem like bad kids, but they don't have jobs or any other activities to do after school.

3. Some of my neighbors have been complaining about one of the houses in the neighborhood. The house is not kept clean. The windows are very dirty and the owner leaves garbage in the yard. The owner is a nice elderly man, but he's having trouble keeping up with everything he has to do.

Role-Playing a Debate

You will role-play a debate about the positive and negative aspects of GM crops. Student A is an advocate for a concerned citizen's group and Student B is spokesperson of a GM company called GM Industries.

A | Work with a partner. Each student will prepare for the debate by reviewing the notes below. Add two more ideas to your notes.

Student A: Leader of Citizen Group

- It's possible that GM crops could harm other insects or animals.
- Insects will get used to GM crops, and become difficult to control.
- Genes from GM plants can flow to other plant populations, creating "superweeds."
- Allergic reactions could occur.
- GM crop seed is expensive for farmers.
- Areas of some other countries have banned GM crops.
- _____
- _____

Student B: GM Industries Spokesperson

- GM crops boost production. They are designed to harm pests, not other animals or insects.
- GM crops grow faster, are larger, and taste just as good as conventional crops.
- We need more scientific information on gene flow and "superweeds."
- GM crops are tested more thoroughly for safety than any other crops.
- With GM crops, farmers save money on fertilizer, pesticides, and farm equipment.
- Agricultural companies often work closely with local farmers to help farmers solve any problems that might arise around GM foods.
- _____
- _____

B | **Role-Playing.** Role play the debate with your partner. Try not to look at your meeting notes as you speak.

> GM crops can be very useful. They are designed to harm only dangerous insects.

> I'm not so sure about that. It's possible that GM foods could hurt other animals as well.

A farm in Greve, Chianti, Italy

Before Viewing

A | Prior Knowledge. In Italy, the Chianti region in Tuscany is known for its beautiful landscape, wine, food, and for its pleasant way of life. What do you think people eat there? Discuss your ideas with a partner.

B | Predicting Content. The Chianti region is also the place where the Slow Food movement began. What do you think the Slow Food movement is? Share some ideas with your partner.

While Viewing

A | Watch the video. Then circle the correct answers.

1. Which sentence best describes the little town of Greve?
   a. It is a traditional place with a comfortable way of life.
   b. It is an innovative place with a fast-paced way of life.
   c. It is a busy place with a hardworking way of life.
2. Which of these criteria would be important to someone following the Slow Food movement?
   a. The export of Italian culture to the rest of the world
   b. Appreciating what is special about each place and its foods
   c. Including more cheese and mushrooms in our diets

Carlo Petrini, founder of the International Slow Food movement

3. In what way did Salvatore Tescano follow the Slow Food movement?
   a. He ran an American-style restaurant in Florence.
   b. He closed his restaurant that served burgers and moved to Greve.
   c. He served more customers in Greve than he did in Florence.
4. How was the *Pecorino* cheese able to make a comeback?
   a. The cheese makers started using the milk of black sheep.
   b. The cheese was put on the menu at several famous restaurants.
   c. A campaign organized farmers and promoted the cheese.

B | Watch the video again. Complete the direct quotations from the video with the words you hear.

Workers make *Pecorino* cheese.

Paulo Saturnini, Slow Cities co-founder:

"Our (1) _____ and our duty is to try to maintain the soul, the essence, the
(2) _____ of Greve in Chianti, and all the other (3) _____."

Sandro Checcuci, Greve resident:

"It's very nice to (4) _____ because we have a (5) _____,
we have a nice landscape. And so when you have nice things to see, a nice place to live in,
it's (6) _____."

Salvatore Toscano, Chef:

"It means taking (7) _____, finding the rhythm that lets you live
(8) _____ in a lot of ways, starting of course, with what you eat."

Luana Pagliai, Cheese Maker:

"It's brought us a kind of fame. Not everyone knew about our (9) _____.
The project is getting us (10) _____."

Luciano Bertini, Farmer:

"From Singapore to Macao, in New York, and in Rome, you always find the
(11) _____, the same hamburgers. Slow Food doesn't want this. Slow Food
wants the specialness of every product to be (12) _____."

After Viewing

Plates of figs and plums will be served to people at a Slow Food event in California, USA.

Critical Thinking. With a partner, discuss the questions.

1. In Lesson A, you learned about GM foods. What would a member of the Slow Food movement think about GM food products? Explain your answer.
2. What could the Slow Food movement do to gain more members? Brainstorm some ideas with your partner.

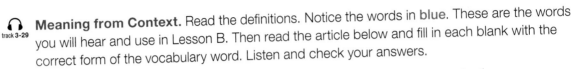

🎧 **Meaning from Context.** Read the definitions. Notice the words in blue. These are the words
track 3-29 you will hear and use in Lesson B. Then read the article below and fill in each blank with the
correct form of the vocabulary word. Listen and check your answers.

1. A **policy** is a plan or set of rules put in place by a government or organization.
2. If one event **coincides** with another, they happen at the same time.
3. An **apparent** situation or feeling is clearly true based on available evidence.
4. An **inclination** is a feeling that makes you want to act in a particular way.
5. If you **presume** that something is true, you believe it is true, although it may not be.
6. A **scenario** is a real or imagined series of possible events or occurrences.
7. The **scope** of a problem or issue tells you how far it reaches.
8. If you say that a situation is **the norm**, you mean that it is usual and expected.
9. **Output** is used to refer to the amount that is produced.
10. **Primarily** means for the most part, mainly, or chiefly.

Egyptians crowd a kiosk selling bread near the Great Pyramids at Giza.
Across the globe, there is rising demand for food but fewer supplies.

In the second half of the 20th century, there was a dramatic increase in the amount of food farmers were able to produce. Thanks to improved farming methods, agricultural (1) _____Output_____ of corn, wheat, and rice increased around 50 percent. It seemed (2) _____apparent_____ that scientists could increase production of food as needed. People (3) _____presume_____ that there would always be enough food to meet the world's needs.

Today, it seems that scientists might have been wrong. In recent years, shortages of important crops such as corn and rice have become (4) _____norm_____, and with these grains in short supply, their prices have been rising. The problem has been particularly serious for people who rely (5) _____primarily_____ on grain to fill their stomachs. The (6) _____scope_____ of the problem has been global, affecting consumers in Africa, Asia, Europe, and the Americas. There is not just one explanation for these shortages, but rather several reasons that (7) _____coincide_____. One reason for the food shortage is that people are eating more meat and dairy products. Both meat and dairy products require large amounts of grain to produce. Another reason is the use of large quantities of grains to produce fuels instead of food. Water shortages and the growing world population have also contributed to the food problems.

There are probably no easy solutions to these problems. It seems very difficult to ask people to fight their natural (8) _____inclination_____ to eat meat. A government (9) _____policy_____ that makes eating meat illegal would likely be very unpopular. However, some experts believe that we have no choice but to take action. If we don't, the future may bring us unpleasant (10) _____scenario_____ of too little food for the world's people.

A | Read the paragraph about the green revolution. Complete the paragraph with the correct form of a word from the box.

apparent	inclination	policy	primarily	scope
coincide	output	presume	scenario	the norm

The Green Revolution

The increase in agricultural (1) _____output_____ of the late 1900s is sometimes referred to as the "Green Revolution." The increase was made possible when four farming technologies (2) _____coincide_____. These technologies are:

- irrigation, a technology that brings water to crops;
- chemical pesticides to help kill or control insects;
- fertilizers, which give plants what they need to grow;
- and smaller plants that produce as much food as larger plants.

In India, workers pull loads of rice stalks to a farm to feed animals.

It would be a mistake, however, to (3) _____presume_____ that these methods will continue to deliver amazing agricultural growth. In fact, now that these four practices have become (4) _____the norm_____ for farmers around the world, it has become (5) _____apparent_____ that the increase in agricultural production can no longer be maintained. In fact, some experts have the (6) _____inclination_____ to help start another "Green Revolution." They hope to avoid future (7) _____scenarios_____ such as food shortages, high food prices, and their consequences.

Scientists and government officials who determine agricultural (8) _____policies_____ are asking, what is the (9) _____scope_____ of the issue? These scientists are trying to figure out if there is any way to improve agriculture. To increase production, they are focusing (10) _____primarily_____ on three different areas: the introduction of GM crops, the improvement of irrigation, and sustainable farming methods. Solving this problem could be the key to our future.

B | **Critical Thinking.** With a partner, discuss the questions.

1. A recent study concluded that science and technology in the past 30 years have failed to improve food access for many of the world's poor. Why do you think this is?
2. Thomas Robert Malthus, an 18th century British scholar, said, "The power of population is indefinitely greater than the power in the earth to produce subsistence[1] for man." Explain what this means in your own words. Do you agree with it?

[1]**Subsistence** is the condition of having enough food or money to stay alive.

Before Listening

Understanding Visuals. Look at the charts. Then answer the questions below. *(See page 216 of the Independent Student Handbook for more information on understanding visuals.)*

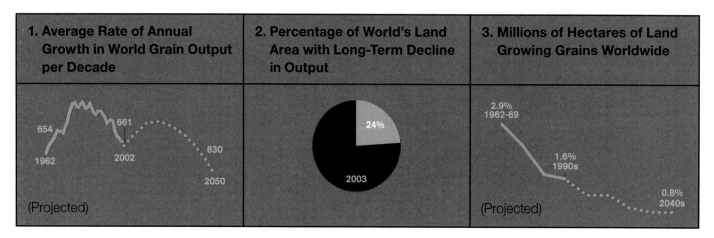

1. Average Rate of Annual Growth in World Grain Output per Decade	2. Percentage of World's Land Area with Long-Term Decline in Output	3. Millions of Hectares of Land Growing Grains Worldwide

1. What will happen to the annual rate of world grain output in 2050?
2. On how much of the world's land was output declining in 2003?
3. How many hectares of land will be dedicated to growing grains in the 2040s?

Listening: An Informal Conversation

track 3-30

A | Listening for Main Ideas. Listen to a conversation about food prices. Choose the best answer to each question.

1. Why don't farmers use more land to produce more food?
   a. They wish to keep prices high.
   b. The government restricted land use.
   c. There isn't any more land to farm.

2. What is the relationship between people eating more meat and the price of grain?
   a. As people eat more grain, meat prices fall.
   b. As people eat more meat, grain prices rise.
   c. As people eat more dairy, meat prices rise.

3. What have governments done to stop rising food prices?
   a. Stopped transporting corn from farm to market.
   b. Used corn in making fuel for cars and trucks.
   c. Placed restrictions on the export of corn.

4. What solution to food shortages do the experts suggest?
   a. They suggest increasing the output on farm land.
   b. They suggest finding more land to use for farming.
   c. They suggest government policies to stop eating meat.

B | Note-Taking. Listen again. Complete the notes with information from the conversation.

Problem:

Rise in food prices over the past ___5 - 10 yrs___, quicker than the norm

Most available land is already ___farmed.___

Reasons for problem:

- Dev. countries have more ___money___ to spend, eat more ___meat & dairy___
- Feeding farm animals requires ___grains___
- Supply and Demand: If only a little food, but many want it: the price ___goes___ ___up___
- Some gov. policies restrict ___grains export___
- Some experts predict that areas of planet ___will become___ ___desert.___

Solutions to problem: Increase ___amount of food grown on land___

- Increase output w/better ___water management___ and fertilizer management; ___GM crops___

After Listening

Critical Thinking. With a partner, discuss the questions.

1. Which of the possible solutions to the global food crisis that you have learned about in this unit are the most appealing to you? Why do you think they might be effective?
2. Some scientists are predicting what they call a "perpetual food crisis" for the world. What do you think this means?

Pronunciation

Syllable Stress
Putting stress on the correct syllable is important. Stressing the incorrect syllable could change the meaning of what you are saying. Look at the words below. When the first syllable of each word is stressed, the words are nouns. When the second syllable of each word is stressed, the words are verbs. For example, **pro**ject is a noun, while pro**ject** is a verb.

conduct   conflict   extract   project   reject

Collaboration. Work with a partner. Write two sentences for each word in the pronunciation box. Use the word as a noun in one sentence, and as a verb in the other sentence. Then read the sentences to your partner. Your partner will monitor your syllable stress.

> Scientists will try to extract a special gene from tomatoes.

> I put vanilla extract into my chocolate chip cookies.

FOOD CONCERNS | 197

Language Function

Giving Recommendations

When discussing a problem, you sometimes want to give advice or a recommendation for how to solve the problem. Here are some expressions you can use to give a recommendation.

Why don't you/they . . .?
If it were up to me . . .
It might be wise (not) to . . .
If I were you I'd/I wouldn't . . .

Have you thought about . . .?
I think he/she/they ought to . . .
It's (probably) a good idea (not) to . . .

🎧 track 3-32 **A** | In the conversation you heard, there were a number of useful expressions for giving a recommendation. Listen and fill in the missing expressions.

1. **Susan:** It seems that over the past five or ten years prices have been rising faster than the norm.

   Andy: Personally, I think ___they ought to_____.

2. **Susan:** When grain prices go up, they'll have very few other options.

   Andy: _____why don't they do something about it_____

3. **Susan:** You know, I heard that some climate experts are predicting a scenario in which large areas in Africa and Asia will become deserts. That might be a problem too, if the land is too dry to grow crops on.

   Andy: Wow. Well, ___if it were up to me_____, I'd try to get the whole world to work together to stop that from happening.

👥 **B** | **Discussion.** Read the statements. Form a group with two or three other students and discuss each statement. Use expressions from the Language Function box to make recommendations.

1. Although they are perfectly delicious and good to eat, many vegetables and fruits are not allowed to be sold in grocery stores because they are considered to be too ugly.
2. Fast-food is becoming more popular throughout the world.
3. Because of high prices they can get for their crops, some farmers are deciding to use land that was once reserved for animals for planting food instead.

An "ugly" carrot cannot be sold in grocery stores.

> It's probably not a good idea to eat at fast-food restaurants more than a couple of times a month.

> Why do you say that?

> Because fast-food can be bad for your health.

Grammar

Subjunctive Verbs in *That* Clauses

The subjunctive verb is the base form of the verb (*be, go, have, bring*, etc.). The form of the verb does not change to agree with its subject.

> He recommended **that each country make** an effort to help agricultural output.
> They insisted **that their food sources be** protected.

Subjunctive verbs are used in *that* clauses (*that* can be omitted) following verbs of advice such as *advise, demand, insist, prefer, recommend, request,* and *suggest.* They are also used following certain expressions such as:

It is best (that) . . .	*It is important (that) . . .*
It is crucial (that) . . .	*It is a good idea (that) . . .*
It is vital (that) . . .	*It is a bad idea (that) . . .*

A | **Discussion.** Form a group with two or three other students. Read about these three people and their situations. Use subjunctive verbs in *that* clauses to make as many recommendations as you can.

1. A small island nation, which is a top exporter of pineapples, has been experiencing a terrible attack of insects. The pests have ruined the pineapple crop for this year, and there is no sign that the problem is going to go away. The president is looking everywhere for advice. What do you recommend that she do?

> It is important that the president eliminate the insects from the island.

2. Pierre loves to cook, and he does it very well. A few years ago, he even took a semester of cooking classes in Paris. Right now he works in a bookstore at a low-paying job, which he doesn't like. When he goes home every night he cooks a wonderful meal for himself. What career advice do you have to help Pierre?

3. Thomas is a young professional living in a big city. He recently got a job, and works six days a week. He usually eats toast in the morning, fast food for lunch, and frozen TV dinners. Imagine that you are a member of the Slow Food movement. What advice can you give to Thomas?

B | **Self-Reflection.** Think of two or three things that you need some advice about. Describe the situation to a partner. Then ask your partner to give you some advice. Your partner will use verbs and expressions followed by subjunctive verbs.

> I would like to learn to speak Spanish.

> It is vital that you practice every chance you get.

People from all parts of the world rely on the same types of foods: grains (such as wheat, corn, or rice), dairy products (such as milk, cheese, or yogurt), meat, fish, and fruits or vegetables. However, people from different places and cultures eat these foods in very different ways. You are going to prepare a poster or PowerPoint presentation about foods of one country.

A | Work with a partner. Choose a country whose food you know about or are interested in.

Country: _____

B | **Researching.** With your partner, research different types of crops that are common in the country you chose. Try to find a grain, a dairy product, a type of meat or fish, and a fruit or vegetable. Then find a food made with each item. Write a description of each food and an interesting fact about it. *(See page 211 of the Independent Student Handbook for more information on researching.)*

C | **Creating Visuals.** Create one slide for each type of food that you researched. Try to include a picture on each slide, if possible. Once you have created your presentation, practice it with your partner.

Country: Ethiopia

Grain: teff (an African grain)

Name of Food: injera

Description: Injera is a type of flatbread that is eaten every day by people in Ethiopia, Somalia, and Eritrea.

Fact: People tear off a piece of bread with their right hand. They then use the bread to eat a bit of stew or salad.

D | **Presentation.** Give your presentation to the class. When finished, ask the class if they have any questions, advice, or comments.

Presentation Skills: Preparing Visuals for Display

When preparing visuals for a presentation, remember that they must be clear to everyone in the room. Keep people in the very back of the room in mind. When you are preparing your visual, ask:

Is the size of the lettering large enough for everyone to see?
Is the language clear and easy to understand?
Will everyone be able to see any photos or graphics clearly?

If necessary, make corrections to your presentation.

Overview

The *Independent Student Handbook* is a resource that you can use at different points and in different ways during this course. You may want to read the entire handbook at the beginning of the class as an introduction to the skills and strategies you will develop and practice throughout the book. Reading it at the beginning will provide you with another organizational framework for understanding the material.

Use the *Independent Student Handbook* throughout the course in the following ways:

Additional instruction: You can use the *Independent Student Handbook* to provide more instruction on a particular skill that you are practicing in the units. In addition to putting all the skills instruction in one place, the *Independent Student Handbook* includes additional suggestions and strategies. For example, if you find you're having difficulty following academic lectures, you can refer to the Improving Your Listening Skills section to review signal phrases that help you to understand the speaker's flow of ideas.

Independent work: You can use the *Independent Student Handbook* to help you when you are working on your own. For example, if you want to improve your vocabulary, you can follow some of the suggestions in the Building Your Vocabulary section.

Source of specific tools: A third way to use the handbook is as a source of specific tools such as outlines, graphic organizers, and checklists. For example, if you are preparing a presentation, you might want to use the Research Checklist as you research your topic. Then you might want to complete the Presentation Outline to organize your information. Finally, you might want to use the Presentation Checklist to help you prepare for your presentation.

Table of Contents

Improving Your Listening Skills
Formal Listening Skills   202

Improving Your Note-Taking Skills   206

Building Your Vocabulary
Independent Vocabulary Learning Tips   208
Prefixes and Suffixes   209
Dictionary Skills   209

Improving Your Speaking Skills
Everyday Communication   210
Doing Group Projects   211
Classroom Presentation Skills   211

Resources
Understanding and Using Visuals:
    Graphic Organizers   214
    Maps, Charts, Graphs, and
        Diagrams   216
Presentation Outline   217
Checklists   218
Summary of Signal Phrases   219

Formal Listening Skills

Predicting

Speakers giving formal talks or lectures usually begin by introducing themselves and then introducing their topic. Listen carefully to the introduction of the topic and try to anticipate what you will hear.

Strategies:

- Use visual information including titles on the board, on slides, or in a PowerPoint presentation.
- Think about what you already know about the topic.
- Ask yourself questions that you think the speaker might answer.
- Listen for specific phrases.

Identifying the Topic:

Let's look at . . .
Today's topic is . . .
What I want to do today is . . .
Today, we're going to cover . . .

Understanding the Structure of the Presentation

An organized speaker will use certain expressions to alert you to the important information that will follow. Notice the signal words and phrases that tell you how the presentation is organized and the relationship between the main ideas.

Introduction

A good introduction includes a thesis statement, which identifies the topic and gives an idea of how the lecture or presentation will be organized.

Introduction (Topic + Organization):

I'd like to focus on . . .   *To begin with . . .*
There are basically two groups . . .   *There are three reasons . . .*
Several factors contribute to this . . .   *There are five steps in this process . . .*

Body

In the body of the lecture, the speaker will usually expand upon the topic presented in the introduction. The speaker will use phrases that tell you the order of events or subtopics and their relationship to each other. For example, the speaker may discuss several examples or reasons.

Following the Flow of Ideas in the Body:

However, . . .   *As a result, . . .*
For example, . . .   *Let's move on to . . .*
The first/next/final (point) is . . .   *Another reason is . . .*

Conclusion

In a conclusion, the speaker often summarizes what has already been said and may discuss implications or suggest future developments. For example, if a speaker is talking about an environmental problem, he or she may end by suggesting what might happen if we don't solve the problem, or he or she might add his or her own opinion. Sometimes speakers ask a question in the conclusion to get the audience to think more about the topic.

Restating/Concluding:

In summary, . . .	*To sum up, . . .*
As you can see, . . .	*In conclusion, . . .*

Listening for Main Ideas

It's important to distinguish between a speaker's main ideas and the supporting details. In school, a professor often will test a student's understanding of the main points more than of specific details. Often a speaker has one main idea just like a writer does, and several main points that support the main idea.

Strategies:

- Listen for a thesis statement at the end of the introduction.
- Listen for rhetorical questions, or questions that the speaker asks, and then answers. Often the answer is the thesis.
- Notice ideas that are repeated or rephrased.

Repetition/Rephrasing:

I'll say this again . . .	*So again, let me repeat . . .*
Let me put it another way . . .	*The most important thing to know is . . .*
What you need to know is . . .	

Listening for Details (Examples)

A speaker will often provide examples that support a main point. A good example can help you understand and remember the main point.

Strategies:

- Listen for specific phrases that introduce an example.
- Notice if an example comes after a generalization the speaker has given, or is leading into a generalization.
- If there are several examples, decide if they all support the same idea or are different aspects of the idea.

Giving Examples:

. . . such as . . .	*. . . including . . .*
The first example is . . .	*For instance, . . .*
Here's an example of what I mean . . .	*Let me give you an example . . .*

Listening for Details (Reasons)

Speakers often give reasons, or list causes and/or effects to support their ideas.

Strategies:

- Notice nouns that might signal causes/reasons (e.g., *factors, influences, causes, reasons*), or effects (e.g., *effects, results, outcomes, consequences*).
- Notice verbs that might signal causes/reasons (e.g., *contribute to, affect, influence, determine, produce, result in*) or effects (often these are passive, e.g., *is affected by*).
- Listen for specific phrases that introduce reasons/causes.

Giving Reasons:

This is because . . .　　　　　　*This is due to . . .*
The first reason is . . .　　　　　*In the first place . . .*

Giving Effects or Results:

As a result, . . .　　　　　　　*Therefore, . . .*
Consequently, . . .　　　　　　*One consequence is . . .*
Another effect is . . .

Understanding Meaning from Context

Speakers may use words that are unfamiliar to you, or you may not understand exactly what they've said. In these situations, you can guess the meaning of a particular word or fill in the gaps of what you've understood by using the context or situation itself.

Strategies:

- Don't panic. You don't always understand every word of what a speaker says in your first language either.
- Use context clues to fill in the blanks. What did you understand just before or just after the missing part? What did the speaker probably say?
- Listen for words and phrases that signal a definition or explanation.

Giving Definitions:

Or . . .　　　　　　　　　*In other words, . . .*
. . . meaning that . . .　　　　*That is (to say), . . .*
(By which) I mean . . .　　　*To put it another way . . .*

Recognizing a Speaker's Bias

Speakers often have an opinion about the topic they are discussing. It's important for you to understand if they are objective or subjective about the topic. Being subjective means having a bias or a strong feeling about something. Objective speakers do not express an opinion.

Strategies:

- Notice words such as adjectives, adverbs, and modals that the speaker uses (e.g., *ideal, horribly, should, shouldn't*).
- Listen to the speaker's voice. Does he or she sound excited, happy, or bored?
- When presenting another point of view on the topic, is that given much less time and attention by the speaker?
- Listen for words that signal opinions.

Opinions:

If you ask me, . . .   *In my opinion, . . .*
(Personally,) I think . . .   *As far as I'm concerned . . .*

Making Inferences

Sometimes a speaker doesn't state something directly, but instead implies it. When you draw a conclusion about something that is not directly stated, you make an inference. For example, if the speaker says he or she grew up in Spain, you might infer that he or she speaks Spanish. When you make inferences, you may be very sure about your conclusions or you may be less sure. It's important to use information the speaker states directly to support your inferences.

Strategies:

- Note information that provides support for your inference. For example, you might note that the speaker lived in Spain.
- Note information that contradicts your inference. Which evidence is stronger—for or against your inference?
- If you're less than certain about your inference, use words to soften your language such as modals, adverbs, and quantifiers.

*She probably speaks Spanish, and she **may** also prefer Spanish food. **Many** people from Spain are familiar with bullfighting.*

Summarizing or Condensing

When taking notes, you should write down only the most important ideas of the lecture. To take good notes quickly:

- Write only the key words.

  dusky seaside sparrow extinct

- You don't need complete sentences.

  That's why the Endangered Species Act, which was passed in the United States in 1973, protects both endangered animals and their habitats

- Use abbreviations (short forms) and symbols when possible.

  info information   dr doctor   w/ with   < less than

  ex. examples   b/c because   = /→ leads to causes   > more than

Outlining

Another way to take clear and organized notes is to use an outline. Like with other types of note-taking, in an outline you should only write key ideas and you should use abbreviations and symbols when possible. To indicate main ideas in an outline, use Roman numerals (I, II, III) and capital letters (A, B, C). Indicate details with numbers. As information becomes more specific, move it to the right.

    I. Background

       A. 1970s & 1980s: Soviet Union developed nuclear technology

       B. 1986: 25 plants w/ safety probs.

    II. Chernobyl disaster

       A. Causes

          1. Mistakes during safety test

          2. No containment building to limit fire and radiation

       B. Result: explosion → people dead

Recognizing Organization

When you listen to a speaker, you practice the skill of noticing that speaker's organization. As you get in the habit of recognizing the organizational structure, you can use it to structure your notes in a similar way. Review the signal words and phrases from the Improving Your Listening Skills section in this handbook.

Some basic organizational structures are:

- Narrative (often used in history or literature)
- Process (almost any field, but especially in the sciences)
- Cause and Effect (history, psychology, sociology)
- Classification (any field, including art, music, literature, sciences, history)
- Problem and Solution

Using Graphic Organizers

Graphic organizers can be very useful tools if you want to rewrite your notes. Once you've identified the speaker's organizational structure, you can choose the best graphic organizer to show the ideas. See the Resources section on page 214 in this handbook for more information.

Distinguishing between Relevant and Irrelevant Information

Remember that not everything a speaker says is noteworthy. A lecturer or presenter will usually signal important information you should take notes on.

Signals for Important Information:

Don't forget that . . .
It is important to note/remember that . . .

Let me stress that . . .
You need to remember that . . .

Instructors and other lecturers may also signal when to stop taking notes.

Signals to Stop Taking Notes:

You can find this in your handout . . .
You don't have to write all this down . . .

This won't be on your test . . .
This information is in your book . . .

In a similar way, they may let you know when they are going to discuss something off-topic.

Understanding Sidetracks:

That reminds me . . .
On a different topic . . .
This is off the subject, but . . .

Incidentally . . .
As an aside . . .
By the way, . . .

Recognizing a Return to a Previous Topic

When a speaker makes a sidetrack and talks about something that is not directly related to the main topic, he or she will often signal a return to a previous topic.

Returning to a Previous Topic:

Back to . . .
To continue . . .
So, just to restate . . .
OK, so to get back on topic . . .
Getting back to what we were saying . . .
To return to what we were talking about earlier . . .

Using Notes Effectively

It's important to not only take good notes, but also to use them in the most effective way.

Strategies:

- Go over your notes after class to review and add information you might have forgotten to write down.
- Compare notes with a classmate or study group to make sure you have all the important information.
- Review your notes before the next class, so you will understand and remember the information better.

Independent Vocabulary Learning Tips

Keep a vocabulary journal.

- If a new word is useful, write it in a special notebook. Also write a short definition (in English if possible) and the sentence or situation where you found the word (its context). Write your own sentence that uses the word.
- Carry your vocabulary notebook with you at all times. Review the words whenever you have free time.
- Choose vocabulary words that will be useful to you. Some words are rarely used.

Experiment with new vocabulary.

- Think about new vocabulary in different ways. For example, look at all the words in your vocabulary journal and make a list of only the verbs. Or, list the words according to the number of syllables (one-syllable words, two-syllable words, and so on).
- Use new vocabulary to write a poem, a story, or an email message to a friend.
- Use an online dictionary to listen to the sound of new words. If possible, make a list of words that rhyme. Brainstorm words that relate to a single topic that begin with the same sound (*student, study, school, skills, strategies, studious*).

Use new words as often as possible.

- You will not know a new vocabulary word after hearing or reading it once. You need to remember the word several times before it enters your long-term memory.
- The way you use an English word—in which situations and with what other words—might be different from a similar word in your first language. If you use your new vocabulary often, you're more likely to discover the correct way to use it.

Use vocabulary organizers.

- Label pictures.

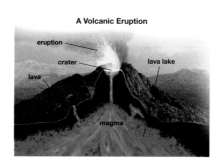

A Volcanic Eruption

eruption

crater

lava

lava lake

magma

- Make word maps.

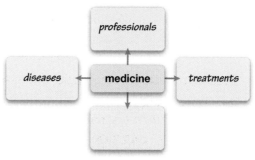

professionals

diseases

medicine

treatments

- Make personal flashcards. Write the words you want to learn on one side. Write the definition and/or an example sentence on the other.

Prefixes and Suffixes

Use prefixes and suffixes to guess the meaning of unfamiliar words and to expand your vocabulary. Prefixes usually change the meaning of a word somewhat. Suffixes usually change the part of speech. If you train yourself to look for the base meaning, or the meaning of the stem of the word, you can understand more vocabulary.

Prefix	Meaning	Example
a-	completely; not	awake; apolitical
bi-	two	bilingual, bicycle
dis-	not, negation, removal	disappear, disadvantages
pre-	before	prehistoric, preheat
mis-	bad, badly, incorrectly	misunderstand, misjudge
re-	again	remove
un-	not, the opposite of	unhappy, unusual, unbelievable

The following are derivational suffixes that change the part of speech of the base word.

Suffix	New Part of Speech	Example
-able	adjective	believable
-ary	noun	summary
-ent	adjective	convergent, divergent
-ful	adjective	beautiful, successful
-ed	adjective	stressed, interested
-ize	verb	summarize
-ly	adverb	carefully, completely
-ment	noun	assignment
-tion	noun	information

Dictionary Skills

The dictionary listing for a word usually provides the pronunciation, part of speech, other word forms, synonyms, examples of sentences that show the word in context, and common collocations.

Synonyms

A *synonym* is a word that means the same thing (e.g., *baby=infant*). Use synonyms to expand your vocabulary.

Word Families

These are the words that have the same stem or base word, but have different prefixes or suffixes.

Different Meanings of the Same Word

Many words have several meanings and several parts of speech. The example sentences in the word's dictionary entry can help you determine which meaning you need. For example, the word *plant* can be a noun or a verb.

Collocations

Dictionary entries often provide *collocations*, or words that are often used with the target word. For example, if you look up the word *get*, you might see *get around*, *get into*, *get there*, and so on.

Everyday Communication

Summary of Useful Phrases for Everyday Communication

It's important to practice speaking English every day, with your teacher, your classmates, and anyone else you can find to practice with. This chart lists common phrases you can use in everyday communication situations. The phrases are listed in this chart from more formal to less formal.

Asking for Clarification: *Could you explain . . . (for me, please)?* *What do you mean by . . . ?* *What (exactly) is . . . ?* *(Sorry,) what does . . . mean?*	**Digressing from the Topic:** *Speaking of . . .* *That reminds me, . . .* *Incidentally . . .* *By the way . . .*
Agreeing: *I agree.* *I think so too.* *I think you're right.* *Exactly!* *You can say that again!*	**Expressing Hopes:** *It would be nice/great/wonderful/ideal if . . .* *I'm hoping (that) . . .* *I (really) hope (that) . . .*
Disagreeing: *I disagree.* *I'm not so sure (about that) . . .* *That's debatable.* *I don't think so.* *That's crazy!* *No way!*	**Apologizing for Interrupting:** *I'm sorry. I didn't mean to cut you off.* *What were you going to say?* *Go ahead.* *Sorry.*
Conceding a Point: *Good point.* *Fair enough.* *I'll give you that.*	**Asking Sensitive Questions:** *Excuse me for asking, but . . . ?* *Do you mind if I ask you . . . ?* *If you don't mind my asking, . . .?*
Expressing Surprise: *That's amazing/astonishing/incredible.* *That's (really) surprising.* *Wow!* *No kidding.* *Imagine that!*	**Congratulating the Group:** *Nice job, everybody!* *Congratulations!* *We make a great team!* *Great going, gang!* *Good for you!* *Way to go, guys!*
Expressing Encouragement: *Good luck!* *Go for it!* *Go get 'em!*	**Expressing Interest:** *Is that so?* *How interesting!* *I didn't know that.*

Expressing Approval and Disapproval:	**Joining a Group:**
(I) think it's fine to . . .	Do you mind if I join your group?
It's OK that . . .	Do you want to work together?
It's not right for (someone) to . . .	Do you need another person?
It's wrong to . . .	
Enumerating:	**Checking Background Knowledge:**
First, . . . Second, . . . Third, . . .	Do you know about . . . ?
First . . . , then . . . , and then . . .	Have you (ever) heard of . . . ?
For one thing, . . . For another, . . .	What do you know about . . . ?
And for another, . . .	What can you tell me about . . . ?

Doing Group Projects

You will often have to work with a group on activities and projects. It can be helpful to assign group members certain roles. You should try to switch roles every time you do a new activity. Here is a description of some common roles used in group activities and projects:

Group Leader—Makes sure the assignment is done correctly and all group members participate. Asks questions: *What do you think? Does anyone have another idea?*

Secretary—Takes notes on the group's ideas (including a plan for sharing the work).

Manager—During the planning and practice phases, the manager makes sure the presentation can be given within the time limit. If possible, practice the presentation from beginning to end and time it.

Expert—Understands the topic well; invites and answers audience questions after the presentation. Make a list of possible questions ahead of time to be prepared.

Coach—Reminds group members to perform their assigned roles in the group work.

Note that group members have one of these roles in addition to their contribution to the presentation content and delivery.

Classroom Presentation Skills

Library Research

If you can go to a public library or school library, start there. You don't have to read whole books. Parts of books, magazines, newspapers, and even videos are all possible sources of information. A librarian can help you find both print and online sources of information.

Online Research

The Internet is a source with a lot of information, but it has to be looked at carefully. Many Web sites are commercial and may have incomplete, inaccurate, or biased information.

Finding reliable sources

Strategies:

- Your sources of information need to be reliable. Think about the author and the publisher. Ask yourself: *What is their point of view? Can I trust this information?*
- Your sources need to be well respected. For example, an article from *The Lancet* (a journal of medical news) will probably be more respected than an article from a popular magazine.
- Start with Web sites with *.edu* or *.org* endings. These are usually educational or non-commercial Web sites. Some *.com* Web sites also have good information, for example www.nationalgeographic.com or www.britannica.com.

Finding information that is appropriate for your topic

Strategies:

- Look for up-to-date information, especially in fields that change often such as technology or business. For Internet sources, look for recent updates to the Web sites.
- Most of the time, you'll need to find more than one source of information. Find sources that are long enough to contain some good information, but not so long that you won't have time to read them.
- Think about the source's audience. For example, imagine that you are buying a new computer and want to read about the different types of computers before you buy one. If the source is written for computer programmers, for example, you might not be able to understand it. If the source is written for university students who need to buy a new computer, it's more likely to be understandable.

Speaking Clearly and Comprehensibly

It's important that your audience understands what you are saying for your presentation to be effective.

Strategies:

- Practice your presentation many times for at least one other person and ask him or her for feedback.
- Make sure you know the correct pronunciation of every word—especially the ones you will say more than once. Look them up online or ask your instructor for the correct pronunciation.
- Try to use thought groups. Keep these words together: long subjects, verbs and objects, clauses, prepositional phrases. Remember to pause slightly at all punctuation and between thought groups.
- Speak loudly enough so that everyone can hear.
- Stop occasionally to ask your audience if they can hear you and follow what you are saying.

Demonstrating Knowledge of Content

You should know more about your subject than you actually say in your presentation. Your audience may have questions or you may need to explain something in more detail than you planned. Knowing a lot about your subject will allow you to present well and feel more confident.

Strategies:

- Practice your presentation several times.
- Don't read your notes.
- Say more than is on your visuals.
- Tell your audience what the visuals mean.

Phrases to Talk about Visuals:

You can see . . .
The main point is that . . .
The line/box represents . . .
This graph/diagram shows/explains . . .

Engaging the Audience

Presenting is an important skill. If your audience isn't interested in what you have to say, then your message is lost.

Strategies:

- Introduce yourself.
- Make eye contact. Look around at different people in the audience.
- Use good posture. *Posture* means how you hold your body. When you speak in front of the class, you should stand up straight. Hold your hands together in front of your waist, if you aren't holding notes. This shows that you are confident and well prepared.
- Pause to check understanding. When you present ideas, it's important to find out if your audience understands you. Look at the faces of people in the audience. Do they look confused? Use the expressions from the chart below to check understanding.

Phrases to Check for Understanding:

OK so far?
Are you with me?
Have you got that?
Does that make sense?
Do you have any questions?

Understanding and Using Visuals: Graphic Organizers

T-Chart
Purpose: Compare or contrast two things or list aspects of two things

GM Food: Pros	GM Food: Cons
pest-resistant crops	could be dangerous

Venn Diagram
Purpose: Show differences and similarities between two things, sometimes three

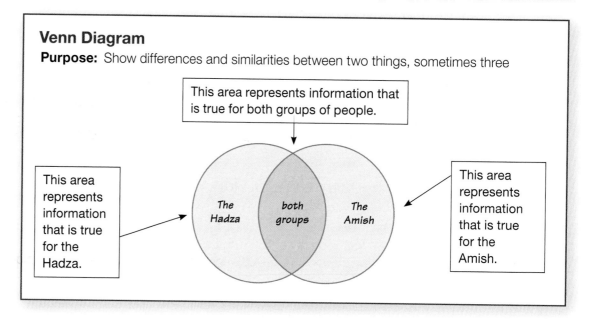

This area represents information that is true for both groups of people.

This area represents information that is true for the Hadza.

The Hadza | both groups | The Amish

This area represents information that is true for the Amish.

Family Tree
Purpose: Organize information about your family relationships

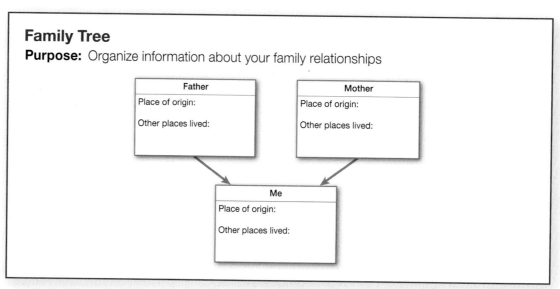

Father
Place of origin:
Other places lived:

Mother
Place of origin:
Other places lived:

Me
Place of origin:
Other places lived:

Flow Chart

Purpose: Show the stages in a process, or a cause-and-effect chain (Flow charts have many different shapes.)

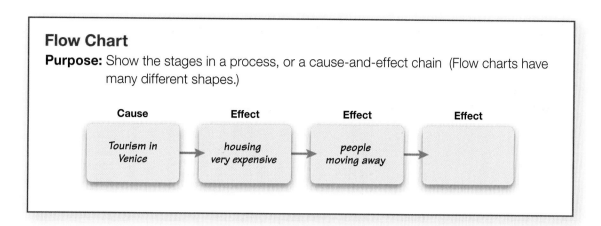

Time Line

Purpose: Show the order of events and when they happened in time

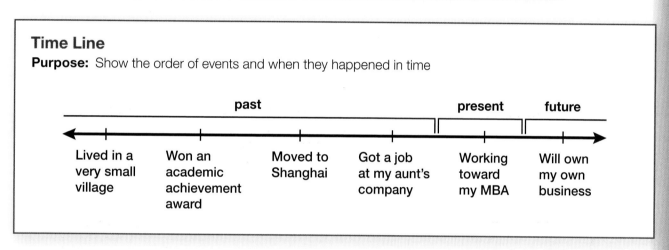

Idea Map

Purpose: Brainstorm ideas or identify main points or themes of a listening or reading. (A Spider Map can also be used for this purpose.)

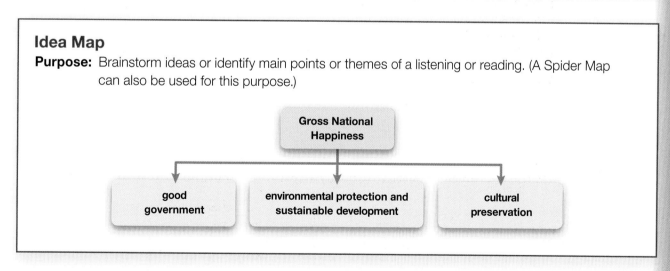

Understanding and Using Visuals: Maps, Charts, Graphs, and Diagrams

Maps are used to show geographical information.

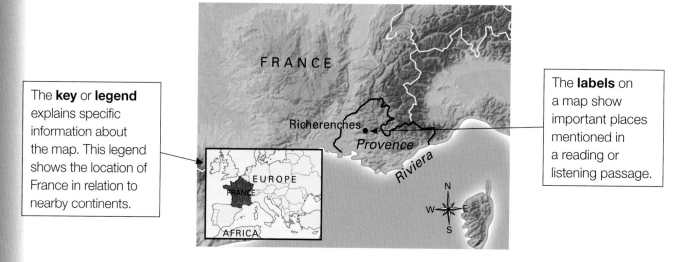

The **key** or **legend** explains specific information about the map. This legend shows the location of France in relation to nearby continents.

The **labels** on a map show important places mentioned in a reading or listening passage.

Bar and **line graphs** use axes to show the relationship between two or more things.

Bar graphs compare amounts and numbers.

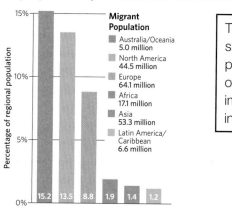

Migrant Population

- Australia/Oceania 5.0 million
- North America 44.5 million
- Europe 64.1 million
- Africa 17.1 million
- Asia 53.3 million
- Latin America/Caribbean 6.6 million

Percentage of regional population: 15.2, 13.5, 8.8, 1.9, 1.4, 1.2

The **y axis** shows the percentage of foreign immigrants in Germany.

Line graphs show a change over time.

Percentage of Foreigners in Germany

Source: www.migrationinformation.org

The **x axis** shows the year.

Pie charts show percents of a whole, or something that is made up of several parts.

Fossil Fuel Use by Sector

This section shows that the Energy Supply sector uses the most fossil fuels.

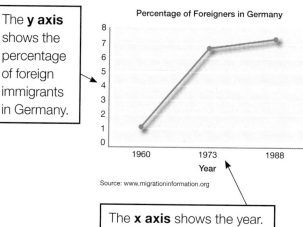

- Waste and Wastewater 3%
- Energy Supply 26%
- Transportation 13%
- Forestry 17%
- Agriculture 14%
- Industry 19%
- Residential and Commercial Buildings 8%

Diagrams are a helpful way to show how a process or system works.

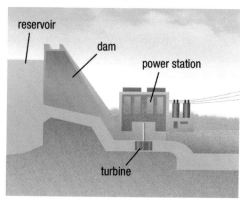

reservoir
dam
power station
turbine

Presentation Outline

When you are planning a presentation, you may find it helpful to use an outline. If it is a group presentation, the outline can provide an easy way to divide the content. For example, someone could do the introduction, another student the first main idea in the body, and so on.

I. **Introduction**

   Topic: _____

   _____

   Hook/attention getter: _____

   _____

   Thesis statement: _____

   _____

II. **Body**

   A. First step/example/reason: _____

     Supporting details:

      1. _____

      2. _____

      3. _____

   B. Second step/example/reason: _____

     Supporting details:

      1. _____

      2. _____

      3. _____

   C. Third step/example/reason: _____

     Supporting details:

      1. _____

      2. _____

      3. _____

III. **Conclusion**

   Major points to summarize: _____

   _____

   Any implications/suggestions/predictions: _____

   _____

   Closing comment/summary: _____

   _____

Checklists

Research Checklist

- ☐ Do I have three to five sources for information in general—and especially for information I'm using without a specific citation?
- ☐ Am I correctly citing information when it comes from just one or two sources?
- ☐ Have I noted all sources properly, including page numbers?
- ☐ When I am not citing a source directly, am I using adequate paraphrasing? (a combination of synonyms, different word forms, and/or different grammatical structure)
- ☐ Are my sources reliable?

Presentation Checklist

- ☐ Have I practiced several times?
- ☐ Did I get feedback from a peer?
- ☐ Have I timed the presentation?
- ☐ Do I introduce myself?
- ☐ Do I maintain eye contact?
- ☐ Do I explain my visuals?
- ☐ Do I pause sometimes and check for understanding?
- ☐ Do I use correct pronunciation?
- ☐ Do I have good posture?
- ☐ Am I using appropriate voice volume so that everyone can hear?

Pair and Group Work Checklist

- ☐ Do I make eye contact with others?
- ☐ Do I pay attention when someone else is talking?
- ☐ Do I make encouraging comments?
- ☐ Do I ask for clarification when I don't understand something?
- ☐ Do I check for understanding?
- ☐ Do I clarify what I mean?
- ☐ Do I express agreement and disagreement politely?
- ☐ Do I make suggestions when helpful?
- ☐ Do I participate as much as my classmates?
- ☐ Do I ask my classmates for their ideas?

Summary of Signal Phrases

Giving Recommendations:
It's (probably) a good idea (not) to . . .
It might be wise (not) to . . .
If I were you, I wouldn't . . .
Have you thought about . . . ?

Showing Understanding:
You must be (tired).
You must have been (glad).
That must be (fun).
That must have been (difficult).

Using Fillers:
Let me think
Just a moment
Oh, what's the word . . .
. . . um . . .
. . . hang on . . .

Expressing Uncertainty:
It appears/looks/seems as though . . .
It appears/seems to me (that) . . .
I'm not quite/altogether sure (that) . . .
*I could be wrong, but it appears/doesn't
 appear (that) . . .*

Paraphrasing:
I mean . . .
In other words . . .
That is (to say) . . .
Let me put it another way . . .
To put it another way . . .

Enumerating Reasons and Examples:
First, Second, Third . . .
First, Next, After that . . .
First, Then, And then . . .
*For one thing, For another, And for
 another . . .*
*In the first place, In the second place,
 And in the third place . . .*

Expressing a Lack of Knowledge:
I had no idea (that) . . .
I didn't realize (that) . . .
I never knew (that) . . .
I wasn't aware (that) . . .

Giving Effects or Results:
As a result, . . .
One consequence is . . .
Consequently . . .
Therefore, . . .
Another effect is . . .

Giving Definitions:
. . . which means . . .
In other words, . . .
What that means is . . .
Another way to say that is . . .
That is . . .

Expressing Opinions:
As far as I'm concerned, . . .
In my opinion, . . .
(Personally,) I think . . .
If you ask me, . . .
As I see it, . . .

Signal to Stop Taking Notes:
You don't have to write all this down . . .
This information is in your book . . .
You can find this in your handout . . .
This won't be on your test . . .

Returning to a Previous Topic:
So, just to restate . . .
Back to . . .
Getting back to what we were saying . . .
*To return to what we were talking about
 earlier . . .*
OK, so to get back on topic . . .

Understanding Sidetracks:
That reminds me . . .
By the way . . .
This is off the subject, but . . .
As an aside . . .
On a different topic . . .

Confirming Understanding:
Are you following me?
Does that make sense?
Have you got that?
Any questions?
Are you with me?
OK so far?

VOCABULARY INDEX

abandon* 64
absorb 84
abstract* 164
abundant 74
accumulate* 144
adjacent* 164
advocate* 184
agriculture 104
alter* 24
alternative* 54
annual* 34
anticipate* 104
apparent* 194
appreciate* 144
approximately* 94
aptitude 174
assess* 144
assist* 134
assume* 84
attribute* 154
authorities* 34

capable* 134
capacity* 164
cease* 124
challenge* 4
classic* 44
coincide* 194
commitment* 124
compatible* 14
compensate* 64
component* 124
conform* 14
consequences* 104
considerably* 54
consistently* 44
constant* 144
constitute* 44
consumer* 134
contaminate 64
contradiction* 104
contrary* 34
contribute* 34
controversy* 64
conventional* 184
convert* 4
convince* 54
correspond* 164
criteria* 134
currency* 134

data* 154
debatable* 14
decline* 84
dedicate 94
definite* 54

demonstrate* 124
derive* 54
devote* 184
diminish* 184
disadvantage 74
displace* 94
display* 104
disturb 44
domestic* 104
dominate* 14
dramatic* 174

economy* 14
eliminate* 144
emerge* 64
enable* 114
encounter* 84
enforce* 14
enhance* 174
ensure* 94
enthusiasm 74
envision 44
equivalent* 154
error* 124
establish* 94
ethical* 174
ethnic* 14
evidence* 24
evolve* 44
exact 174
exhibit* 54
expansion* 154
expert* 64
exploit* 24
expose* 64

federal* 114
fee* 134
finance* 4
flexible* 164
focus* 34
found* 114
framework* 174
funds* 34

generate* 4
global* 154
grant* 114

highlight* 114

ignore* 34
illegal* 94
illustrate* 164
immense 84
implications* 84
incentive* 74

inclination*	194
incredible	84
indication*	24
individual*	134
initially*	154
innovative*	4
insert*	54
integrate*	54
intense*	184
interfere	94
internalize*	14
interpret*	164
invest*	94
isolate*	104
issue*	34
layer*	74
legislation*	154
link*	84
maintain*	34
major*	124
maximize*	4
method*	174
migration*	84
modify*	184
monitor*	184
motive*	164
objective*	114
obviously*	124
offset*	184
ongoing*	24
option*	144
organic	144
originate	174
output*	194
overwhelming	94
perception*	44
period*	104
persist*	144
perspective*	114
pesticide	144
philosophy*	164
policy*	194
portion*	114
precede*	134
presume*	194
primarily*	194
principle*	74
prior to	154
professional*	134
prohibit*	14
promote*	124
purchase*	124
pursue*	74

random*	44
ratio*	44
react*	64
recover*	24
regain*	114
regulate*	4
reject*	104
release*	64
renewable	74
resident*	4
restore*	4
restrict*	94
scenario*	194
scope*	194
shortages	74
statistics*	124
status*	24
strategy*	24
structure*	4
subsequently*	84
sum*	134
sustainable*	34
textile	54
the norm* (norm, the)	194
threat	24
traces*	144
transition*	104
transport*	54
trigger*	64
ultimate*	154
underestimate*	164
undertake*	114
unique*	14
unprecedented*	174
utilize*	74
variation*	44
versions*	154
via*	184
violate*	24
virtually*	174
welfare*	184

*These words are on the Academic Word List (AWL). The AWL is a list of the 570 highest-frequency academic word families that regularly appear in academic texts. The AWL was compiled by researcher Averil Coxhead based on her analysis of a 3.5 million word corpus (Coxhead, 2000).

Critical Thinking

analyzing information, 1, 2–3, 11, 13, 19, 21, 22–23, 35, 37, 41, 42–43, 47, 53, 57, 61, 62–63, 73, 77, 81, 82–83, 101, 102–103, 121, 122–123, 129, 133, 141, 142–143, 161, 162–163, 167, 173, 181, 182–183, 187, 193, 195

arguing a point of view, 38

asking questions for further research, 145

brainstorming, 31, 32, 57, 60, 113, 171, 185, 186

comparisons, 166

creating effective visuals, 200

debates, 40, 191

distinguishing between relevant and irrelevant information, 207

evaluating a lawsuit, 150

evaluating arguments, 36, 40

evaluating numbers and statistics, 116

evaluating pros and cons, 71

evaluating Web sources, 120

explaining choices, 94

explaining guesses, 90

explaining ideas, 27, 29

expressing and explaining opinions, 10, 36, 38, 45, 46, 47, 57, 78, 95, 115, 129, 131, 153, 168, 185

identifying lecture topic, 6, 202

making inferences, 7, 93, 99, 173, 205

meaning from context, 4, 24, 34, 44, 64, 74, 84, 104, 112, 124, 134, 144, 174, 184, 194, 204

memory building, 180

note-taking using an outline, 66, 67, 206

organizing ideas, 11, 40, 171

organizing presentations
    group, 60
    organizing information, 100

paraphrasing, 48–49

predicting content, 6, 12, 16, 26, 52, 56, 66, 86, 106, 146, 166, 192, 202

predictions about future, 70

proposing solutions for problems, 151, 197

questioning results, 167

rating items, 78

recognizing a return to a previous topic, 207

recognizing speaker's bias, 205

recognizing speaker's organization, 206

relating content to personal experiences, 147

relating to personal opinion, 107, 113

remaining objective, 185

responding to and refuting an argument, 38

restating content, 26, 36, 97, 131

summarizing, 127, 189, 206

supporting ideas, 168

survey results, 51

understanding and using visuals/graphic organizers, 206
    charts, 5, 11, 31, 42–43, 91, 100, 122–123, 160, 171, 186, 196, 216
    diagrams, 10, 66, 72, 76, 216
    flow charts, 215
    graphs, 130, 216
    idea maps, 107, 215
    maps, 2–3, 12, 16, 66, 92, 216
    Spider Map, 20
    T-charts, 76–77, 214
    time lines, 87, 215
    Venn diagrams, 214

understanding buzzwords, 109

understanding quotations, 48, 49

understanding scientific theories, 86–87

understanding structure of presentation, 202–203

using new grammar, 9–10, 19, 30, 39, 49–50, 59, 70, 79, 90, 99, 110, 119, 129–130, 139, 149–150, 159, 170, 179, 189–190, 199

using new vocabulary, 5, 15, 25, 65, 75, 85, 95, 105, 125, 135, 145, 155, 175

using notes, 26, 36, 66, 67, 207

Grammar

adjective clauses
    non-restrictive, 39
    restrictive, 30

compound adjectives, 49–50

connectors
    to add and emphasize information, 129–130
    of concession, 139

present participle phrases, 179

relative pronouns
    as object, 30
    as subject, 30

tag questions, 59

verbs
    active voice, 9
    agents in passive voice sentences, 19
    causative, 189–190
    future perfect progressive tense, 79
    future perfect tense, 70
    passive voice, 9–10
    past modals to make guesses about the past, 90
    past modals to make inferences, 99
    phrasal, 149–150
    subject-verb agreement with quantifiers, 170
    subjunctive, in *that* clauses, 199
    three-word phrasal, 159
    verb + gerund, 110
    verb + object + infinitive, 119

Language Function. *See also* Grammar; Pronunciation; Speaking

agreeing or disagreeing, 18, 210
apologizing for interrupting, 11, 210
asking about personal opinions, 51
asking for clarification, 58, 210
asking sensitive questions, 131, 210
asking who will go first, 151
checking background knowledge, 178, 211
conceding a point, 71, 210
confirming understanding, 188–189, 219
congratulating the group, 107, 210
digressing from the topic, 138, 210
emphasizing important information, 68–69
enumerating, 168–169, 211, 219
expressing approval and disapproval, 78, 211
expressing encouragement, 40, 210
expressing hopes, 98–99, 210
expressing interest, 91, 210
expressing lack of knowledge, 118, 219
expressing surprise, 88–89, 210
expressing uncertainty, 148–149, 219
giving definitions, 219
giving effects or results, 219
giving recommendations, 198
introducing a topic, 8
introducing examples, 28–29
joining a group, 171, 211
paraphrasing, 48–49, 219
responding to and refuting an argument, 38
returning to a previous topic, 219
showing that you are following a conversation, 128–129
showing understanding, 158–159, 219
signals to stop taking notes, 219
suffixes, 55
understanding sidetracks, 219
using fillers, 108–109, 219
using gestures, 171

Listening

to conversations, 16, 18, 56, 134
to conversations between classmates, 16, 176-177
to conversations between friends, 96–97, 136-137, 156-157
for details, 7, 16, 47, 87, 137, 156
    examples, 203
    reasons, 204
to a guided tour, 27
to informal conversations, 56-57, 196-197
to a lecture, 186-187
to a news report, 46-47
to a question-and-answer session, 146-147
to a student debate, 36-37
to a student presentation, 106-107
to a study group discussion, 76-77, 116-117
to a TV show, 166-167
for key concepts, 36, 76, 86
for main ideas, 6, 16, 46, 56, 67, 96, 106, 116, 126, 146, 156, 166, 176, 196, 203
note-taking, 26, 27, 36, 56, 93, 117, 133, 147, 167, 187, 197
    in a graphic organizer, 76, 107
    in an outline, 67, 127, 177
predicting content, 6, 16, 26, 56, 66, 86, 106, 146, 166, 202
prior knowledge and, 36, 96, 116, 156
to a radio show, 86–87, 126-127
for specific information, 57

Presentations

audience questions and
    dealing with difficult, 140
    preparing for, 100
budgets, 140
checklist for, 218
debates, 40, 191
demonstrating knowledge of content, 213
engaging the audience, 213
fighting nervousness, 80
getting background information, 100
group
    asking who will go first, 151
    checklist for, 218
    roles, 211
making eye contact, 20
organizing information for, 20, 40, 60, 100, 217
persuasive speeches, 171
planning, 20, 60, 80
    outline for, 217
preparing notes, 60
recognizing speaker's bias, 205
recognizing speaker's organization, 206
relating to your audience, 160
researching for, 100, 200, 211–212, 218
research presentations, 100
sharing advice, 160
speaking clearly and comprehensibly, 212
speaking with confidence, 40
understanding structure, 202–203
varying voice volume, 119
visuals/graphic organizers for
    creating and using, 80, 200
    Spider Map, 20

Pronunciation

of dropped syllables, 157
of letter *t*, 17
linking consonants to vowels, 117
/ŋ/ and /ŋk /, 57
question intonation, 97
-*s* endings, 37
stress
of two-word compounds, 77
on syllables, 197
word stress to clarify information, 177
vowel-to-vowel linking, 137

Resources

checklist for presentations, 218
outlines
for note-taking, 66, 206
for presentations, 217
visuals/graphic organizers, 206, 214–216
cartoons, 7
charts, 5, 11, 31, 100, 122–123, 160, 171, 186, 216
diagrams, 10, 66, 72, 76, 216
family tree, 91
flow charts, 215
graphs, 42-43, 130, 184, 196, 216
idea maps, 107, 215
maps, 2–3, 12, 16, 66, 82-83, 92, 116, 152, 216
pie charts, 122-123
poster or slide presentations, 80, 200
Spider Map, 20
T-charts, 76–77, 214
time lines, 87, 215
Venn diagrams, 214
vocabulary organizers, 208

Speaking. *See also* Language Function; Presentations; Pronunciation

asking and answering questions, 33, 57, 59
brainstorming, 31, 32, 57, 60, 113, 171, 185, 186
conducting a survey, 51
conversations, 10, 11, 139, 177
dialogs, 17
discussion, 2–3, 6, 10, 11, 13, 16, 18, 19, 20, 25, 26, 27, 30, 31, 33, 36, 42–43, 46, 50, 51, 52, 53, 56, 57, 60, 61, 62–63, 65, 66, 67, 73, 77, 78, 79, 80, 81, 85, 86, 87, 89, 90, 91, 93, 95, 96, 97, 100, 101, 102–103, 107, 111, 113, 115, 117, 118, 120, 121, 122–123, 125, 126, 127, 129, 131, 133, 135, 137, 138, 139, 141, 142–143, 145, 147, 148, 150, 153, 155, 156, 157, 160, 161, 162–163, 165, 167, 169, 170, 173, 175, 177, 180, 181, 182–183, 187, 190, 195, 197, 198, 199

and making inferences, 7
and self-reflection, 15, 29, 45, 70, 75, 94, 105, 108, 119, 137, 151, 159, 170, 179, 199
interviewing, 111, 151
role-playing, 33, 59, 71, 98, 140, 158, 191
sharing with others, 110, 115
short answers, 57

Test-Taking Skills

categorizing, 8, 40
checking correct answers, 17, 37, 73, 77
circling correct answers, 96, 131
fill in blanks, 5, 8, 14, 16, 18, 25, 28, 35, 38, 45, 48, 54, 55, 58, 59, 65, 68, 70, 72, 78, 79, 88, 95, 98, 108, 109, 114, 115, 118, 125, 128, 133, 134, 135, 138, 144, 148, 154, 158, 159, 164, 165, 168, 178, 188, 193, 194, 195, 197, 198
matching, 4, 12, 14, 24, 32, 34, 44, 46, 52, 64, 74, 84, 85, 87, 92, 104, 112, 132, 139, 145, 149, 152, 156, 159, 164, 172, 179, 184
multiple choice, 7, 27, 47, 53, 67, 73, 86, 106, 113, 116, 126, 132–133, 146, 166, 173, 176, 186, 192–193, 196
ranking, 126
sentence completion, 9, 10, 13, 15, 29, 30, 39, 55, 79, 113, 125, 145, 155, 170, 179, 185
sequencing, 53, 93, 173
short answers, 59
true/false questions, 15, 16, 75, 76, 96, 137, 153, 157

Topics

Beauty and Appearance, 41–60
Energy Issues, 61–80
Food Concerns, 181–200
Health and Fitness, 141–160
Migration, 81–100
Mind and Memory, 161–180
Money in Our Lives, 121–140
Protecting Our Planet, 21–40
Tradition and Progress, 101–120
Urban Challenges, 1–20

Viewing

Animal Minds, 172-173
The Black Diamonds of Provence, 132-133
and collaboration, 33
and critical thinking, 13, 53, 73, 93, 113, 133, 153, 173, 193
Crocodiles of Sri Lanka, 32-33
and direct quotations, 193
Farm Restoration, 112-113

for main idea ideas, 13, 53, 73, 113, 132, 153, 173, 192

for specific details,13, 112, 153

and note-taking, 32, 93, 133

Paraguay Shaman, 152-153

and predicting content, 12, 32, 52, 132, 173, 192

and prior knowledge, 152, 192

and sequencing events, 53, 93, 173

Skin Mask, 52-53

Slow Food, 192-193

Solar Power, 72-73

Tuareg Farmers, 12-13

using a dictionary, 12, 32, 52, 92, 112, 132, 152, 172

visuals/graphic organizer

    diagrams 72

    maps, 92, 132, 152, 192

Wildebeest Migration, 92-93

Vocabulary

building vocabulary, 4, 14, 24, 34, 44, 54, 64, 74, 84, 94, 104, 114, 124, 134, 144, 154, 164, 174, 184, 194

    dictionary use, 4, 5, 12, 14, 15, 25, 32, 34, 52, 54, 55, 66, 85, 92, 105, 112, 114, 132, 150, 152, 155, 164, 172, 209

    experimenting with new vocabulary, 208

    keeping a vocabulary journal, 208

    meaning from context, 4, 24, 34, 44, 64, 74, 84, 104, 124, 134, 144, 154, 174, 184, 194

    prefixes, 209

suffixes, 55, 209

    using new words as often as possible, 208

    vocabulary organizers, 208

using vocabulary, 5, 15, 25, 35, 45, 55, 65, 75, 85, 95, 105, 115, 125, 135, 145, 155, 165, 175, 185, 195

    choosing the right definition, 85, 115, 125

    dictionary use, 5, 15, 25, 55, 85, 105, 155

Writing

cartoon captions, 7

combining sentences, 30, 39, 139

conversations, 10

forms, 120

idea maps, 107

in charts, 15, 31, 91, 160, 171, 186

lists, 131, 152, 180

notes for presentations, 60

note-taking, 26, 27, 33, 36, 87, 93, 111, 117, 127, 133, 145, 147, 167, 177, 187, 197, 206

    researching for presentations, 80

    using a graphic organizer, 76, 107

    using an outline, 66, 67, 127, 177, 206

questions, 57, 145

sentences, 29, 110, 119, 159, 197

Spider Map, 20

surveys, 128

PHOTOS (continued)

Image Collection, **93:** Ralph Lee Hopkins/ National Geographic Image Collection, **94:** Roy Toft/National Geographic Image Collection Stock, **95:** Iv Mirin/Shutterstock.com, **96:** Randy Olson/National Geographic Image Collection, **96:** Randy Olson/National Geographic Image Collection, **99:** Joe McNally/National Geographic Image Collection, **101:** Paul Nicklen/National Geographic Image Collection, **102:** Bartosz Hadyniak/iStockphoto.com, **102:** Randy Olson/National Geographic Image Collection, **103:** Lightmediation/National Geographic Image Collection, **103:** Schoeller, Martin/National Geographic Image Collection, **103:** Steve Winter/National Geographic Image Collection, **104:** Schoeller, Martin/National Geographic Image Collection, **107:** Lynsey Addario/National Geographic Image Collection, **109:** Melinda Fawver/Shutterstock.com, **109:** Carmen Martínez Banús/Maica/, **110:** Martin Thomas Photography/Alamy, **112:** YinYang/iStockphoto.com, **113:** Bruce MacQueen/Shutterstock.com, **114:** Paul Harris/ John Warburton-Lee Photography/Alamy, **115:** Dave G. Houser/Corbis, **117:** Jack Dykinga/National Geographic Image Collection, **118:** Handout/Reuters, **118:** Mircea Simu/ Shutterstock.com, **121:** Tyrone Turner/National Geographic Image Collection, **122:** StockLite/ Shutterstock.com, **122:** Billy Hustace/Corbis, **122-123:** Tino Soriano/National Geographic Image Collection, **124:** David Mclain/National Geographic Image Collection, **124:** David McLain/National Geographic Image Collection, **126:** Blend Images (RF)/Hill Street Studios/ Jupiter Images, **129:** Fedor Kondratenko/ Shutterstock.com, **132:** Catherine Hansen/

Photononstop/PhotoLibrary, **132:** sutsaiy/ Shutterstock.com, **133:** foodfolio/Alamy, **134:** John Gress/Reuters, **136:** Aaron Lambert/Santa Maria Times/ZUMA Press/ Newscom, **139:** Frank May/dpa/Landov, **141:** Jimmy Chin/National Geographic Image Collection, **142:** Photograph by Peter Essick, **142:** John Stanmeyer LLC/National Geographic Image Collection, **142:** Jimmy Chin/National Geographic Image Collection, **142-143:** Dawn Kish/National Geographic Image Collection, **144:** Photograph by Peter Essick, **144:** Everett Collection, **146:** Peter Essick/National Geographic Image Collection, **147:** Peter Essick/National Geographic Image Collection, **148:** Photograph by Peter Essick, **148:** Peter Essick/National Geographic Image Collection, **148:** Photograph by Peter Essick, **148:** Peter Essick/National Geographic Image Collection, **150:** Rich Legg/iStockphoto, **152:** Michael Nichols/National Geographic Image Collection, **153:** Michael Edwards/Alamy, **153:** Terry Whittaker/FLPA/PhotoLibrary, **154:** dbtravel/ dbimages/Alamy, **154:** Bill Hatcher/National Geographic Image Collection, **154:** Pete McBride/National Geographic Image Collection, **156:** Jimmy Chin/National Geographic Image Collection, **159:** Denis Raev/iStockphoto.com, **161:** Rod Porteous/Robert Harding World Imagery/Corbis, **163:** Vincent J. Musi/National Geographic Image Collection, **163:** Maggie Steber, **163:** Maggie Steber/National Geographic Image Collection, **164:** Uryadnikov Sergey/Shutterstock, **165:** Cohn, Ronald H/ National Geographic Image Collection, **166:** Vincent J. Musi/National Geographic Image Collection, **166:** Vincent J. Musi/National Geographic Image Collection, **169:** Natursports/

Shutterstock, **169:** sjlocke/iStockphoto, **169:** Christina Richards/Shutterstock.com, **172:** sextoacto/iStockphoto, **172:** Joe Raedle/ Newsmakers/Getty Images, **173:** FLPA/Alamy, **174:** Maggie Steber/National Geographic Image Collection, **175:** AP Photo/Primate Research Institute, Kyoto/Tetsuro Matsuzawa, **176:** Maggie Steber/National Geographic Image Collection, **179:** Michael Nichols/ National Geographic Image Collection, **181:** Michael S. Yamashita/National Geographic Image Collection, **182:** Lee Avison/GAP Photos/Getty Images, **182:** Jim Richardson/National Geographic Image Collection, **182-183:** Fritz Hoffmann/National Geographic Image Collection, **183:** John Stanmeyer LLC/National Geographic Image Collection, **184:** Jim Richardson/National Geographic Image Collection, **186:** Jim Richardson/National Geographic Image Collection, **187:** Jim Richardson/National Geographic Image Collection, **187:** Jim Richardson/National Geographic Image Collection, **187:** Colin Monteath/Minden Pictures, **187:** nopporn/Shutterstock.com, **188:** Jim Richardson/National Geographic Image Collection, **189:** Ferran Traite Soler/ istockphoto.com, **189:** Jim Richardson/ National Geographic Image Collection, **190:** Ted Aljibe/Staff/AFP/Getty Images, **192:** CuboImages srl/Alamy, **192:** Marka/ Alamy, **193:** Christine Webb/Alamy, **193:** Eric Risberg/AP Photo, **194:** John Stanmeyer LLC/ National Geographic Image Collection, **195:** John Stanmeyer LLC/National Geographic Image Collection, **198:** tBoyan/iStockphoto, **200:** Otokimus/Shutterstock

MAP AND ILLUSTRATION

2-3: National Geographic Maps; **6:** National Geographic Maps; **7:** www.cartoonstock.com; **10:** Fernando Baptista and Alejandro Tumas, NGM staff; **12:** National Geographic Maps; **16:** National Geographic Maps; **32:** National Geographic Maps; **64:** National Geographic Maps; **66:** National Geographic Maps;

82-83: NGM Maps/National Geographic Image Collection; **85:** Gregory Manchess/ National Geographic Image Collection; **92:** National Geographic Maps; **92:** Map courtesy of Roy Safaris–Tanzania; **102-103:** National Geographic Maps; **104:** National Geographic Maps; **106:** National Geographic Maps; **106:** Atlaspix/ Shutterstock.com; **112:** National Geographic Maps; **116:** National Geographic Maps;

132, 216: Mapping Specialists, Ltd. Madison, WI USA; **152:** National Geographic Maps; **152:** National Geographic Maps; **154:** National Geographic Maps; **162-163:** Roger Harris / Photo Researchers, Inc.; **175:** National Geographic Maps; **190:** National Geographic Maps; **192:** Mapping Specialists, Ltd. Madison, WI USA; **196:** Sean McNaughton, NGM Staff; **208:** Bob Kayganich/ illustrationonline